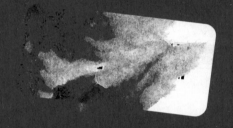

# UTOPIAN
*Audiences*

# UTOPIAN
## *Audiences*
### HOW READERS LOCATE NOWHERE

# Kenneth M. Roemer
*University of Massachusetts Press    Amherst and Boston*

LC 2003013814
ISBN 1-55849-421-9

Designed by Sally Nichols
Set in Fairfield LH Light by Graphic Composition, Inc.
Printed and bound by The Maple-Vail Book Manufacturing Group

Library of Congress Cataloging-in-Publication Data

Roemer, Kenneth M., 1945–
    Utopian audiences : how readers locate nowhere / Kenneth M. Roemer.
        p.  cm. — (Studies in print culture and the history of the book)
Includes bibliographical references and index.
    ISBN 1-55849-421-9 (Cloth : alk. paper)
    1.  American literature—History and criticism. 2.  Utopias in literature. 3.  Authors
and readers—English-speaking countries. 4.  English literature—History and criticism.
5.  Utopias—English-speaking countries. 6.  Reader-response criticism.  I. Title.
II. Series.
        PS169.U85 R64 2003
        810.9'372—dc21

                                                                        2003013814


British Library Cataloguing in Publication data are available.

Utopian Audiences *is dedicated to:*

*733 students, retirees, and book club members, for their willingness to participate in my reader-response utopian community;*

*my former American and Japanese students in "Build Your Own Utopia," "Shapes of Utopia," and "American Utopian Expressions," for their lively discussions;*

*my friends in the Society for Utopian Studies, for encouraging me to finish this book;*

*and my personal utopian audience—Micki, Vonnie, Michael, Kathy, and Alex—for their patience and love.*

# Contents

# Illustrations

# Preface

It may seem strange to preface a preface to a book on a topic as grand as utopia with two humbling images and a humbling fact. But, then again, the process of utopian speculation can be both strange and humbling.

The first image is a gift from the Hungarian photographer André Kertész. It is a photographic extension of a nineteenth-century painting convention: the solitary female reader (Lyons 323). In 1929 Kertész photographed an elderly woman wrapped in a dark shawl and propped up by pillows on her bed. She is reading. She appears absorbed in a book whose identity is beyond our view. In *A History of Reading* (1996) Alberto Manguel imagines several scenarios for this peaceful image. The location is the Hospice de Beaune, in France—an old-folks home in "the heart of Catholic Burgundy" (213). Consistent with the setting, she might be reading her Bible, a devotional, or sermons. But what if, Manguel speculates, she is reading Racine or Voltaire or Cocteau's *Les enfants terribles,* a racy novel published in the mid-1920s? Or we might add, what if she is reading Fourier's utopian visions of the twelve passions fulfilled? And what if his image of a "withdrawn solitary reader" (Long 181) masks the reality of a reader eagerly anticipating talks with friends about her reading? In the privacy of her mind is she isolated or communal? Is she a pious, a cultured, a heretical, a voyeuristic, or a passionate radical reader? The answer is beyond our purview.

The other image comes from a fictional future that is now our past. Edith Leete—the heroine in the most popular and influential American utopia, Edward Bellamy's *Looking Backward* (1888)—hopes to calm the nerves of a nineteenth-century man, Julian West, who has recently arrived in her world of A.D. 2000. She ushers him into a "cosy apartment," the family library. She hopes that a visit with the authors of the past, his "friends," will make him "feel at home." Initially West is delighted; alone he settles into a book by "the most familiar of names before me"—Dickens. Quickly his calm and delight change to intense disorientation and guilt. The striking contrasts between Dickens's world of "misery and poverty" and the equalities of Boston in 2000 heighten his "appreciation of the strangeness of [his] present environment." "Every paragraph, every phrase, brought up some new aspect of the world-transformation that had taken place," a transformation that he "had neither foreseen . . . nor toiled for." It was a world he "so little deserved" (188–90).[1] Edith had hoped reading old friends would bring comfort and reassurance; instead it brought dislocation and guilt.

The "fact" comes from the computer data bank run by the world's leading bibliographer of English-language utopian works, Lyman Tower Sargent. As of February 6, 2003, his bank had holdings of 5,621 titles ("Re: Utopias Count").

The images remind us that it is extremely difficult to know exactly what people read in private and practically impossible to predict exactly how an individual reader will respond to a particular text. The fact reminds us to be suspect of any generalities tendered about such a vast body of particulars as utopian literature. But the images and fact also speak of the fascinating richness and diversity of this literature and of the wonder of how readers can transform themselves (possibly from peaceful old ladies to radical utopians) and their books (from familiar scenes to strange world-transformations) as they bring to life "every paragraph, every phrase."

*Utopian Audiences* cannot pretend to explain how readers locate nowhere. I hope, however, it will help us to understand some of the likely reasons why and how American readers transformed a book by a relatively unknown author into an agent of national and even international change, how these reasons might relate to reading utopian literature in general, and why the study of the literature of nowhere is such a fertile exploration site

for studying the frustratingly inaccessible but perpetually fascinating process of reading.

My first debt of gratitude goes to the 733 readers who completed the
surveys and reading analyses discussed in chapters 7, 8, and 9. Just as
important were the professors, high school teacher, and my liaison with
the retirement community who administered the surveys and analyses:
Jean Stein, Wesley Palms Retirement Community, San Diego; Sandra
Campbell, Arlington High School, Texas; the members of the Arlington
women's reading group; Lavern Prewitt, University of Texas at Arlington;
Csaba Toth, University of Minnesota; Carol Kolmerten, Hood College;
Mickey Abrash and June Deery, RPI; Susan Matarese, University of
Louisville; Howard Segal, Harvard Summer School; Alex MacDonald,
Campion College, University of Regina, Saskatchewan, Canada; Naoki
Onishi, International Christian University, Mitaka, Tokyo, Japan; Heinz
Tschachler, Universität für Bildungswissenchaften, Klagenfurt, Austria.
    Lyman Tower Sargent, Tom Moylan, and David Herman, the three
readers for the University of Massachusetts Press, offered excellent suggestions for revision. I would also like to thank Janice Radway, who gave
me advice during the early stages of constructing the survey questionnaire; Beth Wright, who suggested parallels between Elise Cavanna's illustrations and the work of other modern artists; Victor Vitanza, who invited
me to attend his graduate seminar on reader-response criticism; Jean
Pfaelzer, Daphne Patai, and Arno Heller, who offered substantive and
editorial suggestions for parts of earlier versions of chapters 3, 4, and 5;
Lyman Tower Sargent, Toby Widdicombe, and Arthur O. Lewis, who gave
invaluable bibliographical guidance; and the many members of the Society
for Utopian Studies who offered comments on my papers related to this
book, especially Gorman Beauchamp, Lee Cullen Khanna, Peter Fitting,
Tom Moylan, Phil Wegner, and Naomi Jacobs.
    I have received generous support from the University of Texas at
Arlington: a semester developmental leave in 1999 from the Graduate
School; graduate research assistants, Linda Jackson and Lexey Bartlett, for
several weeks in 1998 and 2002, from the English Department; a summer
grant in 1996 from the College of Liberal Arts; and much assistance from
the Library's Interlibrary Loan Department. I would also like to thank

Christine Murray for her proofreading skills. A Senior Fellowship from the Japan Society for the Promotion of Science in 1988 enabled me to survey students at International Christian University.

I owe a special debt of gratitude to Michael O. Bellamy, the great-grandson of Edward Bellamy, who permitted me to cite material, especially in my chapter 4, from his unpublished critical biography, "'Pleasure Reconciled to Virtue': Edward Bellamy's Utopian Quest."

I thank the following publishers for permission to reprint revised versions of chapters 2, 3, 4, and 5: Universitätverlag C. Winter (Brigitte Georgi-Findlay and Hans-Ulrich Mohr, eds. *Millennial Perspectives: Lifeworlds and Utopias.* Heidelberg, 2002: 55–98); Gunter Narr Verlag (Arno Heller, Walter Hoelbling, and Waldermar Zachariasiewicz, eds. *Utopian Thought in American Literature. Untersuchungen zur literarischen Utopie und Dystopie in der USA.* Tübingen, 1988: 7–24); The University of Rhode Island (*ATQ* 3.1 [March 1989]: 101–22); and the University of Massachusetts Press (Daphne Patai, ed. *Looking Backward, 1988–1888: Essays on Edward Bellamy.* Amherst, 1988: 126–46). I thank the following individual and publisher for permission to reproduce illustrations: Ursula K. Le Guin for the maps she drew in *Always Coming Home* (copyright 1985 Ursula K. Le Guin, New York, Harper & Row); and Easton Press, for illustrations from their 1981 reprint of the 1941 Limited Editions Club edition of *Looking Backward.* I would also like to thank Ursula K. Le Guin for permission to quote from her letters to me and for her continual encouragement.

And, as always, my thanks to Micki.

# UTOPIAN
*Audiences*

# Introduction
*Utopian Studies and Utopian Audiences*

---

Considering all the millennial hype during the close of the twentieth and opening of the twenty-first century—Levi's even advertised their jeans as "apocalyptic tough"—it is not surprising that there was a notable increase in interest in utopia, since utopianism and millennialism are linked "isms." To name a few examples, there were international conferences in England (1999, 2000), Germany, and Russia (both in 2000); a collaborative inter-national exhibition, *Utopia: The Search for the Ideal Society in the Western World,* in 2000 and 2001 at the New York Public Library and the Biblio-thèque nationale de France; important national exhibitions, including the "Utopias & Dystopias" section of the New York Public Library's 1995 *Books of the Century* exhibition; grand reference projects utilizing international teams of scholars, notably the *Dictionary of Literary Utopias* (2000), edited by Vita Fortunati and Raymond Trousson; at least two new anthologies, Gregory Claeys and Lyman Tower Sargent's *The Utopia Reader* (1999) and John Carey's *The Faber Book of Utopias* (1999); bibliographies that expand the horizons of utopian literature to include Australian, New Zealand, Canadian, and Japanese texts; and several books since 2000, including the elaborate *Utopia* exhibit catalogue and works by Sally Kitch, Tom Moylan, Susan Matarese, Phillip Wegner, Patrick Parrinder, and Ralph Pordzik, whose *Quest for Postcolonial Utopia* (2001) examines utopias from many English-speaking countries, including India, Ireland, Nigeria, Scotland, and South Africa.[1]

This recent interest in utopia is much more than a turn-of-the-century academic fad. In the 1960s and 1970s many political and social movements—especially feminism and communal experiments—and the revitalization of American and British utopian fiction inspired by Ursula K. Le Guin, Joanna Russ, Marge Piercy, Samuel Delany, and Doris Lessing contributed to the formation of academic associations in America (the Society for Utopian Studies and the Communal Studies Association) and in Great Britain, Italy, France, and other countries; the founding of journals (for instance, *Utopian Studies* and *Communal Societies* in America and *Notizie A.I.S. U* in Italy); and, in utopian literature, the publication of comprehensive general national and specific author bibliographies.[2]

Despite this impressive growth, one crucial element in the study of literary utopias is frequently omitted—the reader. The great majority of commentators on utopias tend to agree with Krishan Kumar that the fundamental goal of the student of utopia should be the analyses of "the nature and quality of [utopists'] ideas about individuals and societies" (*Utopia and Anti-Utopia,* ix) and that the appropriate avenue to this goal is the study of the texts, the author, and historical/cultural contexts.

Certainly there are significant exceptions. In *Utopianism* (1991) Kumar draws attention to readers by chastising William Morris for concentrating on the author: "William Morris once said that 'the only safe way of reading a utopia is to consider the temperament of its author.' That is very good advice; but it leaves out the problem of the temperament of the reader" (100). Moreover, there are at least two books that place emphases on textual and genre constructions of readers of utopias. Peter Ruppert's *Reader in a Strange Land* (1986) is a provocative study that utilizes Wolfgang Iser's concept of the text as a "network of response-inviting structures" (Iser, *Act* 34) to define ideal readers who approach literary utopias as opportunities to discover questions, ambiguities, and contradictions out of which they imagine their own models of utopia. In one of the most fascinating studies of utopias, *The Boundaries of Genre* (1981), Gary Saul Morson argues that the meaning of a literary utopia "depends upon the readers' assumptions about (1) the appropriate conventions for interpreting the work, and (2) the literary tradition in which it is placed" (172). There are also several excellent article-length reader-response studies of models of utopian readers or of documented readings, especially reviews.[3] Furthermore, if we broaden our scope to include relevant science-fiction criticism, we discover a substantial body of work, including pioneering studies of narrator-reader relationships by Marc Angenot and Kathleen Spencer, and more recent discussions of applications of reader-response theory by Ed McKnight and of definitions of reading protocol by Tom Moylan.[4] As I suggest near the conclusion of chapter 2, even if we restrict our view to criticism focused on utopian literature, we find that recent attempts to define literary utopias imply an elevation of the reader, as scholars and critics shift their interests away from what utopian literature is to what it does. Since, at least in theory, readers are the objects of this functional approach to definition, their position is elevated.

This implied elevation and the few books and articles focused on the reader of utopian literature are, however, still minority reports. In order to gain a better understanding of why particular utopias have become for particular generations important agents of changed perceptions and even changed realities, we need more emphasis on utopian readers and the processes they use to transform authors' "temperaments" and their words into personalized guides and inspirations. Moreover, we need reader-response and reception analyses that draw upon a variety of approaches. As provocative and insightful as the previous reader-oriented studies have been, they—including my own work—tend to emphasize text- or genre-based theoretical models of readers or, less frequently, historical documented readings or, much less frequently, examinations of oral and written responses of "real" late twentieth-century readers. By emphasizing one approach over, or to the exclusion of, others, utopographers miss opportunities to discover correlations between theoretical and documented concepts of readers of utopias, correspondences and contradictions between past and present responses, and generalized concepts of reading grounded in both theory and empirical evidence. They miss opportunities to offer what Jonathan Boyarin and others call ethnographies of reading that explore a variety of "fields of interaction shaping and surrounding the textual remains of the past" (Boyarin 2).[5]

The images of the elderly woman in the Beaune hospice and Julian West's unanticipated responses to Dickens and the "fact" of 5,621 utopian titles temper my ambitions for this book. One book will not "correct the imbalance" and elevate readers to a position equal to the author and text in utopian studies; the variety of approaches I use certainly does not exhaust the possibilities of reader-response/reception studies relevant to literary utopias and most certainly does not reveal the variety of ways "actual" readers have experienced utopias; and, in chapters 3 through 9, my focus on one influential utopia should not be read as a template for interpreting responses to all literary utopias (even if we limit ourselves to the mere 5,621 written in English). I do hope, nonetheless, that my eclectic approach and concentration on Bellamy's *Looking Backward* will offer a combination of breadth and specificity that will suggest the importance of readers in the history of utopian literature and indicate several significant ways of defining and assessing the cultural, literary, and personal processes that enabled and still enable readers to access and transform utopian literature.

To introduce the nature and organization of *Utopian Audiences,* I will offer three brief previews: first, a statement of the assumptions that shape my eclectic approach to reader response and reception theory; second, an explanation of why I decided to focus on the late nineteenth century and especially on *Looking Backward;* and third, an outline of the book's organization.

Three basic assumptions shaped my approach to studying utopian reading audiences: texts invite the creation of meaning, and readers give meanings to the texts (meanings that may or may not coincide with the invitations); before, during, and after the reading experience, this process of meaning creation is constrained, guided, and encouraged by powerful cultural, historical, and personal situations and forces; and the complexities of the textual invitations, the acts of meaning formation, and the situations and forces call for combinations of approaches to reading typically associated with reader-response, reception, and history-of-the-book studies.

To be a bit more specific, the textual invitations can appear in networks of an almost infinite variety of explicit forms (for example, direct address, explanations, descriptions, images) and implicit forms (for example, repetitions or the "gaps" and "inconsistencies" analyzed by Wolfgang Iser or the "absent paradigms" Marc Angenot associates with speculative fiction). Readers can accept, reject, ignore, or transform the invitations, or they may be completely oblivious to some of them. What they do with the invitations depends on an almost infinite variety of variables that constrain, guide, and encourage how they shape or ignore the textual invitations. The forces can be as broad as the millennial eschatologies, the gender roles, the literacy rates, and the concepts of books and reading that shaped late nineteenth-century American responses to utopian literature. During that same period, they could also be related to more specific forces: historical circumstances (for instance, the economic depression of the early 1890s and the increase of reform movements), specific conventions of reading (for instance, travel literature, biblical parables, and sentimental fiction), and technological developments that, on a personal level, made reading less expensive and easier on the eyes and, on a societal level, made the achievement of an alternative reality more believable. Then of course, there are the more immediate situations: the specific interpretive communities that shape "negotiated" responses (to borrow Stanley Fish's and David Bleich's terms), the personal circumstances during the reading, and the—once again—almost infinite varieties of individual psychologies that shape responses to textual invitations.

The complexity of textual invitations and the forces and situations constraining, guiding, and encouraging the creation of meaning calls for response studies that approach the creation of reading from a variety of angles. I certainly cannot pretend to offer the "correct" combination in this book. But I have found several approaches particularly useful for the study of utopian audiences. I'll offer a working overview of these approaches by organizing them into general response categories and by linking them to several of the theorists who shaped my views. Concepts of the implied, competent, and ideal reader; the authorial audience; the audience as stranger in utopia; and the narratee have helped me understand textual invitations. Hence, I'm clearly indebted to Wolfgang Iser, Jonathan Culler, Robert DeMaria, Peter J. Rabinowitz, Peter Ruppert, and Gerald Prince. The general cultural studies and more specific studies of the intersections between history and utopian literature cited in chapter 3 obviously helped me to identify relevant value systems, worldviews and events influencing nineteenth-century readers. Just as important were the essays and books that defined rates of literacy, concepts of books, and technologies of production and distribution. Here I am especially in debt to students of the American book, for example, Carl Kaestle, Cathy Davidson, and Ronald Zboray, and the global book, for example, Alberto Manguel, Guglielmo Cavallo, and Roger Chartier. To understand how knowledge of genre conventions directed readers, I used interpretations that focused specifically on utopias, especially Gary Saul Morson's, but I also benefited from excellent studies of sentimental or domestic fiction (Nina Baym, Mary Kelley,

Susan K. Harris) and general examinations of the impact of a knowledge of general reading conventions, for instance, Peter J. Rabinowitz's *Before Reading* (1987).

Much of this book focuses on actual readers as they are represented either in historical documented readings or in the written responses of living readers who all read one book and expressed their responses in the forms of answers to a questionnaire and in analyses of the influences (which I term transformational associations) that shaped their ability to create meaning from the text's invitations. In the former cases I was obviously influenced by general and specific studies of book reviewers (for instance, Nina Baym's interpretations of American reviewers and Steven Mailloux's comparisons between American and British reviewers), but I was also guided by attempts to place readers in history in collections such as James L. Machor's *Readers in History* (1993) and Cathy Davidson's *Reading in America* (1989) and, in chapter 7, by theorists who examined how modern readers misread unfamiliar historical texts (for instance, Culler, Fredric Jameson, Ruppert, I. A. Richards, Louise Rosenblatt, and Robert Escarpit). My attempts to understand the reading protocols of 733 contemporary readers were influenced more by Janice Radway's studies of romance readers, by the many scholar-teachers mentioned in chapter 7 who used student readers, and by Fish's concept of interpretive communities than by Norman Holland's and David Bleich's psychological models or Pierre Bourdieu's sociological study of 1,217 readers.

What differentiates my approach to reading from other response criticism? Obviously, one distinction is my emphasis on the necessity of using a combination of interpretive viewpoints applied to one popular and influential text. (For the advantages of using such a text, see below.) As compared to the American reader-response criticism of the late 1970s and early 1980s, I also place much more emphasis on representations of actual historical and modern readers. I especially believe in the value of "experimenting" with relatively large samples of living readers who come from different backgrounds—different enough to reflect some of the cultural, historical, and personal variables that constrain, guide, and encourage readers to accept, reject, ignore, or transform textual invitations.

Three considerations inclined me toward the late nineteenth–early twentieth century: the need for more reader-response and reception studies of this period, the dominance of print media, and the abundance of American utopian literature. The past two decades have witnessed the appearance of several excellent studies of American book production, readers, and reviewers, including Nina Baym's *Novels, Readers and Reviewers* (1984), Davidson's *Revolution and the Word* (1986) and her edited volume *Reading in America* (1989), William Gilmore's *Reading Becomes a Necessity of Life* (1989), Ronald Zboray's *A Fictive People* (1993), David D. Hall's *Culture of Print* (1996), and Hugh Amory and David D. Hall's *The Colonial Book in the Atlantic World,* volume 1 of *A History of the Book in America* (2000). As different as these books are, they all share a focus on eras before 1860. Even the excellent collections edited by James L. Machor (*Readers in History: Nineteenth-Century American Literature and the Contexts of Response* [1993]), Michele Moylan and Lane Stiles (*Reading Books: Essays on the Material Text and Literature in America* [1996]), James P. Danky and Wayne A. Wiegand (*Print Culture in a Diverse America* [1998]), and Barbara Ryan and Amy M. Thomas (*Reading Acts: U.S. Readers' Interactions with Literature, 1800–1950* [2002]) focus on earlier or later periods, the notable exceptions being essays on responses to Dickinson's published poetry in *Readers in History,* on Twain, Helen Hunt Jackson, and Houghton Mifflin's Biographical Series in *Reading Books,* on reading in an Iowa community context in *Print Culture,* and on middle-class Victorian readers— Barbara Sicherman's revealing study of readers who created "cultured" identities by buying, reading, and displaying books in *Reading Acts.* Carl Kaestle's comprehensive *Literacy in the United States* (1991) does include some discussion of the late nineteenth century, and the special Victorian culture issue of *American Quarterly* (27 [December 1975], published in book form as Daniel Walker Howe's *Victorian America* [1976]), John Thomas's *Alternative America* (1983), and the other studies of Victorian America mentioned in chapter 3 do offer important information about book production and reading attitudes at the close of the century. Christine Pawley provides a detailed study of late nineteenth-century reading in a small Iowa community context in *Reading the Middle Border* (2001), and in *Getting at the Author* (2001) Barbara Hochman examines how readers questioned the belief that a book revealed authorial identity as realism gained favor. Martyn Lyons's "New Readers in the Nineteenth Century" in Cavallo and Chartier's *A History of Reading in the West* (1999) does focus on the late nineteenth century, but Lyons's primary interests are British, French, and

German readers. There are relevant cultural studies, notably Susan K. Harris's investigations of British and American literary hostesses.[6] For the twentieth century, literacy studies and detailed examinations of the publishing industry and readers are plentiful. These include Janice Radway's studies of the Book-of-the-Month Club and modern romance readers and Molly Abel Travis's *The Construction of Readers in the Twentieth Century* (1998). But Kaestle laments the fact that in contrast to the twentieth century, evidence relating to literacy for the late nineteenth century is sketchy and unsystematic and studies of readers are less available (64–65). I hope *Utopian Audiences* will contribute to the efforts of Kaestle, Thomas, Harris, Pawley, Hochman, Sicherman, and others to develop a fuller portrait of late nineteenth-century reading experiences, especially since this period was a golden era, two times over.

It was the golden era of print media and the golden era of the literary eutopia in America. (Throughout the book, I will follow common usage and use *utopia* to indicate the "good place," even though it literally means "no place" or "nowhere." Occasionally, as in this case, when I want to emphasize the "good place" as opposed to the "bad place," dystopia, I will use *eutopia*.) As discussed in chapter 3, Kaestle and Sicherman link important economic, technological, and educational developments to dramatic increases in production, distribution, circulation, and literacy from 1880 to 1920. (The popularity and influence of the period's newspapers and magazines is an area that has received substantial attention.) The reading audience was large, books were plentiful, and access to them had increased as libraries multiplied, prices dropped, and distribution systems improved. By 1897 the Sears Roebuck catalogue even included "twelve pages of book ads" (Sicherman 140–41). True, print media were not the only communication forces available. The telegraph and telephone, and more recently the phonograph, carried messages across rooms, towns, and regions. As early as 1878 the editor of *Publishers' Weekly*, frightened by Edison's predictions about recording books, envisioned a dystopian future with libraries filled "with nothing but sheets of tin foil grooved with simple lines" (qt. in Hayes 82). I'm sure he would be gratified to know that never happened and that it wasn't until the twentieth century that silent and talking films, radio, television, videos, and the computer reduced the dominance of the printed page (Sicherman 152). As Lyons proclaims in Cavallo and Chartier's *A History of Reading in the West*, the 1890s "was the 'Golden Age' of the book in the West: the first generation which acceded to mass literacy was also the last to see the book unchallenged as a communication medium" (313).

Considering this dominance, it is not surprising that many of the utopian works published during the period made brief mention of books and reading experiences, and at least eighteen included extended discussions of improved books of the future, whose features included varied pastel margins, illustrations more realistic than photographs, covers so beautiful they are displayed as paintings, and new forms of typefaces and written symbols that soothe the eye and speed comprehension (Hayes 64–85). At least twenty-two utopists also imagined books that had inspired reform movements (Roemer, *America as Utopia* 321), and, as West's experience with Dickens demonstrates, several included transformative reading experiences.

Beginning with Allyn Forbes's 1927 survey and continuing with twentieth-century scholars up through more recent surveys in James Simmons's "Utopian Cycles" (1998) and Susan Matarese's *American Foreign Policy and the Utopian Imagination* (2001), the consensus has been that more literary eutopias—at least two hundred—were published from 1888 through the early years of the twentieth century than in any other period of American (or possibly any other country's) history (Simmons 201). The obvious reason for the 1888 beginning date is the publication of *Looking Backward, 2000–1887* in that year. Of nineteenth-century American titles, only *Uncle Tom's Cabin* and, possibly, *Ben Hur* outsold *Looking Backward*. The book's popularity inspired numerous book-length fictional responses, some with titles that played off of Bellamy's title, characters, and ideas (*Looking Backward and What I Saw, Looking Further Backward, Looking Further Forward, Looking Beyond, Looking Within, Looking Upward, A.D. 2000, Young West, The Industrial Army*). There were approximately one hundred American reviews of *Looking Backward;* reform journals, including Bellamy's *Nationalist* and *New Nation* sprang up, inspired by *Looking Backward;* numerous literary, social, labor, and reform leaders as different as William Dean Howells, Mark Twain, Upton Sinclair, Samuel Gompers, Eugene Debs, Charlotte Perkins Gilman, and Elizabeth Cady Stanton voiced public support; and at least 165 Nationalist or Bellamy Clubs appeared in America and grew into the Nationalist Party that influenced the national Populist Party. During the twentieth century many socialist, Progressive, and New Deal politicians cited Bellamy as an important influence, and translations of *Looking Backward* inspired reform movements around the world, with especially strong impacts on England, Europe, Russia, Canada, Australia, and New Zealand, where a minister of education and a prime minister reviewed *Looking Backward*.[7] Thus it is not surprising that in 1935 the philosopher John Dewey, the historian Charles Beard, and the editor of *Atlantic,* Edward Weeks, contended that of books published since 1885 only Marx's *Das Kapital* had done more to shape the thought and action of the world (Shurter, "Introduction" xv).

Today this high estimation of the impact of *Looking Backward* may seem puzzling to many readers, since Bellamy's utopia may be an unknown nowhere to them. Since *Looking Backward* may also be unfamiliar to some of the readers of this book, a brief overview may help to orient them to my comments about *Looking Backward* in part 1 and to the extended discussions of the book in parts 2 through 4. (For an extended overview by a Bellamy contemporary, see Michael Maher's 1891 review in the *Month* [pt. 1, 1–10]; for a thorough twentieth-century summary, see Darko Suvin's *Metamorphoses of Science Fiction* [170–78].) Like most literary utopias, *Looking Backward* is a combination of narrative and argumentative discourses. Bellamy combines narratives of estrangement (to borrow the term Suvin popularized), romance, and conversion with arguments presented in guide-visitor dialogues and a sermon. Time travel creates the initial sense of estrangement from the "present"; the evolving love between the estranged visitor, Julian West, and the utopian guide's daughter, Edith Leete, creates the love interest; and the conversion dramatizes the transformation of a rather selfish wealthy individual (West) into a supporter of a centralized, socialized, egalitarian economy and a concept of self that merges the individual and society. The guide-visitor dialogues (which are notoriously monologic; the guide, Dr. Leete, is clearly the "man with the answers") provide most of the explicit intellectual arguments that convince the visitor to convert, though a long sermon by Rev. Barton near the conclusion of the book helps West to comprehend the just appeal of the social self.

To be more specific about the combinations of narrative and argument: In the Boston of 1887, thirty-year-old Julian West's "wedding bliss" with his wealthy fiancée, Edith Bartlett, is delayed by labor strikes that halt the building of their new home (102). His anger about this situation exasperates his chronic insomnia. In his secret subterranean, fireproof sleeping chamber (the silence helps him sleep), he is hypnotized into a deep sleep.

That night the house burns; West's family assumes that he perished. In 2000 Dr. Leete discovers the chamber and gently awakens West. West spends almost all of the next days in the home and company of Dr. Leete, his wife, and their blue-eyed daughter, Edith. In the tradition of sentimental fiction, separation, intrigue, and circumstance shape the romance between West and Edith. Edith Leete is actually the great-granddaughter of Edith Bartlett; she knows the story of the tragic separation of the lovers but delays telling West until it is clear that they are in love, and thus the two Ediths on symbolic (and genetic) levels merge. Dr. Leete is the primary force behind West's cognitive conversion. Edith Leete's nurturing sympathies are the primary forces behind his emotional and psychological conversion process, which is often plagued by severe bouts of physiological (burning eyes, crying, and nausea) and psychological (split identity and guilt) suffering. Even at the conclusion of the narrative, after West has awakened from a horrible dream that placed his converted self back in 1887 (where he finds himself painfully estranged from the Bartletts and their wealthy friends), even then as he awakes and returns to the year 2000, he is tortured by a guilt that drives him to "confess . . . with tears" to Edith Leete his unworthy presence in utopia (311).

Except for a visual overview of Boston from Dr. Leete's rooftop, visits to an enormous distribution center and a public dining facility with separate family rooms, and a brief and traumatic street-level walk, West's visual confirmation of the new world is limited to the Leetes' home, where he listens to long explanations offered by Dr. Leete and to a long sermon transmitted by a respected minister. Hence, West's experience of the "outside" utopian world is almost exclusively a verbal-construct experience. Some of the key elements of this construction are the following: The evolution of utopia was natural and peaceful. Huge separate corporations gradually grew into one Great Trust, which, without revolution by the people or great antagonism from the capitalists, became an enormous people's trust—a nationalized public system of production and distribution (the industrial army) administered by ten national departments. This economic engine is the real government. There are no state governments, and Congress rarely meets. All basic issues are settled. There is little for legislators to do. Groups of three judges try the few court cases; most of the accused plead guilty. The many ranks of the industrial army (a meritocracy of skill and effort) encompass the entire labor-management force, which is headed by a president elected by the retired members of the industrial army. Economic equality is a crucial element of the new America. Everyone receives a lifelong (and quite generous) annual credit allowance (credit cards are the means of exchange; each year each citizen receives an equal allotment of the national product). After a free and excellent public education and with a few exceptions, everyone serves in the industrial army from twenty-one to forty-five. The first three years are unskilled labor positions; the rest are for further education, training, and work. Citizens choose their careers; a sliding work-hour scale (more hours for popular work, fewer for less popular) ensures an even distribution of the labor force. Exceptions to the time served include mothers (but not fathers) who opt to raise their children for several years (they still receive a full annual allotment for this essential work); those who retire as early as thirty-three at a reduced annual allotment; infrequent recalls of specific individuals up to fifty-five; and artists and writers who can support themselves if their creations attract enough buyers. (Dr. Leete does indicate several forceful restrictions: only wives and mothers can achieve the highest ranks in the women's branch of the industrial army, and any able person who refuses to serve leads a solitary, bread-and-water existence.) The retirement years are years of indulgence. This can mean travel and entertainment, but Leete stresses the freedom to pursue intellectual and spiritual interests. Actually, Rev. Barton implies that a citizen's entire life is a spiritual pursuit, in the sense that the concepts of honor, patriotism, and duty that motivate him or her to serve with excellence are fueled by a powerful identification with the human race, a profound desire to associate individual achievement with the elevation of the entire human brotherhood and sisterhood.

Today *Looking Backward* is certainly not a household term, and there is some truth to a prediction made by a *Literary World* reviewer in 1889: "The man of the year 2000 a.d. will consider its wide sale one of the curiously interesting but transitory phenomena of the last quarter of the nineteenth century" ("Philanthropic Fiction" 176). Nevertheless, editors and scholars still remember Bellamy. In *Edward Bellamy* (1988) Toby Widdicombe needed 587 pages to list and index all the studies of Bellamy through the late 1980s. For his new collection, *Revising the Legacy of Edward Bellamy* (2002), Widdicombe needed 542 more pages to gather unpublished fiction, critical comment, and bibliography. New editions of *Looking Backward* continue to appear, most recently Alex MacDonald's Broadview Press edition. Another sign of remembrance: *Looking Backward* was one of only eight American works of fiction selected as supplements to the 1998 edition of the *Heath Anthology of American Literature*. Of special relevance to this study is the abundance of documented responses to *Looking Backward* and the fundamental questions that this abundance and the book's impact raise: Why was this book so popular and so influential? What does the popularity ask/tell us about literary utopias, books and readers, and reader-response criticism and reception theory?

*Utopian Audiences* addresses significant aspects of these questions from a variety of critical viewpoints. In part 1, I offer an overview of the characteristics that make literary utopias and the documented responses to them especially worthy sites of reader-response/reception interpretations. In chapter 1, I focus on relevant characteristics of utopian texts, especially their variety and their hybrid nature. In chapter 2, I discuss the multiple forms of documented responses, including those typically associated with other forms of literature, such as reviews, interviews, autobiographical comment, websites, and reader surveys, and especially those more particularly associated with utopian literature: fictional "answers," behavioral interpretations (communes and reform movements), and illustrators' imaginings. Chapter 2 concludes with a call for making readers integral elements in the definition of literary utopias, whether the definitions stress a traditional descriptive approach (What is a utopia?) or a poststructuralist process viewpoint (What does a utopia do?).

Chapters 3 through 9 focus on responses to late nineteenth- and early twentieth-century utopian literature, especially Bellamy's *Looking Backward*. I begin with broad cultural and historical constructions of Bellamy's readers and conclude with analyses of a specific sample of 733 "real" late twentieth-century readers. Chapter 3 surveys forces that prepared late nineteenth-century readers to perceive utopian literature as a meaningful guide to the realities and potentialities of past and present American experience. The forces examined include particular historical events; modes of perception (especially seeing in contrasts); attitudes about large-scale organization; broad reform, economic, and technological developments; shared intellectual and literary traditions and value systems; and strongly held beliefs about books and reading. Chapter 4 examines in greater detail the specific relationships between knowledge of one popular fictional genre (the sentimental or domestic novel) and nineteenth-century readers' ability to transform the estranged regions of utopia into places as familiar as their homes, while simultaneously altering their perceptions of those homes. In particular I emphasize the impact of the narrative structure and its invitations to experience constructive guilt; the domestic settings that create sometimes reassuring, sometimes disruptive overlying images of the familiar and unfamiliar; the implications of offering a slightly modified sentimental heroine as the primary dramatization of the utopian woman; and the potential appeal of an androgynous first-person utopian narrator.

Chapter 5 offers a transition from the construction of culture- and text-based models of reading processes to interpretations of documented historical readings. The focus of the chapter—the relationship between utopia and stasis—raises fundamental questions about utopianism and responses to utopias. Does utopia imply/mandate changelessness? Can any static vision be appropriate for modern societies? Is a preference for dynamism a reflection of privilege—a life so secure that stability becomes a bore? Since readers are changing in the very act of reading, is it even possible to imagine, write, or communicate a static utopia? I examine the issue of stasis from the viewpoints of two contrasting "ideal" readers and my reconstruction of the first "real" reader of *Looking Backward*. The first construction is a traditional "content" reader who sees the text as fixed and perceives meaning as "intrinsic and objective, something to be extracted from the text" (Steig 23–24). The second is a reader implied by the connections and indeterminacies between overlapping present-future images and between the fictional readers Julian West addresses and Bellamy's contemporary readers. The third is my reconstruction of the first reader of *Looking Backward*, Edward Bellamy, based on his published comments about the composition process, his revisions for the second edition, and his "rereadings" in the form of articles, comments, and the fictional sequel *Equality* (1897). Each construction or reconstruction defines significant responses to the crucial utopian dialogue between stasis and dynamism.

Chapters 6 through 9 concentrate on the documented responses of late nineteenth- and late twentieth-century readers. Chapter 6 examines the strategies of almost one hundred professional readers—reviewers—writing more than one hundred years ago. Although their reviews were certainly not representative of the population (I could identify only a few women and no "minority" reviewers), their reviews reached thousands of readers in different socioeconomic classes and of widely varying political, economic, and religious orientations. Their constructions of model readers of literary utopias and their adopted personae of urgently needed guides to reading utopias reflect the assumptions of many late nineteenth-century readers about the potential power of utopian texts to alter, constructively or destructively, personal perceptions, individual behavior, and the nation's future.

I concentrate on the written and, in some cases, spoken responses of 733 late twentieth-century readers in chapters 7, 8, and 9. In terms of gender, ethnic representation, and socioeconomic and regional distribution, this group of readers is much more representative of the American population than the nineteenth-century reviewers were—much more but still not truly representative. Despite the presence of high school readers, a significant number of thirties-plus college students, a middle-to-retirement-age women's reading group, and a California retirement community, the sample was primarily college students in their twenties. The sample was, nevertheless, large enough and diverse enough to allow tentative speculation about the nineteenth-century language and conventions that are accessible and inaccessible to modern readers, the types of personal experiences that incline readers toward empathetic reactions to utopian narratives, the impact of the hybrid nature of utopian texts upon the variety of the responses, and the hierarchy of transformational associations that readers use to make a hundred-year-old utopia their personal utopia. The more than 3,100 transformational associations described also reflect how the readers shaped Bellamy's utopian visions of religion, women, equality, and the concept of utopia, especially how reading a utopia relates to self-perceptions and national identity.

The afterword covers a story that somehow eluded French newspapers. In April 2000, there was a secret preview of the magnificent *Utopie* exhibit held at the Bibliothèque nationale de France in Paris. Julian West and many of his fictional colleagues who had visited utopia attended, as did all the readers discussed in this book: the textual and cultural constructs, the first readers (the authors), the reviewers, the illustrators, the critics, the scholars, and the 733 students, reading group members, and retirement community residents. The polyvocality of the assembly verged on cacophony. The disagreements underline the importance of the personal, literary, cultural, and historical forces discussed in the book that shape reading experiences. The agreements point toward consistent appeals of utopian invitations that cut across these shaping forces.

One aspect of my afterword is not fictional. I draw upon the previous chapters and the responses of readers as different as Bellamy's living descendants, Japanese students, rural Texans, and long-deceased book reviewers to reaffirm my belief that any interpretation of utopia that fails to stress how readers have or can potentially transform the invitations of utopian literature is at best a partial story. We can never "get" the whole story of utopia. If, however, we make conscious attempts to include the reader in all our discussions of utopian literature, we may understand more about how utopia gets to us and how we reshape its nowhere dimensions to suit our needs.

# Part One

*Placing Readers at the
Forefront of Nowhere*

# The Nature of Utopian Invitations

# One

Part 1 of *Utopian Audiences* takes the form of a promotional catalogue—an inventory of reasons and examples designed to portray utopian literature as an inviting arena for reader-response theory and criticism. In this chapter I offer a selective overview of the nature of utopian literature, emphasizing characteristics particularly relevant to potential and actual responses of readers. Specifically, I examine the implications for reader-response criticism of the great number and variety of literary utopias and of the hybrid nature of most utopias. In chapter 2, I focus on the numerous forms of documented responses to literary utopias, stressing the textual and visual expressions that are especially associated with utopian literature. I conclude chapter 2 by arguing that concepts of readers should be integrated into the fabric of both traditional descriptive and poststructuralist process definitions of utopian literature.

As some of the latter brief subsections of Book Two of More's *Utopia* demonstrate, there are disadvantages to overview catalogues. Catalogues rarely devote enough space to each topic covered. Articles and even book-length studies could be and in some cases have been devoted to the areas I discuss. I hope, however, that my overviews will offer enough detail and sufficient breadth to suggest why the reader should be elevated in the study of utopian literature.

## Utopian Diversities

There is no contesting the abundance of literary utopias, though there is much debate about how to define them. At the conclusion of chapter 2, I will focus on the definition issue. For the purposes of these opening comments, my working definition is a fairly detailed narrative description of an imaginary culture—a fiction that invites readers to experience vicariously an alternative reality that critiques theirs by opening cognitive and affective spaces that encourage readers to perceive the realities and potentialities of their culture in new ways. If the author or reader perceive the alternative imaginary culture as being significantly better than the "present," then the work is a eutopia or, in the more popular usage, a utopia; if significantly worse, it is a dystopia.[1] In this book the focus is on [e]utopias.

Not all of the 5,621 English titles in Lyman Tower Sargent's computerized listing and published bibliographies conform to this definition. The same can be said of the extensive international bibliographies compiled by Glenn Negley and Michael Winter, as well as Arthur O. Lewis's wonderfully useful and fully annotated *Utopian Literature in the Pennsylvania State University Libraries* (1984).[2] But regardless of which definition a bibliographer uses, utopographers agree that thousands of these texts have been written and that they are distinguished by a great variety and by a fascinating mix of literary genres.

Why are the diversity and the hybrid natures of the texts relevant to reader-response criticism? They are not if we adopt a simplistic notion of subjectivist criticism that eliminates any significant role for the text in the reader's creation of meaning or if we adopt a simplistic notion of the projection of identity themes that dominate response. But it is a disservice to both David Bleich's subjectivist criticism and Norman Holland's concepts of identity themes to eradicate the significance of the nature of the text. Furthermore, in this book, despite its eclecticism, I do advocate an interactive model of reading, though as chapters 6 through 10 make clear, the ways readers transform utopian texts have (or theoretically would have) astounded and even disturbed utopian authors. Since I do assume that the characteristics of the textual invitations are significant, it is highly relevant to highlight the variety and hybrid natures of utopias. The former suggests the possibility of studies that would rest on a valid basis of comparison (responses to imaginary better worlds) while exploring the degrees of different responses to differing utopias. As discussed in chapter 8, the latter suggests possibilities for comparing responses to hybrid utopian texts and nonutopian texts that conform more precisely to established generic conventions.

To students of utopian literature the diversity of literary utopias is taken for granted. Unfortunately, those outside the field may have been misguided by the stereotypical image of utopias as the monolithic and static authoritarian alternatives so effectively attacked in numerous twentieth-century dystopias, most notably those written by Zamiatin, Huxley, and Orwell. Even a brief glance at four of the most frequently commented-upon issues discussed in documented responses—socioeconomic organization, religion, industrial and technological development, and the role of women—reveals an impressive diversity.[3]

It is true that most of the utopias and many of the most influential utopias—those authored by Plato, More, Cabet, and Bellamy, for instance—emphasize a collectivist, even socialistic socioeconomic organization. But as Sargent, Peter Fitting, and others have demonstrated,[4] there is a long tradition of individualist and capitalistic utopias extending back at least to Aristophanes' play *Ecclesiazusae* (produced in 392 B.C.), which criticizes Plato's collectivism, and extending up through nineteenth- and twentieth-century utopias that advocate individualism (James Fenimore Cooper's *The Crater* [1847] and Ayn Rand's *Atlas Shrugged* [1957] and includes direct responses to socialistic utopias (notably the many fictional critiques of Bellamy's *Looking Backward*), as well as utopias written by well-known entrepreneurs, in particular, John Jacob Astor (*A Journey in Other Worlds* [1894]) and H. L. Hunt (*Alpaca* [1960]).

Many of the best-known utopias of Western civilization either imply a foundation of Christian beliefs, as does More's *Utopia* (1516), or explicitly associate their utopias with Christianity, as illustrated by traditional Christian utopias such as Andreä's *Christianopolis* (1619) and utopias that integrate Christian and secular beliefs—works as different as Campanella's *City of the Sun* (1623) and B. F. Skinner's *Walden Two* (1948), whose guide, Frazier, compares positive reinforcement to Jesus' command to love thine enemies. But there are also significant utopias that draw upon non-Christian religions: Theodor Herzl's *Altneuland* (1902), which built upon Herzl's earlier book *The Jewish State* (1896), played an important role in the establishment of the Zionist movement and the nation of Israel. Tao

Yuanming's fourth-century "Record of the Peach Blossom Source" and Liu
Shilong and Huang Zhouxing's seventeenth-century accounts of idealistic,
fictive gardens reflect Confucianism and other Far Eastern religions,[5] and
Huxley's *Island* (1962) is grounded in Tantric Buddhism. Moreover, many
utopian authors have promoted idealized or more realistic depictions of
Native American belief systems. The latter include Marge Piercy's *Woman
on the Edge of Time* (1976) and Ursula K. Le Guin's *Always Coming Home*
(1985).

At least since Bacon's *New Atlantis* (1627), the ties between technological development and utopian ideals have been firmly established. But
even if we ignore the hundreds of antitechnology dystopias, there is a
substantial body of utopias that are highly critical of technological development. Samuel Butler's *Erewhon* (1872) is a well-known instance of
an antitechnology utopian satire; Austin Tappan Wright's *Islandia* (1942) is
a prime example of an agrarian, antitechnological utopia. There is also a
substantial body of utopias that argue for carefully controlled (often be-
hind-the-scenes) use of technology, as in William Morris's *News from
Nowhere* (1891), Piercy's *Woman on the Edge of Time*, and Le Guin's *Always
Coming Home*.

Even readers with a slight acquaintance with utopian literature should
know that the depiction of women can range from virtual invisibility or
definitions limited to reproductive capacities, as in Plutarch's idealized depiction of the Spartans, to various feminist depictions ranging historically
from Margaret Cavendish's seventeenth-century writings, to the utopias
envisioned by Charlotte Perkins Gilman in the late nineteenth and early
twentieth centuries and the influential feminist utopias of the 1970s and
1980s, to portraits of androgyny as subdued as the feminine characteristics
of Bellamy's Julian West, as ambiguous as the illustrations of the main guide
in John Uri Lloyd's *Etidorhpa* [*Aphrodite* backwards] (1895), and as explicit
as the biological cycles of the hermaphrodite characters in Le Guin's *The Left
Hand of Darkness* (1969).

Of course, the diversity of utopian literature is not limited to differing
positions advocated in relation to significant issues. Most utopias take
the form of fictional prose narratives, but, routinely, utopian bibliographies
include some drama, poetry, and speculative essays. Furthermore, the implied attitude of the author about the feasibility and/or desirability of

making nowhere somewhere can become a crucial factor in the interaction between reader and utopian text. Again there is great variety.

At one extreme there is the utopian narrative as detailed blueprint just waiting to be applied. In *Common-wealth of Oceana* (1656) James Harrington's meticulous creation of alternative political systems influenced the writers of American colonial constitutions and the United States Constitution. King Camp Gillette (inventor of the safety razor) in *Human Drift* (1994), *"World Corporation"* (1910), and *The People's Corporation* (1924) offered detailed written plans, illustrations, and stock certificates that would help promote the economic and demographic unification of America (the population would move near Niagara Falls). In *The Harrad Experiment* (1966, 1990), *Proposition 31* (1968), *The Premar Experiments* (1975), and other novels that often come complete with detailed bibliographies, Robert Rimmer outlined his step-by-step processes for achieving sexual, intellectual, and social better worlds.

Satirists, as well known as Jonathan Swift (*Gulliver's Travels,* 1726) and as obscure as Ryunosuke Akutagawa (*Kappa,* 1927), offer a view of utopia radically different from the blueprint creators by alternately criticizing existent cultures and implying better worlds with their fantastic settings and creatures. Somewhere in between the extremes of blueprint and satire are the ambivalent and ambiguous utopias. Mark Twain's *Connecticut Yankee* (1889) is a paradigm of the former. Twain utilized the satirist's technique of displacement, in this case to King Arthur's England. From this vantage point he could use Hank Morgan's voice to undermine romantic illusions of the past and to promote an idealized and Americanized vision of a democratic and technologically advanced utopia. But as he worked out the implications of transforming feudal England (and struggled with financial and other personal problems), the burlesque and utopianism turned to bitter and horrid dystopian fantasies of exploded, drowned, and electrocuted knights, body counts, darkness, and loneliness. *Connecticut Yankee* remains one of the most ebullient and tortured expressions of American utopianism.

During the 1980s, the ambiguous or critical utopias attracted much attention and at least one book-length study (Tom Moylan's *Demand the Impossible,* 1986). The focus was on contemporary works by Le Guin, Piercy, Joanna Russ, and Samuel R. Delany; Kim Stanley Robinson is a more recent addition to the list. The protagonists, narrators, and authorial voices of these works often maintain a complex polyvocal dialogic that alternately and sometimes simultaneously critiques the present, sincerely hopes for a better world, and questions our ability to articulate or even imagine such a world. These works have impressive predecessors: Fyodor Dostoyevsky's *Notes from Underground* (1864), Nathaniel Hawthorne's *The Blithedale Romance* (1852), H. G. Wells's, *A Modern Utopia* (1905), and, of course, More's *Utopia,* whose concluding paragraph could stand as a motto for the ambiguous utopia: "Meanwhile though he [Raphael Hythloday] is a man of unquestioned learning, and highly experienced in the ways of the world, I cannot agree with everything he said. Yet I confess there are many things in the Commonwealth of Utopia which I wish our own country would imitate—though I don't really expect it will" (91).

In *Scraps of Untainted Sky* (2000) Tom Moylan has identified a recent variant of the critical utopia, the critical dystopia. Focusing on works by Kim Stanley Robinson (*The Gold Coast,* 1988), Octavia Butler (*The Parable of the Sower,* 1993, and *The Parable of the Talents,* 1998), and Marge Piercy (*He, She, and It,* 1991), he defines a form of utopian literature that, like the classic dystopias, is firmly grounded in extrapolations of disturbing trends in the present that could lead to frightening developments in the future. But unlike the earlier dystopias, these are more self-reflexive and imply or even represent signs of hope, for example, the ability of a countermovement to thwart an international corporate power play near the conclusion of *He, She, and It.* Other works, not typically discussed within the context of utopian literature and not discussed by Moylan, also exhibit traits of the critical dystopia—for example, Gerald Vizenor's *Bearheart* (1978, 1990) and Leslie Marmon Silko's *Almanac of the Dead* (1991) offer self-reflexive, near-future, nightmarish worlds that conclude with hopeful signs. Like the works Moylan examines, they communicate a "scrappy utopian pessimism" (160).

## Variegated Hybrids

The reviewers analyzed in chapter 6 and the late twentieth-century readers discussed in chapters 7 through 9 did indeed respond to key "issue positions" articulated by utopian guides and their visitor about socioeconomic critiques and models, religion, industrial-technological development, and women's roles, and they also responded to the implications of

Bellamy's narrative and his authorial voice (in the postscript) that place him closer to the Harrington-Gillette-Rimmer blueprint utopia than to the distancing of satire, the fracture of ambivalence, or the meta-critical gaze of critical utopias and critical dystopias. As suggested in chapters 4, 6, and 8, they also responded to a characteristic of utopian literature that has fascinated and frustrated readers for centuries—its hybrid nature. In passing or in greater detail reviewers, scholars, and utopian authors often write of the "mixing of genres in many literary utopias" (Fitting, "Concept of Utopia" 11) or, more specifically, the combinations of fable and manifesto (Pfaelzer, *Utopian Novel* 18). In a "Note to the Reader" of *A Modern Utopia,* the authorial voice of H. G. Wells offers one of the most convincing descriptions of the hybrid nature of the literary utopia: "I am aiming throughout at a sort of shot-silk texture between philosophical discussion on the one hand and imaginative narrative on the other" (xxxii).

From century to century, culture to culture, reader to reader, the nature and meanings of this shot-silk mix will of course change. There are, nonetheless, recurrent patterns to the texture. At the core of the "philosophical discussion" mixture are the dialogue and the various normative discourse forms. The former invites the reader to vicariously experience utopia step-by-step. The author hopes to keep a step ahead of the reader by anticipating his or her doubts and objections as the discussions unfold. Thus a typical utopian text stages "an implicit debate with the objections and ideologies and political prejudices of its readers (Fitting, "Concept of Utopia" 15). The most frequently cited paradigms for the utopian dialogue are the exchanges in Plato's *Republic* and More's *Utopia,* but the familiar figures of visitor(s), guide(s), and foil(s) occur in varied configurations. More's Hythloday combines visitor, guide, and, in Book Two, narrator roles. More's persona is a secondhand visitor who (like the reader) experiences Utopia through Hythloday's words. Sometimes the foil is a character (Skinner's Professor Castle); sometimes the foil is a disembodied implication (in *Looking Backward,* Leete's references to past Americans who failed to see the natural evolution of Nationalism). The normative discourse forms are grounded in oral (sermons, speeches) and nonfictional written forms (treatises, manifestos, petitions, proclamations, legal documents). Striking examples of the former include Rev. Barton's sermon in *Looking Backward* and the thirty-eight-page speech by John Galt in *Atlas Shrugged.* The oral-derived forms can invite strong affective responses for readers moved by sermons and speeches; part of their vicarious utopian experience is "hearing" utopia. Or these sections can seem distant and boring, especially to readers, like the late twentieth-century readers presented in chapter 7, who are not accustomed to hearing or being moved by sermons or speeches. A striking example of the written normative discourse form noted by Fitting is the constitution appended to H. L. Hunt's *Alpaca Revisited* (1967) ("Concept of Utopia" 11). Such "documents" can add verisimilitude to an imaginary world or become tedious, pretentious, or ridiculous obstacles to the reader's ability to enter the utopian worldview.

At the core of the "imaginative narrative" are at least three stories: various strategies that facilitate displacement, estrangement, and defamiliarization; the conversion dramas; and the romance narrative structures. The most common forms of displacement are travel adventures in space or time. The former date back at least to Hellenistic journey "novels" (Manuel and Manuel 1); the latter are typically traced back to Louis Sébastien Mercier's *L'an deux mille quatre cent quarante* (1771), though Lise Leibacher-Ouvrard has called attention to an earlier example, Jacques Guttin's *Epigone, histoire du siècle futur* (1659) (Leibacher-Ouvard). Some narratives combine space and time displacement and mix degrees of real and imaginary times and places, as in the cases of Hank Morgan's removal to sixth-century England in *Connecticut Yankee* and Connie's transference to Mattapoisette, 2137 A.D. in *Woman on the Edge of Time*. Darko Suvin would link these displacements to "cognitive estrangement"; Louis Marin would emphasize spatial play. From either critical perspective the removals invite readers to distance themselves from familiar worldviews. They create openings; opportunities for (silent readerly) dialoguing with the guides, visitors, and foils; invitations to imaging and thought experiments.

The conversion dramas and romantic narrative structures invite empathetic reading experiences. In the typical utopian plot the displaced visitor to utopia is closer (in terms of worldview and experience) to the readers than to any other character. (Obviously, there are many variations. In More's *Utopia,* for example, the persona "More" listens and discusses rather than visits, and the readers are not permitted to witness the actual guide-visitor dynamic, since Hythloday is a returned, and mostly converted, visitor/narrator.) The visitor is frequently the reader surrogate; both are experiencing strange new worlds. The fundamental emotional and psychological drama of most utopias that offer extended portrayals of the visitor is, Will he or she convert to the utopian worldview? In some instances this dramatic question is explicitly answered, as when Professor Burris abandons his university life and makes his pilgrimage back to Walden Two. In other utopias the final commitments are more obscure. In either case the implied reading dynamic is clear. If readers allow visitors to be their surrogates, and if those visitors begin to doubt their self-concepts and worldviews and to desire alternative selves and worlds, then it is more likely that the readers will allow themselves to be fellow travelers on the route toward conversion, even though this traveling will most likely be temporary and qualified.

The degree to which readers identify with the visitor's conversion drama can be strongly affected by the presence of a romantic narrative, an element that became an important part of utopian literature during the nineteenth century. (These effects will be discussed in chapters 3 and 8.) A romantic plot can offer readers welcome relief from dialogues and speeches and enhance the humanization of otherwise pasteboard characters. Depending upon a reader's viewpoint, romances can become convincing, contrived, or contradictory testing grounds for gender issues in utopias as suggested by Piercy's *Woman on the Edge of Time* (Connie's attraction to Bee), Gilman's *Herland* (the triple marriage), and Bellamy's *Looking Backward* (West's love for and dependency upon Edith).[6]

Many other forms of expository, argumentative, and narrative discourses "move in between" the utopian realms of "philosophical discussion" and "imaginative narrative"—notably the realism of exposé, the cultural anthropology of utopian daily life, and the framing discourses that comment on the internal discussions and narratives. Exposés of the horrors of the present against which the wonders of utopia are compared can approach the vividness of muckraking realism. This tactic may shock some readers into desiring a different world or risk angering others fond of the present who would perceive the descriptions not as realism, but as gross distortions.

To answer the horrors of the present, utopists need to create their imaginary better world with the descriptive discourse of "touches of prosaic detail," to borrow Wells's words (*Scientific Romances* viii). The quality of these descriptions ranges from the chaotic cataloguing of the deservedly obscure *Milltillionaire* (1895) by Albert Waldo Howard and *Sub-Coelum* (1893) by Addison Peale Russell to the highly sophisticated fictionalized cultural anthropology of Le Guin's *Always Coming Home*. Depending on the quality of the descriptions and the ability of readers to visualize fictional environments, the detailed descriptive discourse can enhance the readers' ability to experience the utopias vicariously, bore them, or confuse them. There is, nevertheless, one constant. As the narrator of Le Guin's "The Ones Who Walk Away from Omelas" openly admits, no writer can satisfy the readers' desire for all the details they need to construct convincing images of entire alternative cultures. There are always enormous indeterminacies or gaps, to use Iser's terms, that leave ample room for the readers' affirmative and/or critical projections and for multiple questions.

The verbal frames that house all the various utopian discourses can take the form of narrative explanations of mysteriously discovered manuscripts, as in Twain's *Connecticut Yankee;* explicit guidelines about how to interpret the text, as in Bellamy's postscript to the second edition of *Looking Backward;* twists in character development, as in Miles Coverdale's revealing-obscuring confession that "I-I myself-was in love-with-Priscilla!" in Hawthorne's *Blithedale Romance* (251); glimpses of alternatives to the primary alternative world couched in footnotes, as in the notes describing a eutopia beyond the dystopia of Jack London's *The Iron Heel* (1907); complex introductions to historical and cultural contexts as in Book One of More's *Utopia;* or complex fictional or nonfictional meta-comments before, after, or throughout the texts, as in Wells's *A Modern Utopia,* Samuel R. Delany's *Triton* (1976), or Le Guin's *Always Coming Home.* The frames can invite rather straightforward relationships between authorial voice and reader or introduce ambiguous, even contradictory, relations, as in these introductory comments in Nikolai G. Chernyshevsky's *What Is to Be Done?* (1863): "I am angry at you because you are so wicked to people, and the people are, after all, you. But you are wicked from a certain mental impotence, and so while reviling you, I am obliged to help you" (qt. in Morson 100).

The frames have the potential to define how closely or how distantly readers position themselves to or from the utopian text, and a changed frame may create a different book. For instance, B. F. Skinner's "Walden Two Revisited," a long introduction to the 1976 edition of *Walden Two,* invites readers to experience utopia much more as a blueprint projection than as the thought experiment presented in the unintroduced 1948 edition. Gary Saul Morson offers an even more striking example. He argues that over the past four centuries there may have been so much disagreement about More's *Utopia* because readers "may *literally* have read different works." In part he is referring to the impact of different translations, but he also stresses the fact that More supervised the publication of three editions, "each of which contained different framing material." He goes on to note that approximately one-fifth of the version of *Utopia* in the Yale Complete Works edition is framing material, the inclusion or deletion of which in previous editions could significantly alter how readers approached Hythloday's accounts and More's persona's responses (164–66).

Whether particular readers perceive the hybrid nature of utopian literature as a "loose and baggy monster" cacophony (Morson 176) or a compelling symphony depends upon a complex network of personal, literary, and cultural variables. Despite the impossibility of predicting how specific readers will respond to the mix, there is a constant to be taken from the mixing. Such a conglomerate literature is a fascinating site for examining how readers create meanings and experience feelings, especially since some of the key elements of the mix pose contradictions. Morson defines utopian literature as a primary example of "threshold art"—"works designed to be interpreted according to contradictory sets of conventions" (x). The most obvious contradictions are reflected by the tensions between the genres utilized by utopists that demand an outrageous degree of "willing suspension of disbelief" (miraculous time and space travel to nowhere, radically reformed humans, etc.) and the genres that present themselves as eminently, even self-evidently believable (the "nonfictional," "factual" descriptions, critiques, arguments). How or why do readers perceive these different strains of language as contradictory, complementary, or puzzling? Does reading this type of hybrid text draw on a greater variety of reading interactions than does reading texts that are more easily defined within traditional conventions? Has the mix of conventions existed long enough so that the mix itself is perceived by readers as conventional? In chapters 4, 6, and 7, I will address specific aspects of these questions with regard to Bellamy's *Looking Backward*. This is obviously a small response to a large set of questions. My intent in this opening chapter is not to promise conclusive resolutions to the questions but to emphasize that literary utopias offer abundant possibilities for investigating reading processes.

# TWO

## Documenting, Visualizing, and Defining Utopian Reception

The number, variety, and hybrid nature of literary utopias make them excellent testing grounds for reader-response critics who construct models of readers and reading processes from close examinations of texts. Utopian literature should also be inviting to reception theorists, cultural and social critics, and critics who emphasize subjective responses. Because of their controversial nature and the tremendous popularity and influence of several of the utopias, there is an enormous body of documented readings recorded in an impressive variety of written, behavioral (communities and movements), and visual forms. As I argue in chapters 5 through 10, these readings can be used to help us understand which historical, cultural, literary, and personal forces enable readers to or deter them from using utopias as temporary escape routes, as disturbing or hopeful catalysts for perceptual changes, and even as inspiring guides to individual and social change. These understandings should in turn enhance our comprehension of reading processes in general and of readings of didactic literature in particular. The abundance of documented responses should also remind utopographers to include discussion of potential and actual responses in any attempt to define utopian literature. I turn to this issue at the conclusion of the chapter.

## Textual Audiences

Many of the documented utopian responses are similar to documented reactions to other forms of literature, and most were written by "professional
readers"—reviewers, authors, and editors. Reviews of popular works are
abundant. Toby Widdicombe has discovered more than a hundred reviews
of Bellamy's works, most of them on *Looking Backward* ("Edward Bellamy's
Utopian Vision"). Reviews of the popular works often appeared in major
magazines. The most extreme censure of *Walden Two,* for example, appeared in an anonymous *Life Magazine* review. The reviewer, John K.
Jessup, asserted that the only freedom in Skinner's utopia was the freedom
of "Pavlovian dogs" and that *Walden Two* was a "menace," a "slur upon a
name [Walden]," and "a corruption of an impulse [utopian idealism]" (qt.
in Skinner, *Shaping of a Behaviorist* 247–48). This widely read review
helped to shape the negative tone of much of the reception among hu-
manists. There were also reviews of obscure works in important journals,
especially during the late nineteenth century in America. For example,
the *Unitarian Review* covered *An Experiment in Marriage* (1889), written
by Bellamy's brother Charles; the *Literary World* reviewed Arthur Vinton's
*Looking Further Backward* (1890), Amos Fiske's *Beyond the Bourn* (1891),
and many other utopias; the *New York Times* reviewed J. W. Roberts's
*Looking Within* (1893).[1] Extended reviews—in the forms of prefaces, introductions, afterwords, and postscripts—often appear as important parts
of the reading experience of well-known utopias, for example, in the cases
of Bellamy's postscript to *Looking Backward* and his son Paul's introduction
to the 1945 World Publishing Company edition.

The types of documented responses to reading studies examined in
recent collections such as James Machor's *Readers in History* (1993),
Michele Moylan and Lane Stile's *Reading Books* (1996), James P. Danky
and Wayne A. Wiegand's *Print Culture in a Diverse America* (1998), and
Barbara Ryan and Amy M. Thomas's *Reading Acts* (2002) are, of course,
available to students of utopia. There are interviews recording the responses of famous authors: Twain thought the first edition of *Looking
Backward* "was about as scrofulous-looking and mangy a volume as I have
set eyes on," but he knew and liked Bellamy and recognized the book's
status as a "new Gospel" (qt. in Budd 76). Comments in autobiographies
reveal how reading utopias changed lives. Charles H. Kerr, the influential
Chicago publisher of socialist works, recalled being "charmed" by *Looking*

*Backward* (qt. in Rosemont 166); Bella Visono Dodd, an Italian immigrant who became a leader in the Communist Party, remembered that Charles Sheldon's *In His Steps* (1897) "made a profound impression on me" (qt. in Kaestle 242). There are published comments by the first readers, the authors, in the forms of the frames previously discussed, in essays and interviews, and in multiple revisions of the text; Arthur O. Lewis points to Butler's frequent revising of *Erewhon* as a prime example of this literary phenomenon (*Utopian Literature* 34). Letters, textual marking, and marginalia often express more private responses than do the reviews and interviews, and the latter two offer physical evidence of immediate responses, as in the case of Leo Tolstoy's heavy markings in the nightmare return section of *Looking Backward* (Kumar, *Utopia and Anti-Utopia* 135). Survey evaluations of scholarship and surveys of "living readers" are obvious complements to the documented responses appearing close to the utopia's publication date. The former are numerous; the latter scarce.[2] The most recent forms of written response are electronic: there are many listservs and websites related to utopia in general and to specific authors.[3] For utopias still in print or recently published, the author and reader comments at Amazon.com can offer fascinating hints, sometimes robustly biased, about readers' responses.

All of the foregoing sources of documented readings are, of course, available for most types of published literature. There are, however, at least three forms of response that are more particularly (though certainly not exclusively) associated with literary utopias: fictional responses, efforts to "act out" the text, and visual renderings of nonexistent better worlds.

It is not uncommon for the authors to answer themselves in sequels (e.g., Bellamy's *Equality* [1997], Butler's *Erewhon Revisited* [1901]), in prequels (e.g., Ernest Callenbach's *Ecotopia Emerging* [1981]), and in "answers" that offer alternatives (e.g., *Island*'s [1962], utopian answer to the dystopias of *Brave New World* [1932] and *Ape and Essence* [1948]). Most of the fictional responses, such as Mark Saxton's sequel to Wright's *Islandia* (*Isar* [1969]), have not been written by the author. I've already mentioned one of the striking examples of fictional dialogues: the many late nineteenth- and early twentieth-century responses to *Looking Backward,* including works by William Morris, William Dean Howells, and Charlotte Perkins Gilman. As Andrew Karp has observed, fictional responses to Bellamy can even be found in late nineteenth-century children's fiction, particularly in parts of

L. Frank Baum's "Oz" books and his "Mrs. Bilkins" short story (Karp 104–05, 119). Fictional responses have continued into the late twentieth century, notably Mack Reynolds's sequel to *Looking Backward, Equality* (1977) and Robert Rimmer's *Love Me Tomorrow* (1978), which he wanted to entitle *Looking Backward II.* (His publisher objected, arguing that few readers today would recognize the allusion to Bellamy.[4]) One of the most interesting derivatives of *Looking Backward* is *Edward Bellamy Writes Again* (1997), "an updated narrative on the philosophy and goals of Bellamy's writings" (Kopp, "Looking Back" 12). In his preface the author, Joseph R. Myers, suggests that he may well be a reincarnation of Bellamy.

Authors of fictional sequels hope to capitalize on the popularity or notoriety of the original work. They can piggyback their criticisms, support, or alternative ideas on the existing interest in the original work. They can also explicitly or implicitly claim that they are answering the previous utopia on its own terms, testing it by its own mixes of "philosophical discussion" and "imaginative narrative." In most cases a critical response takes the form of an extrapolation that demonstrates the dangers hidden in the original narrative or the form of an alternative setting that answers the original. Richard C. Michaelis's *Looking Further Forward* (1890), with its emphasis on the corruption and favoritism spawned by the industrial army system described in *Looking Backward,* is a good example of the former. William Morris's *News from Nowhere* (1890), with its emphasis on small communities and craftsmanship instead of Bellamy's urban setting and mass production, is a good example of the latter. Less frequently, the sequel writer focuses on psychological extrapolation. In *Young West* (1894) Rabbi Solomon Schindler supported many of Bellamy's economic and social stances. But through the eyes of Julian West's son we discover that the psychological transition for a person suddenly thrust into utopia, as his father was, can be traumatic. Schindler's fictional response was in many ways more sophisticated than the responses of most twentieth-century critics who ignore or downplay West's anguish at the conclusion of *Looking Backward.*

## Acting Out Utopia

One of the basic claims of reader-response criticism is that readers complete texts. Typically the implication of this claim is that texts do not have meanings or emotional experiences "in" them. The interactions between textual invitations and readers' responses create the "thoughts" and "feelings" of the reading experience. In the case of utopian literature, there are a significant number of striking examples demonstrating that readers can not only create but act out their interpretations, often in groups as small as an urban extended-family commune or as large as a national movement.

The relevant scholarly studies of intentional community responses can take the form of comprehensive histories, such as Carl J. Guarneri's *The Utopian Alternative: Fourierism in Nineteenth-Century America* (1991), or more specialized studies, such as Carol A. Kolmerten's *Women in Utopia: The Ideology of Gender in the American Owenite Communities* (1990), which makes excellent use of letters that document the ways women responded to how several communities acted out their interpretations of Owen's visions of utopian living. The complex history of acting out Étienne Cabet's *Voyage en Icarie* (1839) is particularly fascinating. Cabet's text itself was in part a fictional response to his reading of More's *Utopia* and Robert Owen's writings (and to personal contacts with Owen) while he was exiled from France and living in London from 1834 to 1839 (Lewis, *Utopian Literature* 35; Fogarty 22). More than 150 years of written "primary source" documentation of the responses to the acting out of Icarian egalitarian principles and regulations of daily life is available in nineteenth-century letters, journals, and community publications and the twentieth-century records and publications (including the newsletter *Reflections of Icaria*) of the National Icarian Heritage Society, the core of which is descendants of Icarian communities.

Possibly the most interesting late twentieth-century examples of acting out responses to literary utopia are the intentional communities inspired by Skinner's *Walden Two*. According to Hilke Kuhlman, during the 1960s and 1970s more than thirty communities described themselves as Walden Two–inspired, and these communes formed the early stages of today's Federation of Egalitarian Communities (2–6). And yet these communities represent very selective "readings." With the notable exception of Comunidad Los Horcones in Mexico, none of them have adopted the behaviorist child-rearing systems at the core of Skinner's imaginary community. Instead, Kuhlman argues, they followed the lead of the best-known *Walden Two* community, Twin Oaks, which emphasized particular parts of Skinner's vision, including the planner-manager governance, sharing income and work, and the labor credit system. Hence, the first communal interpretation of Skinner's text became the "real" text to which other communities responded with various adaptations. As is the case with varying responses to texts in general, the differences between the acted-out readings of members of Los Horcones and the other communal members can be, to a large degree, explained by differences in personal backgrounds: the founding members of Los Horcones had helped to operate a school for children with behavioral problems. Unlike many of the other *Walden Two* communal members, they were mainly attracted to Skinner's behavioral science, which for them constituted the foundation for a better society (Kuhlman 158).

The larger the scale of acting out a utopia, the more difficult it is to trace particular responses. There are, nevertheless, provocative opportunities. Some involve textual comparisons. For example, comparing the similarities and differences between the colonial constitutions of Pennsylvania and Massachusetts to the guidelines in Harrington's *Common-wealth of Oceana* suggests which parts of Harrington's political system received favorable and unfavorable receptions among colonial legislators (Lewis, *Utopian Literature* 80). Similar comparisons could be made on a broader scale between the concepts of Zionism and a Jewish state depicted in Herzel's *Altneuland* and the actual development of the movement and state during the twentieth century.

Considering its popularity and impact, it is not surprising that there is an abundance of primary and secondary material relating to the acting out of Bellamy's *Looking Backward.* The primary materials include writings produced by and descriptions appearing in the *Nationalist* of the California Kaweah community inspired by Bellamy's ideas; numerous articles about reform activities appearing in the *Nationalist,* the *New Nation,* and in at least eleven other magazines inspired by *Looking Backward* (Shurter, "Utopian Novel" 160–61). Secondary studies of activist reception include examinations of the attempts to implement Bellamy's ideas on an international scale by Csaba Toth in "The Transatlantic Dialogue," Francis Shor in "Ideological Matrix," and the contributors to Sylvia Bowman's *Edward Bellamy Abroad.*

Much of the attention has been focused on the activities of the American Bellamy and Nationalist Clubs. If Janice Radway and Elizabeth Long had been living in Boston during the 1890s, they might have been tempted to write group reading studies of Bellamy Clubs using the techniques developed in *Reading the Romance* and "Textual Interpretation." Though we are not fortunate enough to have such a study, we do have Everett MacNair's and Arthur Lipow's book-length analyses of American Nationalism and some interesting new research by Ronald Howe.

In "Reconsidering Edward Bellamy" Howe utilizes information from the *Nationalist* and other late nineteenth-century magazines, newspaper obituaries, biographical dictionaries, and census figures from 1890 and 1900 to offer an interesting portrait of the type of person who was moved so deeply by *Looking Backward* that he or she wanted to transform reality to conform more closely to Bellamy's imaginary world (417–32). The similarities shared by the members suggest important cultural, religious, and geographical influences that inclined particular readers to strong positive responses. For example, the religious affiliations of the Boston Nationalists were overwhelmingly Protestant, and the majority of these were "humanistic" Protestants, in particular Unitarians, Universalists, and Transcendentalists. Even though the more than 160 American Clubs extended beyond the Northeast and across the country, with good representation in the Midwest and particularly strong concentrations in California, most of the Nationalists had northeastern, especially New England, family roots. These were not poor, but also not wealthy, readers. Over 45 percent of the male leaders of the clubs were boarders or rented their homes or farms. The employment levels of the male and female leaders suggest middle- or upper-middle-class status. Many of the male leaders were either "high status white collar" (36%) or "low status white collar" (30%). Defining the socio-economic status of the women leaders is more difficult, since slightly more than half of them (56%) were not employed outside the home. Those who were employed fit the pattern of the male leaders. Forty-four percent of the Nationalist women leaders found in the 1900 census held white-collar positions. As I argue in chapter 3, these general portraits suggest that many of the religious, socioeconomic, and geographical forces that shaped how someone like Bellamy conceived of his utopia also prepared many of these readers to receive his vision.

But when he moved beyond the broad portrait, Howe discovered that there was substantial diversity among those acting out Bellamy's utopia, with the significant exception of racial diversity. Twenty percent of the Nationalist leaders were women; this figure compares favorably even with political parties today. Howe also found that there were more "blue collar" workers (21%) and farmers (12%) among the Nationalist leaders than had previously been reported, and, of course, these figures could be and probably were even higher for the general membership.[5] Furthermore, as John L. Thomas would remind us, there was significant diversity of viewpoint within the general portrait. For instance, the first Nationalist Club in Boston included reform editors, retired generals infatuated with Bellamy's industrial army, Theosophists, Christian Socialists, feminists, and self-proclaimed "cultural radicals" (Introduction 1, 20–21). The reading and post-reading processes these Nationalists used to project and activate their projections of utopia at Nationalist Club meetings and elsewhere certainly make for fascinating reception case studies.

For example, the initial published response of one of the Christian Socialists, the influential editor and novelist William Dean Howells, suggests a mixture of admiration for Bellamy's allegorical skills and attacks on inequality (Howells praised the coach analogy) and a fear that Bellamy's clever literary "tricks" and the "very charming condition of things" in his utopia could delude readers into accepting the "poison" of socialism ("Editor's Study" 154–55). Even a decade later, in his laudatory obituary for Bellamy, Howells had not been won over by Bellamy's emphasis on urban settings, advanced technology, and massive centralization of the economy. But there was enough room, enough openings, in Bellamy's utopian text to encourage Howells to accept the invitation of Bellamy's literary tricks and ethical stances and to project his own Christian, family, and village utopian visions, which eventually took the printed form of Howells's *Altrurian Romances*. Howells's angle of vision inclined him to downplay Bellamy's secular, industrialized socialism and to embrace what he perceived to be the "distinctive [family] virtue" of Bellamy's "imagination which revived throughout Christendom the faith in a millennium" ("Edward Bellamy" 254).

## Eyewitness to Utopia

Written texts, in the forms of direct responses or description of attempts to act out utopia, are the most obvious and most abundant forms of documented responses to utopian literature available to reader-response critics. Visual forms can also offer provocative insights into how readers place nowhere. Occasionally the visual cues used in attempts to direct readers take the form of the physical appearance of the book itself. In 1950 the

Limited Editions Club of New York published an edition of *Gulliver's Travels* that included a large volume for the Brobdingnag travels and a tiny one for Lilliput (Manguel 145–46). Another example comes from the nineteenth century. The margins of the first edition of Rabbi Solomon Schindler's *Young West* (1894) were pastel-colored, providing a demonstration of the beauty and medical benefits of reading in utopia (less glare from the pages).

There are also examples of literary utopias that are so dominated by visual images that, for many readers, the illustrations become the primary text. For example, in 1524 the Chinese painter Wen Zhengming created a scroll entitled "Peach Blossom Spring," inspired by Tao Qian's ancient prose poem depicting an idyllic world. A transcription of Wang Wei's eighth-century poem "Peach Blossom Spring" appears in a small space at the end of the scroll. Thus the experience of opening the scroll invites the viewer/reader to project Wen Zhengming's images into the poem. For some viewers/readers (even if they can read Chinese), the poem will be reduced to a small sidebar to the dominant images (Atkinson, "Visions").

An American husband-and-wife team created another striking example, the virtually forgotten eutopian-dystopian *Ultimo* (1930). The book originated in a cold bedroom. In the late 1920s, during a severe New England winter, John Vassos, a respected industrial designer, painter, and illustrator, dreamed of a future civilization forced by an ice age to inhabit gigantic underground cities. Life was secure, comfortable, and egalitarian, but "the very perfectness"—the "monotony" (30)—stifled the hero, who by the end of the narrative undertakes a space mission in hopes of beginning human history anew. Ruth Vassos encouraged her husband to "put it down" on paper (John Vassos, letter). The forceful illustrations of frozen landscapes and streamlined cityscapes in black, white, and grays were completed first. Then Ruth Vassos wrote brief corresponding narrative commentaries that the book designer shaped into small justified blocks (typically eight lines) facing the full-page illustrations. Because the text regularly "interrupts" the illustrations, John Vassos's images do not dominate the viewers'/readers' responses to the extent that Wen Zhengming's images do. Still, unless a reader is especially unreceptive to visual imagery, it is likely that the illustrations, not the text, will dominate his or her reaction to Vassos's underground world.

Though the physical appearance and visual images may dominate

readers' responses to a few literary utopias, the inclusion of a few illustrations is a more typical visual approach to shaping the gaze of utopian
reading—typical and ironically persistent. As Laurent Gervereau has
noted, utopia "has first and foremost been textual. It is told, not seen; it
is 'Nowhere.' . . . And yet from very early on, utopian works have been
complemented by illustrations" (357). Illustrations are, of course, found
in practically all forms of literature, and the illustrators of literary utopias
experience many of the same opportunities and problems as the illustrators of science fiction, fantasy, or fantastic works as unclassifiable as *Codex
Seraphinianus* (1981), which Luigi Serafini constructed out of invented
words and images. Illustrators of utopias do, nonetheless, face challenges
particular to the genre: they must depict a world that does not exist in the
readers' reality; one that is presumed to be better than the readers' world;
and yet one that is believable enough to move readers to reevaluate the realities and potentialities of their world.

Several English and architecture professors have asked their students
to take on these challenges, and the results constitute interesting forms
of reader response.[6] For example, at Georgia Institute of Technology and
Mississippi State University, W. A. McClung challenged students to
render designs for More's Utopian buildings (9–10), and at SUNY Buffalo
one of Lynda H. Schneekloth's students, Jo-Anne Charron, focused on
Piercy's *Woman on the Edge of Time*. She had a strong negative reaction
to the impersonality of Piercy's concept of out-of-womb birth. Her visual
response was to add a ritual space to Piercy's no place. She transformed
Piercy's "brooder" into an Ectogenic Birth Center that included an area
where "parents" could perform rituals that celebrate "the birthing of a new
life" and establish personal bonds between adults and fetus (Schneekloth
19–20). Charron's drawing is a striking example of how a reader can transform a utopian text, combining elements of the text with her personal notions of the importance of ritual.

Many of the illustrations that appear in literary utopias reflect such
transformations. Of the tens of thousands of illustrations relevant to the
reception of utopian literature, I will discuss a selection that suggests four
of the many different ways to approach the relationships between readers
and visual representations: how changes in illustrations from edition to
edition can potentially transform a utopian vision; how an illustrator can
attempt to "rewrite" a utopia gone out of control; how illustrations can

attempt to update and humanize a utopia; and how illustrations can suggest the complexities of the authors' responses to their sources and can reveal insights about their identities.

It is not surprising that the cover of the journal *Utopian Studies* displays the first (1516) version of a map of More's *Utopia*. The most familiar images associated with utopia are maps of the island of Utopia that appear in various editions of More's *Utopia*. I do not need to belabor the importance of these illustrations, since they have already received ample attention, especially in the excellent "Mapping of Utopia" subsection of Marina Leslie's *Renaissance Utopias and the Problem of History* (1998: 33–53). But even if we concentrate briefly on one small section of three of the map versions, we can imagine the potential effects of the changes, from edition to edition, especially if the map appears early in the reading experience.

The foregrounds of the two best-known versions invite different readings. In the anonymous woodcut of the first edition (1516), the ship faces right and is accompanied by a smaller boat facing left toward the ship (fig. 1). In the more elaborate third edition (1518), created by Ambrosius Holbein, the ship faces left; the boat, right (fig. 2). Leslie offers several provocative interpretations of the reversal (38, 40); I would add another possibility that supports her arguments. The reversal creates a frame for and a complement to the diagonal lines (the garlands) pointing toward what is missing in the 1516 version—two figures. Even the tiny figure in the boat faces these figures. One of the figures speaks using his extended arm and pointing finger (to the map) to delineate his words. The other faces the speaker, has his back to the map, and watches/listens. The visual highlighting of these representations of Hythloday and More's persona (and the further addition of a third figure in the lower right, another listener, whose military attire suggests that he is probably not the other listener in the book, Peter Giles), changes the view of the book from being "about" a (fantasy) place to a drama of the teller-listener narrative, "the staging of the rhetorical moment" (Leslie 42–43).

In a much later edition not discussed by Leslie—*Insul Utopia*, published in 1704 (Frankfurt am Main)—the two figures in the lower left are replaced by a representation of a Native American posing behind a corner sign labeled "Utopia" (fig. 3). Again the figure is the focal point, but now the emphasis is not on the drama of narrative performance. Instead the figure invites connections: More's Enlightenment vision with New World

Figure 1. *"Vtopiae Insvlae Figvra," from Thomas More,* Utopia *(Louvain, 1516).*

*Figure 2. Ambrosius Holbein, "Vtopiae Insvlae Tabvla," from Thomas More, Utopia (Basel, 1518).*

*Figure 3. "Vtopia," from Thomas More, . . . Insul Utopia (Frankfurt am Main, 1704).*

locales and peoples, a relationship that Arthur E. Morgan argued for in *Nowhere Was Somewhere* (1946).

The degree to which these three maps influence particular readers will of course depend upon how much they allow illustrations to guide their reading. The three do, nonetheless, signal three related yet different types of utopian readings: an unmediated, vicarious visit to an imaginary world that invites a willing suspension of disbelief with a mapping; a mediated visit that elevates the position of the teller and listener(s) (which by implication puts the reader/listener in the utopian picture); and a visit that associates nowhere with real places and people (though they are "exotic" and distant from European readers). One of the most recent mappings of Utopia, James Cook's illustration for the expanded edition of Alberto Manguel and Gianni Guadalupi's *Dictionary of Imaginary Places* (2000), makes realistic linkages even more explicit. Cook labels the water "Atlantic Ocean" and the land adjacent to the island, "South America" (673). The unmediated fantasy of 1516 has evolved into a South American road map. If they allowed the various maps of Utopia to be their guides, the sixteenth-, eighteenth-, and twentieth-century readers would indeed be viewing different utopian books.

The contrasts between the text and the illustrations in the closing chapters of the first edition of *Connecticut Yankee* suggest a case of an illustrator who wanted to (and hoped the readers would) read a different book, one not limited to the words on the page. Henry Nash Smith has called Dan Beard, the illustrator, the "first reviewer of *Connecticut Yankee*" (Twain 16), and Beverly R. David, M. Thomas Inge, and others have examined the friendly relationship between Twain and Beard.⁷ Beard's line drawings often take on the style of political cartoon, demonstrating how an illustrator can invite readers to see specific comparisons between the text's imaginary world and the real world that the text implies. Beard used explicit labels on images, e.g., "LABOR" and "FREE TRADE," and caricatures, e.g., Jay Gould and possibly Bellamy (Inge 190), to make clear visual statements about the links between Twain's imaginary England and the realities of late nineteenth-century America. Twain enthusiastically approved of Beard's extrapolations. He rejected only one of the 220 drawings submitted: "two knights preparing to charge each other" (Inge 180).

In the concluding chapters, however, the text and image seem to part company. After failing to create a democratic and technologically advanced American utopia in sixth-century England, Hank Morgan decides to tame the ungrateful and rebellious Authorians with futuristic weaponry. As mentioned previously, the results are some of the most horrifyingly dystopian scenes in utopian literature. In chapter 42, "War!," Beard does include several melodramatic battle scenes. But as the war progresses, it seems as if Beard's goal is to divert attention away from the unfolding destruction. In chapters 42 and 43 he inserts drawings of comic fat priests and of Hank dreaming of his sixth-century lover and wife, Sandy. When Beard does offer visual impressions of the slaughter, he reduces the carnage to a dehumanized, disembodied comedy of disconnected body parts, a visual counterpart of a technique sometimes used by southwestern humorists, including Twain.

In the last illustration (fig. 4) Beard obscures the nightmare carnage, the pathetic death of Hank, and the dark implications about technology and the imposition of American ideals by offering late nineteenth-century readers an allegorical tableau celebrating the Victorian family, sentimental

*Figure 4. Dan Beard, "The End," from Mark Twain,* A Connecticut Yankee in King Arthur's Court *(New York, 1889).*

love, and an ahistorical triumph over time and death. In his detailed examination of the Twain-Beard collaboration M. Thomas Inge observes that Beard "decided to give the novel another ending": "As [Beard] commented in a hand-annotated edition of *Connecticut Yankee,* 'It was only a few centuries which separated the Yankee from his wife, Sandy, and his little baby. I had not the heart to kill him as did the author; so I put death at the throat of time, thus killing all that separated the man from his wife and uniting them again'" (217).

Twain's enthusiastic approval of Beard's illustrations suggests not only his enjoyment of the caricature, satire, and social commentary Beard drew into and out of the text, but also his willingness to have readers' attention diverted from his American utopia gone sour. Beard's attempts to avoid eyewitness accounts of dystopia represent a vivid response of one reader and by implication an assumption by that reader about what other readers of the period would like to avoid seeing as potential American futures.

Considering the popularity and influence of *Looking Backward,* we would expect early visual representations of Bellamy's utopia. In the May 4, 1890, issue of the *Boston Globe,* there was indeed a series of futuristic and comic renditions, including an aerial view featuring an enormous transparent umbrella protecting Boston from rain and a portrait of a high-tech policeman on rollerskates (25). Another series of illustrations appeared in 1890. A Boston architect, J. Pickering Putnam, wrote a sixty-four-page book *Architecture under Nationalism.* Almost all the illustrations represent classical Greek or Gothic buildings, and a few that are classical Roman. Putnam's point was that Nationalism would (re)create the best of the social and economic conditions that inspired the great architects of the past. The result would be a renaissance of grand public buildings and the creation of practical and comfortable cooperative apartments.

Buyers of the first edition of *Looking Backward* could select from five different colored covers; as early as 1889 in Stockholm and 1890 in London, Melbourne, and New York, cover illustrations appeared, and there have been several foreign illustrated editions.[8] And yet James J. Kopp, who maintains what may be the world's largest private collection of Bellamy's books, and Nancy Snell Griffith, a Bellamy bibliographer, would both agree that illustrated English editions of *Looking Backward* are surprisingly rare. There is, nevertheless, one truly remarkable example—the "first significant fine press edition" (Kopp, "Looking Back . . . Exhibit" 10)—with illustrations that invite readers to see the modern and personal qualities of a nineteenth-century blueprint utopia. On a word-association experiment few readers would link Bellamy with the forces that helped create this edition: Hollywood, modernism, and visual intimacy. In 1941 fifteen hundred copies of *Looking Backward* were designed and printed by Merle Armitage in Hollywood for The Limited Editions Club in New York. Irwin Edman, of Columbia University, wrote the introduction. He admitted that Bellamy's utopia was in some ways dated. Technology had surpassed several of his predictions, and the regimentation of his society and his "evangelical" tone might seem out of step with the 1940s (l).[9] But the accuracy of many of Bellamy's predictions, his criticisms of inequality, and his hope for a world of brotherhood and justice made the utopia "a vision with an edge" relevant to "a streamlined age" (l, e). At the beginning of each chapter, illustrations by Elise Cavanna (Armitage's wife, who is listed simply as "Elise" on the title page) invited readers to perceive this nineteenth-century utopia as both modern and intimate.[10]

Cavanna's line drawings have the crispness of linoleum block prints. (In 1950 her lithographs shown at Los Angeles's Forsyth Gallery were praised for "the beauty of near mathematical lines and forms" [Millier 21]). The background colors alternate: red, green, blue, black, gray, maroon, and brown. With two exceptions, the lines are white. There is some variety in the styles. A classical rendering of the Venus de Milo begins chapter 25 on the role of women; chapter 1, which includes West's laments about labor strife, opens with the red outline of a fist superimposed over a Boston street scene suggesting social realism. Most of the illustrations, however, fall into two categories. The first is a combination of European Futurism, American Streamlining, and an emphasis on abstract geometric shapes celebrated by artists like Vassily Kandinski and in the famous sphere and spire of the 1939 World's Fair poster. Cavanna frequently used this composite style to represent machines, for example, a rocket ship (259) and a majestic electronic transmitter of music (121, fig. 5). Adding an austere classical motif to this mix, she combined a simple outline of a lyre with a radio dial to represent the receiver of the transmissions (283, fig. 6).

The other style is rare, possibly unique, for utopian illustrations. Cavanna used, more than any other style, an austere yet intimate simplicity reminiscent of Picasso's *The Love of Jupiter and Semele* (1931). To be more accurate, it is as if we are viewing enlargements of specific sections from *The Love*. Most of these drawings are close-ups depicting a full or partial face or hand during or just before a crucial experience. For instance, the hand of the mesmerist hovers above the face of the insomniac West (15, fig. 7); West first opens his eyes to the future (23); and West's hand rests on a Dickens volume that will inspire a strong emotional response (153). In an especially poignant example of this style, Edith's full-faced sympathetic gaze rests on a partial view of West's face. West's one eye that we can see suggests his sadness and detachment (339, fig. 8). This illustration opens chapter 27. West is distraught. Rev. Barton's sermon

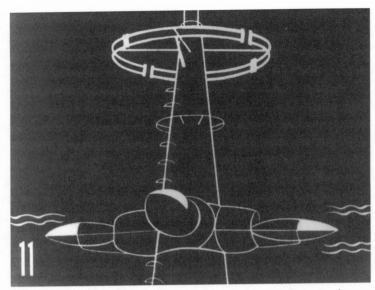

Figure 5. Elise Cavanna, A Transmitter, from Edward Bellamy, Looking Backward, 2000–1887 (Norwalk, 1981). By permission of Easton Press.

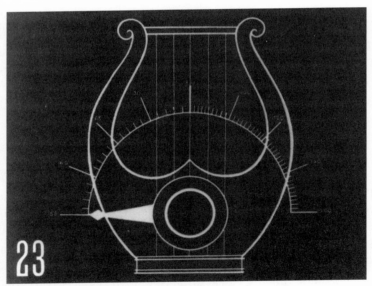

Figure 6. Elise Cavanna, An Electronic Receiver, from Looking Backward. By permission of Easton Press.

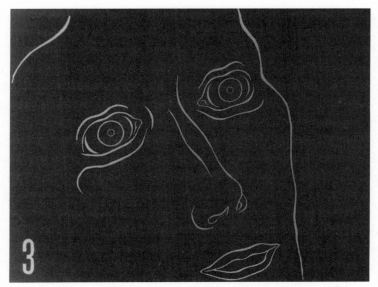

*Figure 7. Elise Cavanna, The Awakening, from Looking Backward. By permission of Easton Press.*

*Figure 8. Elise Cavanna, Edith Leete's Gaze, from Looking Backward. By permission of Easton Press.*

(ch. 26) has made him feel that his "position is so much more utterly alone than any human being's ever was before" (288).[11] In chapter 27 Edith Leete consoles West and (finally) subtly reveals her love for him.

Possibly Cavanna's illustrations are the first modern feminist "readings" of *Looking Backward*—feminist in the sense that she, like the feminist authors of literary utopias in the 1970s and 1980s, emphasizes the significance of intimate personal relationships instead of the typical blueprint overview (as in the *Boston Globe* mega-umbrella or utopian maps in other utopias). One could also argue, of course, that the intimacy is a throwback to nineteenth-century sentimentality. But the modernist style of Picasso and the viewing context of the other Futurist/Streamlined/Kandinski images does suggest how creative illustrators and publishers can give vital visual expression to their responses to utopian literature. Certainly for "Elise" *Looking Backward* was transformed from a nineteenth-century blueprint into a modern and intimate utopia. Her images invite the readers to participate in a similar transformation.

Up to this point my emphasis has been on the visual evidence of responses by very important readers, professional illustrators, and how their images might shape the responses of readers. My last example focuses on a nonprofessional illustrator: an author whose drawings suggest complex intellectual and personal relationships to the "sources" she was transforming into her utopian narrative.

I have already mentioned Ursula K. Le Guin's *Always Coming Home* several times. It is one of the most interesting and complex literary utopias ever written. Because of their implicit and explicit criticism of traditional utopianism, Sally Kitch perceives *Always Coming Home* and other critical utopias of the 1970s and 1980s as "rejections of utopianism" (76). Like Tom Moylan and Lucy Sargisson, I prefer to see the critical utopias, in particular *Always Coming Home,* as a revitalization and redefinition of literary utopianism (Moylan, *Demand* 1–12; Sargisson 20).

At the core of the narrative of *Always Coming Home* is the story of the Kesh people, who "might be going to have lived a long, long time from now in Northern California" (xiii). As is the case with many of the critical utopias of the 1970s and 1980s, these citizens of utopia do not inhabit a perfect world. They must endure the legacies of natural disasters, past wars, pollution, and toxic accidents and the potential of hostilities mounted by the patriarchal, militaristic culture of the Condors. On a more personal level, we discover some mean-spirited and jealous citizens of utopia and family tensions as intimate as a daughter's struggle to establish dual allegiance with a Kesh mother and a Condor father. (The protagonist of the central story—whose names at different stages of her life are North Owl, Terter Ayatyu, wife of Retforok, Woman Coming Home, and Stone Telling—is raised as a Kesh but travels with her father to Condor country, where she marries and lives for several years before returning to her homeland without her husband.) Despite the imperfections of Kesh life, Le Guin's essays make it clear that in her opinion a culture like the Kesh culture points toward an alternative superior to the realities and potentialities of mainstream American culture.[12] The Kesh worldview offers a complex blending of steady-state economy/ecology, the enriching closeness of tribalism, and an egalitarian and nonhierarchical social organization, all of which is reflected in rich ceremonial cycles.

The form of *Always Coming Home* distinguishes it from the other ambiguous or critical utopias of the 1970s and 1980s. It looks much more like an anthropological collection or handbook than a novel. The central narrative of North Owl is interrupted, framed, and surrounded by songs, chants, short tales, poems, dramas, elaborate clan and kinfolk charts, life stories, cooking recipes, and a series of commentaries and self-ruminations by the "editor" of the collection, Pandora, who takes on attributes of both guide and visitor in this utopia. The book concludes with more than a hundred pages of descriptions of significant ceremonies, details about eating habits and other daily activities, information on the Kesh alphabet and numbering system, and a fourteen-page, small-print glossary. The original Harper & Row cloth and paper editions came boxed with an audiotape of Kesh songs and stories.

Throughout all the text, including the glossary, there are illustrations. Margaret Chodos, a professional artist, provided most of the line drawings. But, as is announced on the title page, the maps were "drawn by the Author." By themselves the maps are not remarkable. These simple, hand-drawn images are nonetheless exceptionally useful guides that help readers to place North Owl among the family, clan, and ceremonial houses and buildings of her hometown, Sinshan (182, fig. 9), and help readers to trace her short trips through the nine towns of the Kesh along the Na River (374, fig. 10) and her long journey to the land of the Condors (140, fig. 11).

When I placed the maps, along with the accompanying text and

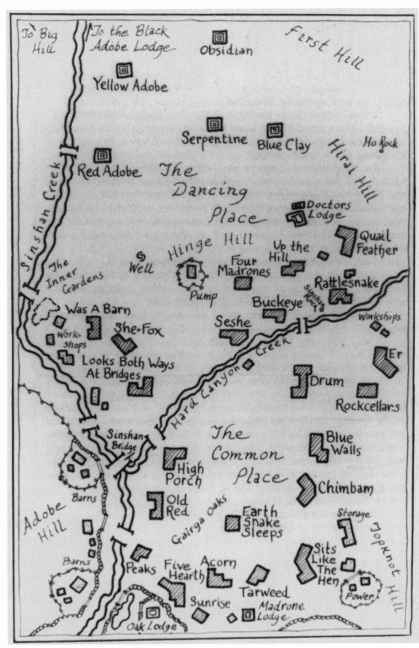

Figure 9. Ursula K. Le Guin, "The Names of the Houses of Sinshan," from Always Coming Home (New York: Harper & Row, 1985). By permission of Ursula K. Le Guin.

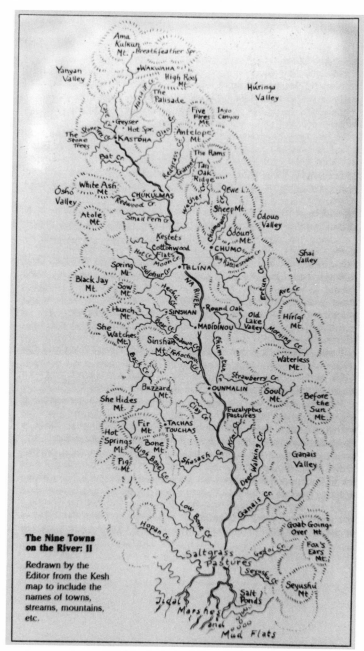

Figure 10. Ursula K. Le Guin, "The Nine Towns of the River: II," from *Always Coming Home. By permission of Ursula K. Le Guin.*

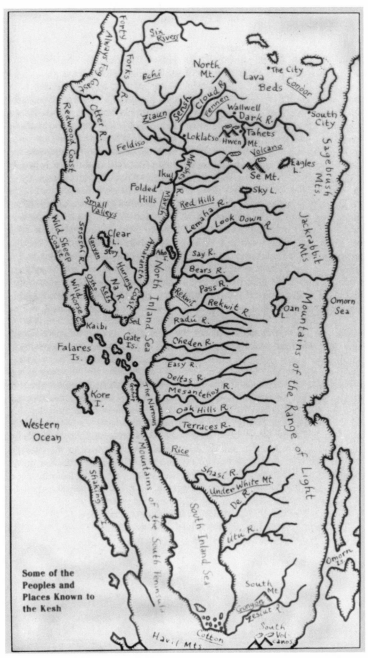

*Figure 11. Ursula K. Le Guin, "Some of the Peoples and Places Known to the Kesh," from* Always Coming Home. *By permission of Ursula K. Le Guin.*

illustrations, beside the maps, text, and illustrations of A. L. Kroeber's *Handbook of the Indians of California* (1925), something remarkable did happen. (For examples, see the stylistic similarities between Le Guin's maps and Kroeber's maps of the "Yurok towns and territory" [9, fig. 12], and "plan of Hupa town of Takimitlding" [129, fig. 13].) I am not going to reduce *Always Coming Home* to a fictional "imitation" of her father's *Handbook* or to a 525-page textual/visual response to her father's 995-page *Handbook.* There are significant differences in the physical appearance. For instance, Kroeber used many photographs; Margaret Chodos included numerous spirals, gyres, condors, and other iconographic images. Furthermore, in preparation for writing *Always Coming Home,* Le Guin read many other studies about California and northwestern Native Americans.[13] Nor do I intend to restrict the nowhere landscape of the Kesh to the Napa Valley, a familiar region to the A. L. Kroeber family. Certainly there are obvious physical, climactic, and cartographic similarities between the Kesh Na Valley and the Napa Valley. In a letter to me, Le Guin notes that "if you look at the USGS maps of the area, the Na Valley is unmistakably and explicitly the Napa Valley; and even the names of several towns can be decoded back to present-day local placenames" (29 February 2000). Despite the striking similarities between the Na and Napa Valleys, Le Guin obviously intended her no place to suggest realities and possibilities of many American and non-American locales. In one of her maps Le Guin even suggests visually that her Kesh country is a metaphor for the vitality of organic growth. It is a terrain relief map of the same area mapped in her "Nine Towns II" map (374, fig. 10). Without the mountain, river, creek, and town names, the "map" now looks like a tree or shrub, with the Na River as a trunk whose roots extend toward the bottom of the image (362, fig. 14). Finally, I lack the space and expertise necessary to define the complex relations suggested by the daughter of a famous anthropologist creating a massive tome that details the lifeways of an imaginary culture with the care of a seasoned cultural anthropologist.

Despite all my necessary qualifications, it is still obvious that Le Guin's decision to personally draw the lines of her utopia and to use her father's work as a guide to the visual and verbal mapping of her utopia suggests intricate lines of reader response—of dependence and transcendence. In private letters to me, Le Guin indicated that the *Handbook* was one of her most important sources of information and inspiration. In preparation for

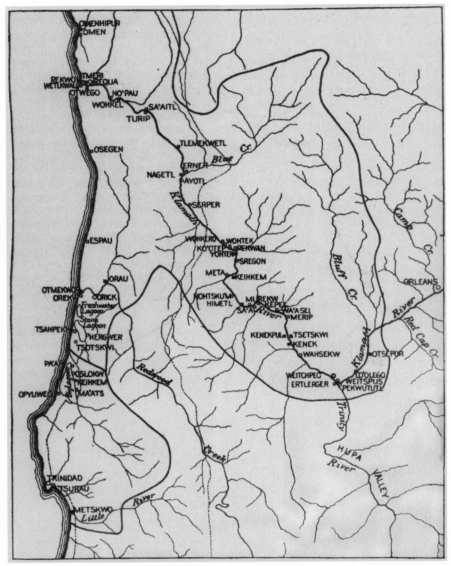

Figure 12. A. L. Kroeber, *Yurok Towns and Territory, from* Handbook of the Indians of California *(Washington, 1925).*

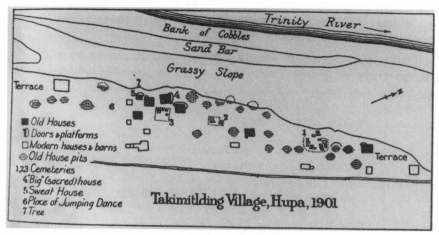

*Figure 13.* A. L. Kroeber, Plan of Hupa Town of Takimitlding, from Handbook of the Indians of California.

writing, she "reread all the *Handbook*" (19 May 1991). She was especially impressed with the sections on the Yorok (1–97) and the Mohave (726–95). Although she did base a few specific characteristics of Kesh life on the lifeways of California tribes (e.g., the "style of warfare" [25 June 1995]), she believes that the strongest influence—i.e., the part of her father's text that she responded to most positively as she wrote *Always Coming Home*—was the "idea of there being no hierarchy and no center," an "idea that was profoundly supported and validated for me by the existence of the pre-white California nations" (19 May 1991). In "A Non-Euclidean View of California as a Cold Place to Be," Le Guin celebrates this nonhierarchical worldview of many California tribes and quotes extensively from the *Handbook*, though she calls the author "A. L. Kroeber" rather than "my father" (97).

There is a central irony to this incidence of father and daughter mappings of nonhierarchical cultures. On the one hand, it is clear that both of them wanted to give voice—at great length and in great verbal and visual detail—to cultures that had something of great value to say to "mainstream" American culture but who were silenced. And yet to "preserve" (anthropological voice) or "express" (literary voice) the truths of great value that they learned from descendants of California tribes or from books about them, both father and daughter had to participate in the centuries-old drama of "speaking for the Other."

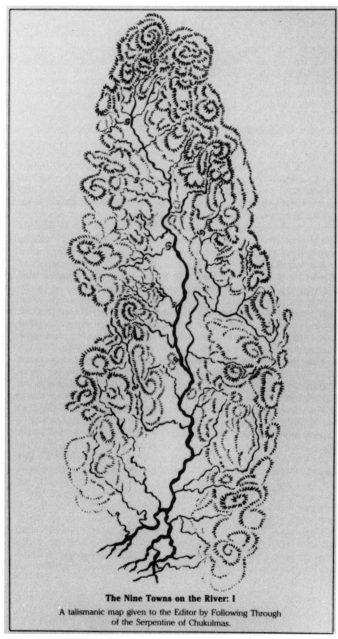

**The Nine Towns on the River: I**

A talismanic map given to the Editor by Following Through
of the Serpentine of Chukulmas.

*Figure 14.* Ursula K. Le Guin, "*The Nine Towns on the River: I,*"
from Always Coming Home. *By permission of Ursula K. Le Guin.*

Another irony: in "A Non-Euclidean View" part of the nonhierarchical, non-Euclidean worldview that Le Guin celebrates, using quotes from her father's *Handbook,* is that: "Coyote country has not been mapped. . . . In the *Handbook of the Indians of California,* A. L. Kroeber wrote, 'The California Indians . . . usually refuse pointblank to make even an attempt [to draw a map], alleging utter inability'" (97). In contrast in Euroamerican utopias, utopia is mapped: "The euclidean utopia is mapped; it is geometrically organized, with the parts labeled *a, a', b:* a diagram or model, which social engineers can follow and reproduce" (97). And yet both Kroeber and Le Guin—like the Kesh, who love to spin words and draw maps (*Always* 450)—metaphorically (with their numerous words and illustrations) and literally, with their personally prepared maps, carefully map out their views of alternative cultures.

But as a daughter, a reader, and a writer, Le Guin had a tremendous advantage over her father, which she stated concisely in a personal letter: "Well, I had a kind of advantage over my father—he couldn't use my book, but I could use his!" (25 June 1995). In the early twentieth century the professional models—the social science discourses—to which Kroeber responded dictated a form and style that organized, detailed, and mapped so that the "reality" of the Other could be communicated with authority to the people (e.g., anthropologists and ethnographers) in mainstream culture who were in charge of speaking for and preserving voices of peoples who, they assumed, would soon vanish. (Indeed, the turn of the century marked the low point of the Native American population in the United States, approximately 250,000 [Utter 39].) Le Guin lives in an era that has witnessed a tremendous increase in Indian populations and the vital growth of Indian literary voices, many of whom she admires.[14] Moreover, as a respected writer of utopian, science fiction, and fantasy literature and especially as a writer known for impressive experiments in form,[15] Le Guin could (indeed might be expected to) blend the "facts" and "maps" of cultural anthropology with the polyvocality of a collection gathered from nonexistent peoples edited by a complex persona whose name (Pandora) is full of ironies, especially for a utopian narrative. In other words, Le Guin could have her maps and Coyote non-maps simultaneously. She could speak (indirectly) about, but not "for," Native Americans. She could celebrate a nonhierarchical utopia with a nonhierarchical, conglomerate form. She responded to her father's *Handbook* with a brilliant form that addressed and even transcended many of the contradictions and ironies of mapping the utopian ideals of the Other.[16]

## Readers Defining Utopia

Certainly the rich history of illustration in utopian literature makes the literary utopia a prime site for reader-response critics like Ellen J. Esrock, who emphasizes the role of visualization in the reading process. In *The Reader's Eye* (1994) Esrock stresses the connections between visualization and the text's believability: "Some readers . . . find sight to be a particularly powerful marker of reality" (183); "seeing what is described makes the textual fiction more real" (184); visualization "sharpens cognitive grasp of the fictional world" (192). Since one of the primary challenges for a utopian author is to convince readers that his or her imaginary better world is believable enough to invite perceptual or even behavioral changes, a key function of a utopian text is its ability to encourage readers to visualize the nonexistent. Viewing utopias from this perspective raises a series of questions about the illustrations. Do the images enhance, limit, or discourage visualization? Which types of readers' visualization skills are activated by detailed realistic images (the *Boston Globe* aerial view of Bellamy's Boston), by impressionistic glimpses (Elise's Picasso-like encounters), by iconographic symbols (Margaret Chodos's gyres and spirals), or explicit social commentaries (Beard's labeled caricatures)? These and related questions could be addressed using Esrock's approach applied to past documented responses to illustrations and to written or (in the cases of the architecture students) visual responses by modern readers to utopian texts and images.

As my previous comments and the eclectic nature of parts 2 and 3 of this book suggest, Esrock's approach to reader response is only one of many that can be fruitfully used to understand how readers transform no place into their own someplace. Even some theoretical orientations that might at first seem inappropriate can and have been used successfully. For example, it is obvious that for Wolfgang Iser all "networks of response-inviting structures" are not equal (*Act* 34). Because he assumes that they will lessen the degree of reader participation, he disdains texts that lay "things out before the reader in such a way that he can either accept or reject them." Iser is particularly bothered by texts that are "structured according to a principle of contrast or opposition" (*Prospecting* 10, 15). Since, as Shakespeare's

Gonzalo reminds us, utopias "by contrast execute all things" (*Tempest* II, i, 143), it would seem that literary utopias would be poor fare for his implied reader studies. And yet, even if we ignore the potential for strong emotional responses to contrasts, which Iser downplays, there are still multiple opportunities for readers to respond "between" the contrasts. The challenge of imagining an entire alternative culture and of anticipating and answering all the "objections and ideological and political prejudices of readers" to that alternative (Fitting, "Concept of Utopia" 15) is so immense that readers are bound to perceive not only the inconsistencies in their reality as contrasted to the utopia, but also contradictions and gaps in the author's arguments and imaginary world that will invite readers to imagine their own alternatives to the author's alternative. This is certainly the case in ambiguous utopias such as *Always Coming Home,* but, as Peter Ruppert has shown, it can also be the case in a book as didactic as *Looking Backward* (62–68).[17]

The utopian authors' attempts to anticipate and answer readers' questions, the abundance of documented written and visual evidence of readers' responses, and the exciting potential for text-based reader-response studies suggested by the number, variety, and hybrid nature of the texts all point toward the necessity of placing the reader at the forefront of the study of utopian literature, including any attempts to define a literary utopia. Previous attempts vary greatly; Darko Suvin's and Lyman Tower Sargent's excellent overviews of definitions make that clear (*Metamorphoses* 37–52; "Three Faces" 5–13, respectively). As Ruth Levitas observes, this diversity is in part explained by what various utopographers are seeking: "One of the reasons why people work with different definitions of utopia is because they are asking different questions" (*Concept of Utopia* 179). For example, if we ask "What is a literary utopia?," our answers will probably take the form of descriptions that focus on "content," genre, and other textual characteristics. If we instead concentrate on function by asking "What does a literary utopia do?," then our orientation would shift toward impact rather than textual characteristics. Of course, there is overlap. To define what a literary utopia "is," we must give some idea of what it "does"; and to explain what it "does," we need some idea of what it "is" that is "doing."

As I indicated in the preface, much of the criticism about utopian literature still focuses on the "content" of the text and on biographical and historical contexts. It is significant, however, that since the last quarter of the twentieth century there have been shifts in emphasis in theoretical discussions of the definition of utopian literature from both the "what it is" and "what it does" orientations that imply an elevation of the reader. There is a long tradition, still manifest in many dictionaries, that answers the question "What is utopia?" with words such as *perfect* or *ideal*. Many utopographers today prefer *better*. In part this is a reflection of the influential ambiguous and critical utopias of Le Guin, Piercy, Lessing, Delany, Robinson, and others who offer us flawed alternatives that still suggest "better alternatives" to our present. But it also reflects a belief among critics and utopian authors that—after witnessing the horrors of world wars and tragically failed attempts by Hitler and Stalin to impose utopian blueprints, and after reading the powerful dystopian visions of Zamiatin, Huxley, and Orwell—late twentieth- and early twenty-first-century readers cannot and will not believe that humans can create perfect worlds or that writers are capable of envisioning a perfection that would appeal to many more than one reader, the author. The (modern) classic expression of this assumed skeptical reader is the voice of Le Guin's narrator in "The Ones Who Walk Away from Omelas." She repeatedly questions the readers' ability to accept the possibility of a better world ("Do you believe? . . . No? Then . . ."); admits her inability to articulate such a world ("How can I tell you about the people of Omelas?"); and gives the readers freedom to imagine their own Omelas, since she knows her words will never satisfy the readers (1–8).

From the functional orientation there have been two significant changes that elevate the reader's importance. First, more critics and scholars are emphasizing the "What does it do?" question.[18] Since this question implies the obvious prepositional phrase—"to whom"—and the "whom" of that phrase is the reader, the shift toward a functional orientation implies the necessary inclusion of the reader in any definition of a literary utopia. Thus it is not surprising that what "the author intended" for a "contemporaneous reader" is a recurring element in Sargent's definitions of various types of literary utopias ("Three Faces" 9). Often such mention of readers in definitions does not, however, specify whether readers will be included as passive recipients of the utopian agency, or as co-creators, or as powerful, even dominating, transformers of the utopian message.

The second shift suggests a move away from the passive end of that spectrum. Typically, utopian functions have been identified as iconoclastic and normative. Utopias disrupt assumptions about the reader's present. The disruptions cause confusion, but they can also create room: (1) for the development of critical perspectives about the present hitherto unexamined by the reader and (2) for the potential acceptance of the utopian models or norms implied by or stated "in" the imaginary better world. An emphasis on the normative-prescriptive functions privileges the author and text as creator and transmitter of representations of better worlds that "correct" the evils of the present and "fill in" the void caused by the disruptions. This could be termed the conversion experience model of utopian reading. A necessary period of confusion and inadequacy precedes and is secondary to the acceptance of the true way accepted as gospel. On the other hand, emphasizing the disruptions—the shifting of perceptions—places more emphasis on the reader. The text (and author) is still important, since the text invited the reader's confusion. Nevertheless, if we emphasize the disruptions, reading a utopia becomes more of a "hinge" experience; there is more emphasis on opening up or out than on filling in and acceptance.[19] The real utopian drama becomes not whether readers will accept the given-gospel of the text, but how they will respond to and use the potentially unhinging experience of reading a utopia. Of course, one option after the unhinging might be to accept the utopian model as gospel and to act accordingly. But that is only one of many options, including that of readers fashioning their own utopian models that combine elements of the textual model and many other models from their past readings and experiences, or the option of remaining in a state of befuddlement.

During the past three decades there has been some shift toward emphasizing the disruptive functions and, thus, an enhancement of the reader's stature. The specific articulation of the unhinging varies. Lee Cullen Khanna and Gary Saul Morson speak of varieties of "defamiliarization"; Darko Suvin favors "cognitive estrangement" that can lead to the development of new perceptual skills; Jean Pfaelzer modifies this and uses "cognitive dissonance"; Louis Marin prefers "neutralization"; Peter Ruppert refers to "disturbing and unsettling effects"; Peter Fitting and Phillip Wegner stress how utopias can "open up" spaces for conceptualization;[20] and in perhaps the best-known articulation, Fredric Jameson claims that the literary utopia's function "is to provoke a fruitful bewilderment, and to jar the mind into some heightened but unconceptualized consciousness of its own powers, functions, aims, and structural limits" ("Of Islands and Trenches" 87–88).

There are significant differences among these articulations, and there are pronounced differences among the preferred results of the unhinging. For Jameson the fruitfulness of the bewilderment is that it invites readers to acknowledge the "imperative to imagine" alternatives ("'If I find'" 231), while simultaneously teaching them the impossibility, or at least the pronounced improbability, of conceiving of utopia: "My modest recommendation was simply that we use the Utopian visions we are capable of projecting today in order to explore the structural limits of such imaginings, in order to get a better sense of what it is about the future that we are unwilling or unable to imagine" ("Comments" 76). Fitting, who is thoroughly familiar with and admires Jameson's emphasis on the disruptive powers of utopias, nevertheless stresses a different response to the unhinging. Although he has argued convincingly against closed, given-gospel notions of utopia, he still hopes for readers who will be open to "the look and feel and shape and experiences of what an alternative might and could actually be, a thought experiment or form of "social dreaming" (Sargent ["Three Faces"] 3) which gave us a sense of how our lives could be different, not only in our immediate material conditions, but in the sense of an entire world or social system" ("Concept of Utopia" 15). In *The Concept of Utopia* (1990) Ruth Levitas offers a middle ground between Jameson and Fitting. Like Ernst Bloch, who strongly influenced her, Levitas advocates the anticipatory rather than the representational functions of utopian literature. Nevertheless, the anticipations should go beyond hope for an awareness of our limitations. The disruptive impact of utopia can enhance our longing and educate our "desire for a better way of being" (8).

Despite the significant differences in terminology and in the range of preferred responses to utopian bewilderment, the shift in emphasis advocated by some critics away from the normative-representational and toward the iconoclastic functions places the utopian drama more firmly in the hands, eyes, and mind of the reader. It is also obvious that the shift from "perfect" to "better" in literary utopias and in the criticism reflects the power of the skeptical eye of that reader. That reader's eye should be visible in every element of a definition of utopian literature. To a greater degree than most critics, I did include the reader in the working definition of a literary utopia offered at the beginning of chapter 1. This is appropriate, since one of my primary goals is to enhance greatly an awareness of the role of the reader in the study of utopian literature. But it should be clear by the end of this chapter that my opening definition (which included both descriptive and functional elements) understated the reader's role. To repeat the definition: A literary utopia is a fairly detailed narrative description of an imaginary culture—a fiction that invites readers to experience vicariously an alternative reality that critiques theirs by opening cognitive and affective spaces that encourage readers to perceive the realities and potentialities of their culture in new ways. If the author or reader perceives the imaginary culture as being significantly better than the "present," then the work is a eutopia or, in the more popular usage, a utopia; if significantly worse, it is a dystopia.

To suggest how readers could be highlighted in definitions of utopian literature, I will discuss several elements of my definition in the contexts of a text and a reader rarely included in discussions of literary utopias.[21] The text is the "Great Vision" chapter (20–47) in John G. Neihardt's and Nicholas Black Elk's *Black Elk Speaks* (1932); the "reader" is Black Elk. The vision fulfills most of the requirements of the definition. It invited Lakotas during the late nineteenth century to experience vicariously an imaginary alternate reality that encouraged them to see the realities and potentialities of their present in new ways. There are both dystopian and eutopian episodes, though by the end of the narrative the eutopian prevails.

Nevertheless, the vision seems woefully inadequate with regard to a "fairly detailed description" and the presentation of a "culture." Where are the "detailed" descriptions that Krishan Kumar and Lyman Tower Sargent call for in their definitions of a literary utopia (*Utopianism* 31; *Utopia Reader* 1)? Where is the information about "sociopolitical institutions" that Darko Suvin requires for his imaginary cultures (*Metamorphoses* 49)? These questions are certainly valid, but if we change viewpoints, the questions and answers change radically. Suppose that Black Elk could read English well, and he read Wells's *A Modern Utopia* and Harrington's *Common-wealth of Oceana*. The former includes much detail about the parallel imaginary world visited by the Owner of the Voice; the latter offers abundant detail about political systems. Still, Black Elk might complain that Wells was much too vague, since he didn't include essential details about symbolic directionality and color and number systems. Such details were absolutely essential to the telling of a Lakota Thunder Being's vision.

Similarly, Harrington did not provide the detailed information about important holy beings and spirituality that would give authority and verisimilitude to a Lakota vision. My point in forcing Black Elk to read Wells and Harrington is to emphasize that what constitutes important detail and significant aspects of culture is often culturally and historically conditioned.

"Narrative," another key element of the definition (since it distinguishes a literary utopia from a treatise) is also conditioned. Modern non-Lakota readers could no doubt perceive the journey motive in the Great Vision, but the sudden transformations of horses into all types of animals and the abundant repetition might obstruct their ability to experience vicariously the imaginary alternative. Again switching perspectives, Black Elk would not be bothered by the transformations and repetition, since they were expected, indeed prescribed by the divine origin of the vision. But he would be greatly disturbed with the inclusion of the words "imaginary" and "fictional" in the definition. In Neihardt's version of the telling, Black Elk begins by stressing that the vision is "not a story," which in this particular context indicates that it is not made up; it really happened (20). Using words that would please Ellen Esrock, Black Elk later reemphasizes this point when he declares that "nothing I have ever seen with my eyes was so clear and bright as what my vision showed me" (49). Both the non-Lakota's confusion about narrative conventions and Black Elk's probable objection to labeling his vision as "imaginary" underline how previous assumptions about conventions and genre boundaries can shape reactions to utopias.

As can learned interpretive strategies: Black Elk had the advantages of family history (holy men), an oral tradition, and expert advisors (for example, Black Road) to help him understand the socially approved meanings of the four directions and colors of the horses; the directions, gifts, and natures of the Grandfather holy beings; and the hoop, flowering tree, and journey. And yet Black Elk experienced/constructed several very different interpretations during his life. As a young teenager he did not share the vision; he was terrified of it. Using my definition, this receiver/author/reader might have perceived his vision as a dystopia. In his late teens and early twenties, when he had shared parts of the vision, portions had been performed, and he had begun to cure people under the inspiration of the vision, he would have perceived the vision as eutopian. By the early 1930s when Neihardt interviewed him, his interpretation would again change.

The military defeat of his people, their poverty, his declining health, and his continuing faith in the vision (and the opportunity to tell the entire vision for the first time), would probably turn the vision into an ambiguous utopia for Black Elk.

A crucial element in my definition and in most recent concepts of utopia is the potential for an opening-up, unhinging experience, that leads to new perceptions and possibly changed behavior. The oppressive historical situation, the strong belief in Thunder Being visions, and in Black Elk's personal case, a severe illness helped prepare Black Elk and the Oglala Lakota to be open to a new vision and then to see this vision as a guide to ceremonial and daily life. Lacking these crucial historical, cultural, and personal experiences, twentieth-century non-Lakota readers would have great difficulty opening up to the vision as a life-altering force, even though they might appreciate it as spiritually uplifting poetic literature.

My two-sentence definition has now grown into several paragraphs, and I have highlighted only one "reader," noting a few actual and hypothetical responses. Again I am reminded of the humbling images that opened the preface of this book. A definition that took into account all the important historical, cultural, reading convention, and personal contexts relating to how readers respond cognitively and emotionally to literary utopias would be an infinitely long definition. I suppose we could appropriate and modify Jameson's approach to reading utopias and admit that the primary function of attempting reader-response studies of utopian literature is that they teach us the limits of our abilities to understand how readers create meanings and feelings. Probably the best we can do with regard to defining utopian literature and to exploring the reader's role in the history and future of that literature is to offer what we consider to be convincing combinations of "what it is" and "what it does" definitions that explicitly include the reader and to consistently include discussion of hypothetical and actual responses in all our interpretations of the texts we define as literary utopias. I will focus on this goal in the following chapters.

I hope my decision to enlist Black Elk to test my definition also suggests three other characteristics of the rest of the book. First, the Black Elk test implicitly offers further justification for the organization and foci of the chapters. The issues briefly mentioned above are the same issues that I examine in greater depth in chapters 3 through 9: the impact on readers' responses of historical and cultural conditioning (chapter 3), of literary conventions and genres (chapters 4 and 6), of shared interpretive strategies (the first sections of chapter 5 and chapter 6), of experiences that change the interpretive viewpoint of the first reader, the author (the last section of chapter 5), and of past and current personal experience that can close or open up a utopian text, and reinforce or unhinge a reader of utopias (chapters 7 through 9). The fact that these reader-response contexts are significant to texts and readers as different as *Black Elk Speaks* and *Looking Backward* and Black Elk and Bellamy's readership also suggests that my concentration on Bellamy's utopia should help us to understand why and how readers respond to many different types of utopias. Finally, I hope that my experiment with Black Elk and the remaining chapters demonstrate that emphasizing the reader's role in the history of utopian literature can provoke new and revealing ways to perceive utopian texts and lead to a greater appreciation of why and how readers transform utopian invitations to imagine better worlds.

# Part Two

*Culturally, Genre(ly), and
Textually Constructed Utopian Readers*

# Three

# Perceptual Origins
*Preparing American Readers to See Utopia*

Long before Darwin's famous voyages, origin hunting was a common intellectual pursuit commonly justified by commonly held assumptions about cause and effect, linear time progressions, and the notion that no entity could be fully understood unless we knew its beginnings. Unfortunately, in their attempts to define coherent patterns of influences, origin seekers sometimes ignore or misrepresent sources that do not fit their patterns and thus reduce the complexity of origins to a parade of objects, people, and events that line up neatly pointing toward an end product. Even careful utopographers attempting to explain the impact of late nineteenth-century utopian literature can give the impression of reductionist cause-and-effect relationships. Unfortunately, as Kumar cautions us, it "is impossible to establish with any degree of precision the appearance of any utopia and its social contexts" (*Utopianism* 101).

One possible way to minimize the tendency to posit simplistic cause-and-effect relationships while still recognizing the crucial importance of relevant contexts is to pay close attention to the circumstances, values, traditions, and attitudes that enable readers to recognize and to give meaning to particular literary phenomena. In many ways this approach is similar to Hans-Robert Jauss's focus on the "horizon of expectations"—the literary, cultural, historical, and ethical expectations of a text's readers "in the historical moment of its appearance" (14). Of course, concentrating on multifaceted dynamic perceptual processes does not ensure the elimination of reductionist studies. Furthermore, an emphasis on contexts and perception may require us to go over similar grounds and reach some of the same conclusions as would be covered and concluded during the course of more traditional cause-and-effect studies of utopian literature. Stressing the importance of perceptual origins does, nevertheless, allow us to see familiar contexts in new and interesting ways. Specifically, it may allow us to see new functions for literary, cultural, and historical contexts and to see that some influences have been overemphasized and other important influences either obscured or ignored. A contextual-perceptual approach to origins also helps us to understand why certain ideas that seem so obvious and meaningful to one generation can be invisible to other generations.

The pre-twentieth-century origins of American utopian fiction offer a provocative arena for an investigation of the junctures between circumstance and perception. Despite the importance of many forms of religious, social, and literary utopianism in early American culture, including a body of utopian and speculative fiction written by authors such as Charles Brockden Brown, James Fenimore Cooper, Edgar Allan Poe, Nathaniel Hawthorne, and Herman Melville,[1] it was not until the appearance of Edward Bellamy's *Looking Backward* in 1888 that a large number of American readers "saw" utopian fiction and that a significant number of these readers perceived of reading and discussing utopian fiction as meaningful ways of understanding past, present, and potential realities and as involving urgent and just appeals for action. Identifying significant historical, cultural, and literary origins as agents that allowed American readers to recognize, give meaning to, and even act out late nineteenth-century utopian fictions helps us to gain a better understanding of why utopian fiction became highly visible for thousands of Americans.

The following overview takes this approach and begins with a discussion of immediate historical circumstances, which is followed by examinations of more general historical and cultural influences, literary genres, and attitudes about reading. I certainly cannot pretend that I cover "all" possible perceptual origins. Furthermore, a thorough discussion of American perceptual origins would include cross-cultural comparisons that drew upon the contributions to Sylvia Bowman's *Bellamy Abroad,* Francis Shor's observations about New Zealand ("Ideological Matrix"), and

Csaba Toth's "Transatlantic Dialogue." I do hope, however, that my approach helps us to comprehend the evolution of an interpretive community of readers that transformed utopian fiction from an obscure form of American letters into an important literary, cultural, and political force.

## Historical Sightings

Since the appearance of early reviews of *Looking Backward* in the 1880s and the first scholarly studies in the 1920s (e.g., Forbes), specific events and trends during the post–Civil War period have been presented as explanations for the existence and popularity of American utopian fiction. Certainly this is a plausible approach. Understanding contemporary responses to *Looking Backward* depends to a large degree upon "our ability to reconstruct the 'question[s]' to which the work itself is an 'answer'" (Eagleton on Gadamer 71). The turmoil of the late nineteenth century forced consideration of numerous questions that inspired Bellamy to "answer" with visions of past, present, and future. Why are terrible things happening? What can be done about this? These were the basic catalysts of *Looking Backward*'s dialogue with its early readers.

Included in the typical litany of events and trends that raised painful questions for these readers are the financial panic of 1873 and the depression of 1893, the Haymarket riot of 1886, and the numerous strikes and labor disturbances, especially those at Homestead and Pullman; and trends such as political corruption, unrest among women and farmers, new immigrations from southeastern Europe, rapid urban sprawl, challenges to traditional intellectual and religious beliefs, and an unequal distribution of wealth. (The 1893 Census Bureau statistics indicated that 9 percent of the families owned 71 percent of the nation's wealth [Pfaelzer, "Immanence" 52]. ) Scholars who emphasize the historical connection to utopian fiction often justify their approach by pointing to references to historical contexts within the utopian texts and to theories about the social functions of utopian fictions. For example, Charles Rooney's content analyses of explicit statements in utopias published from 1865 to 1917 demonstrate the high frequency of references to contemporary economic, social, and political problems (41–86), and Pfaelzer and I have argued that the utopias served the dual purpose of offering dramatic articulations of anxieties about historical conditions and of presenting hopeful future possibilities that promised escape from the present, which was often depicted as a transitional stage leading to a permanently better future (Pfaelzer, *Utopian Novel* 3–25; Roemer, *Obsolete Necessity* 15–34).

The disturbing questions and hopeful possibilities raised by historical circumstances could, for many readers, create a "desire for a better way of being" (Levitas, *Concept of Utopia* 199). In late nineteenth-century America this desire was fueled especially by a sense of unjust contrasts and a perceived need for order. Henry George's popular book *Progress and Poverty* (1879) certainly helped readers to see the contradictions of unequal distribution of wealth. When placed within the contexts of many familiar American attitudes and expectations, the above-mentioned events and trends highlighted economic and numerous other contrasts: thousands of men and women unable to find work or even refusing to work in the land of opportunity that celebrated the work ethic; the loss of influence by the farmer and rural America in Nature's Nation; and the swelling numbers of urban immigrants who declined to dissolve into the Protestant melting pot of American lifestyles. As historians and political scientists have argued, many middle-class, late nineteenth-century Americans perceived these contrasts as signaling a basic loss of order.[2]

Writing orders reality, and most writing involves contrast. But very few forms of writing emphasize the desirability of order and organization to the degree seen in the descriptions of physical and human relationships found in the typical late nineteenth-century American utopia.[3] And few forms of writing depend so heavily upon explicit and implicit contrasts, particularly between what is and what should be, to the degree found in the descriptions and the visitor-guide dialogues of utopian fiction. Hence, historical circumstances were important origins of utopian fiction, not only because they provided familiar topics that would both ground and energize utopian narratives and because they helped readers to desire a better world, but also because they sensitized readers to the meaningfulness and usefulness of a literature that viewed the world as a cruel and senseless collage of contrasts—contrasts that spoke urgently for orderly resolutions to contemporary problems.

This sensitivity was heightened and the utopias rendered more believable by the successes of nineteenth-century reform organizations that appeared to demonstrate that specific historical problems could be solved in an orderly and organized way. The extent of the reform impact might be as limited as the effects of a small temperance group assailing the local representatives of liquor manufacturers, the saloon, and politicians or as large as the crushing impact of Grant's industrialized military forces that, from a Northern viewpoint, assailed the evils of slavery. But the basic message was the same: specific problems could be resolved by reform organizations. This message would allow readers to find meaning in the numerous descriptions of reform organizations found in the utopian fictions, and it is not surprising that, as discussed in chapter 2, a significant response to the most popular utopian work was the formation of Bellamy Clubs and Nationalist Clubs from coast to coast and the eventual participation in national reform organizations, especially the Populist and Democratic parties.

The faith in reform organizations reflected a broader faith in large organizations. Modern readers are frequently repulsed by the highly centralized bureaucracy of Bellamy's industrial army. They read this fictional institution through their knowledge of real history—world wars, Soviet Socialism, and huge government and corporate bureaucracies. As Jonathan Auerbach and Kumar argue, many of Bellamy's Northern contemporaries perceived the industrial army through their idealized visions of "the nation" and of the successful (from a Northern viewpoint) Civil War machine that combined large-scale industrial and military forces.[4] The most pronounced expression of this faith was a series of fictional and nonfictional utopian projections written by King Camp Gillette, inventor of the safety razor, who was in part inspired by Bellamy. In books such as *The Human Drift* (1894) and *"World Corporation"* (1910), Gillette imagined a gigantic people's corporation and the concentration of most of the American population in an enormous national city near Niagara Falls, which would supply a practically limitless source of energy (Prettyman; Roemer, "Technology, Culture, and Utopia").

## Machines and Values Focus the Utopian Gaze

If we step back from specific historical conditions and the faith in reform movements and large organizations, and broaden our view of influences to include technological developments, middle-class value systems, and general American and European attitudes often depicted as "sources" of utopian thought, we can again see how these forces helped to develop an interpretive community inclined toward recognizing and giving meaning to utopian fiction. The inventions of the eighteenth and nineteenth centuries in combination with developing production and distribution systems (and the imaginations of early science fiction writers such as Jules Verne) inspired late nineteenth-century utopists to envision various degrees of technological utopias. There were flashy gimmicks tacked on to the narratives (e.g., prototypes of Polaroid cameras), complex communication and distribution systems (e.g., Bellamy's audio transmission and pneumatic tubes), and enormous urban complexes such as those imagined by King Camp Gillette and in Chauncey Thomas's *The Crystal Button* (1891) and Will N. Harben's *The Land of the Changing Sun* (1894).[5] As Neil Harris, Mulford Q. Sibley, and Howard Segal have argued convincingly, technological developments also helped readers to see utopia as a "real" possibility. Actual developments may not have always "rescued far-reaching schemes from improbability" (Harris 219), but only when "technology advanced sufficiently to offer the prospect of an 'affluent society' for many did most utopian schemes begin to appear at all realistic" (Segal 56). There was a shift in emphasis in the perception of the traditional functions of utopian fiction—the critical, contemplative, and prescriptive functions. The reality of technological developments made the prescriptive functions of the utopias more believable, more applicable, more visible.

During the past twenty-five years, there has been a revival of interest in the study of American Victorian middle-class value systems in America, inspired in part by the appearance in December 1975 of "Victorian Culture in America," a special issue of *American Quarterly*. According to Daniel Walker Howe, the guest editor, specific values frequently stressed by Victorian spokesmen and spokeswomen included cleanliness, punctuality, repression of sexual urges, postponement of gratification, specialization, efficiency, hard work, devotion to duty, competitiveness, seriousness, self-improvement, a future orientation, rationality, orderliness, emphasis on order and stability, and a Christian (notably Protestant) outlook (Howe, especially 521–28). Many of these values were implied in the responses to nineteenth-century historical events and technological developments already discussed. These values helped middle- and upper-middle-class readers (i.e., the bulk of the reading audience and of the Nationalist Clubs' membership) to recognize utopian fiction in the sense that they invited these readers to see numerous elements of the fictions—the clean and quiet streets, the efficient department stores and warehouses, the stable family relationships and controlled desires, the loyalty to industrial organizations and to the future America, the orderly administration of the economy and the government—as signs that signified a reinforcement of cherished values.[6] This reader-text relationship is especially obvious when we compare the Victorian values to most of the values implied by *Looking Backward*. But we don't have to restrict our view to this one utopian fiction. Rooney's content analysis of approximately one hundred works published between 1865 and 1917 and my examination of 160 late nineteenth-century works reveal a striking congruence between the Victorian and utopian values, especially in the areas of efficiency, hard work, seriousness, self-improvement, future orientation, rationality, emphasis on order and stability, and a Christian outlook (Rooney, 141–65; Roemer, "Utopia and Victorian Culture" 315–17).

Nevertheless, as I have argued elsewhere ("Utopia and Victorian Culture" 317–24), there was not an exact correspondence between the Victorian and utopian values. If there had been, then the utopias would not have been truly utopian; they would not have functioned as "opening spaces" or as critiques of the status quo, nor would they have offered truly alternative models of a better world. There are two areas where the differences seem especially obvious: the utopists' emphasis on cooperation and equality (versus the Victorian celebration of competition) and the near-future settings of many utopias (versus the Victorian stress on postponement of gratification). (The near futures are especially obvious in *Looking Backward* and in the technological utopias examined by Howard Segal in *Technological Utopianism in America* [1985].)

But even in these two areas the influences of the Victorian values can be seen; or rather the values invited the readers/authors to see/present the critiques in ways that could be perceived as being compatible with competition and postponement of gratification. First of all, as noted in chapter 1, beginning in 1836 with Mary Griffith's "Three Hundred Years Hence," there has been a significant tradition of American utopian fiction that advocates the preservation of most elements of a competitive free-enterprise system.[7] Furthermore, even though the majority of nineteenth-century American utopists advocated economic cooperation and some form of a more equitable distribution of wealth, their utopias were not devoid of competition, though the motivation for the competition had changed. The goal was not profit; the goals were self-improvement, public esteem, and a sense of an expanded identity gained through the experience of contributing, to the best of one's ability, to the public good. We find the culmination of this view of competition in *Looking Backward* in a series of observations by Dr. Leete and Julian West about motivation in A.D. 2000. Leete notes that administrators are "overrun with volunteers" for "'extra hazardous'" duty because the "young men are very greedy of honor, and do not let slip such opportunities" (135). Later he adds that it is certainly not money (since all receive equal wages) or even awards and badges that motivate workers. The "higher motives" of "service to the nation, patriotism, passion for humanity" spur the workers on to compete (154). West eventually concludes that the incentives and competition were almost "too strong" and "too hot" (176–77).

Both before and after the publication of *Looking Backward,* there were American utopists who envisioned the postponement of the gratification of experiencing utopia to the distant future. These predictions ranged from Mary Griffith's three hundred years to a few thousand years in David A. Moore's *The Age of Progress* (1856), Milton Worth Ramsey's *Six Thousand Years Hence* (1891), and Chauncey Thomas's *Crystal Button.* But most of the nineteenth-century American utopias were set either only fifty to a hundred years in the future or in the present. The present-time utopias were located in isolated communities, on distant islands, on other planets, and even inside the earth. (In these latter cases the conventions of travel literature, the existence throughout the eighteenth and nineteenth centuries of American utopian communities, the increase in transoceanic travel facilitated by the steamship, and John Cleves Symmes's theories about the inner earth all were important perceptual origins that enabled readers to recognize these utopias of the present.) Another characteristic of the utopias that suggests an unwillingness to postpone gratification is, as Jean Pfaelzer has convincingly pointed out, the tendency of the utopists to avoid detailed descriptions of the transition to utopia (*Utopian Novel* 3–25, 112).

Still, the Victorian value of postponement of gratification did help readers to see and to feel the negative effects of swift and apparently easy transitions to utopia in at least two important works. In Rabbi Solomon Schindler's previously mentioned utopia, *Young West,* Julian West's son finds his father's "Confessions." As he reads them, he is surprised to discover that his father had been very unhappy in utopia. He simply could not adapt to the sudden transition. The implication in this text is that a sudden gratification without proper preparation can be too much of a shock for most humans.

The moral dimension of quick gratification, complete with all the connotations of a disturbing and "undeserved" conversion experience, is clearly implied in the final sentences of the most popular American utopia, *Looking Backward*. West is delighted to "return" from his nightmare visit to the Boston of 1887 and overjoyed to find that his love, Edith Leete, is still with him. But, as I will discuss in greater detail in the next chapter, this return is strongly and painfully colored by the culmination of nagging doubts about how unworthy he is to be in utopia. Instead of ending with a celebration of the nearness and inevitability of utopia (themes frequently sounded by Dr. Leete), Bellamy chose to leave the reader with the image of a guilt-ridden narrator who wishes that he could have postponed his gratification by transporting himself back in time so that he could work for utopia:

> *But in that moment, while yet I mused with unspeakable thankfulness upon the greatness of the world's salvation and my privilege in beholding it, there suddenly pierced me like a knife a pang of shame, remorse, and wondering self-reproach, that bowed my head upon my breast and made me wish the grave had hid me with my fellows [nineteenth-century Americans] from the sun. For I had been a man of that former time. What had I done on the deliverance whereat I now presume to rejoice? . . .*
>
> *"Better for you, better for you," a voice within me rang, "had this evil dream been the reality, and this fair reality the dream; better your part pleading for crucified humanity with a scoffing generation, than here, drinking of wells you digged not, and eating of trees whose husbandmen you stoned"; and my spirit answered, "Better, truly."*
>
> *. . . Kneeling before [Edith], with my face in the dust, I confessed with tears how little was my worth to breathe the air of this golden century.* (310–11)

It is clear that even after a brief stay in utopia, West has begun to compose his confessions.

To begin to grasp *Looking Backward* as a "text-as-read," to use Janice Radway's term, we must be aware of Bellamy's ability to create episodes that invited nineteenth-century American readers to see their value system supported even when he is explicitly or implicitly criticizing it. Of course, this type of reader-text relationship could never have occurred without generations of readers learning a shared value system. Only then could readers see an attack on competitive economics and a sudden and unearned trip to utopia as signifying a reinforcement of familiar and just American values.

## Transatlantic Origins

The perceptual origins of late nineteenth-century American utopian fiction were not, of course, limited to American events, American technological developments, and American values. European influences were crucial—influences such as the legacy of the Enlightenment, scientific and social evolutionary theories, socialism, and Christianity. All of these have received attention from Frank and Fritzie Manuel and many other students of utopia;[8] and all can be viewed as perceptual origins. The continuing influence of Enlightenment thought and the newer impact of popular evolutionary ideas encouraged middle- and upper-middle-class readers to perceive humans as being basically good, though corruptible by "bad" environments, and to perceive time as a linear process leading toward improvement. Both these perceptions would help readers to recognize what Pfaelzer calls "progressive utopias" and Segal labels "technological utopias."

The word *socialism* carried such strong negative connotations for nineteenth-century American readers that almost none of the nineteenth-century American utopists, including Bellamy, used it. Still, an awareness of European socialism, however misinformed, helped readers to imagine the possibility of national systems of production and distribution that represented alternatives to capitalism. This awareness made the utopias depicted by late nineteenth-century utopists—most of which involved cooperative, planned economies—more blessedly or terrifyingly believable (depending on the reader's economic biases) than if Americans had shared no knowledge of socialism.

Many American studies scholars and utopographers have emphasized the connections between American utopianism and the Christian heritage of millennialism.[9] This heritage enabled Americans to perceive their history as a "specially commissioned" drama of "elect" actors and to see specific historical events as signifying or at least foreshadowing an alternative, better history, which might, however, be preceded by apocalyptic disasters. These habits of perception would certainly help readers to recognize the warnings and hopes encoded in West's nightmare return and awakening, in books such as Ignatius Donnelly's *Caesar's Column* (1890) and other apocalyptic utopias identified by Pfaelzer (*Utopian Novel* 112–40, 174–75), in Twain's *Connecticut Yankee* (1889), and in the volcanic imagery and all-or-nothing historiography of many late nineteenth-century utopias (Roemer, *Obsolete Necessity* 22–34). More important, millennial expectations conditioned readers to accept both the nationalism of the utopias[10] and the tendency of utopian narrators and guides to present the past and present of America primarily as pre-texts leading to more significant times. Even the "conservative" utopias, with the possible exception of David H. Wheeler's nonfictional *Our Industrial Utopia* (1895), incorporated some improvements that were grounded in the past and present and would blossom in the future.

The popular nineteenth-century American historiography was replete with contradictions that juxtaposed notions of logical evolutions with ancient millennial expectations and more recent ahistorical pronouncements, such as Emerson's declaration in "The Young American" that America "has no past; all has an onward and perspective look" (230). This historiography certainly did not prepare late nineteenth- or twentieth-century Americans to formulate realistic appraisals of their nation's place in history. It was, nevertheless, a splendid preparation for recognizing the appeals of American utopian historiography. Popular views of America's past and how that past predicted the future would help to render Bellamy's utopian vision "familiar" and authentically American.

## Reading Conventions and Book Power

Centuries-old millennial expectations, clusters of Victorian values, technological developments, and specific historical events and trends helped to create an interpretive community of readers ready to accept Bellamy's invitation to utopia. So did their previous reading experiences and their culture's preferred notions of the act of reading. One does not have to be an avid promoter of intertextuality to assume that the educated Victorian readers' exposure to a few classic utopias, perhaps an early American utopia, and most probably adventure, conversion, and romance narratives, as well as the other elements of the utopian hybrid mix discussed in chapter 1, would help them to recognize the potential importance of utopias. At the very least this prior literary knowledge would help them to recognize the primary conventions of utopian fictions, notably the "flat" characters, the guide-visitor dialogues, the various fantastic and coincidental ways of transporting visitors to utopia, and the general form of the apologue— Wells's "shot-silk" mix of "philosophical discussion" and "imaginative narrative" (*Modern Utopia* xxxii).

Although the most obvious literary precursors to late nineteenth-century American utopias were earlier utopias, we should be careful not to overemphasize their importance as perceptual origins. The authors of the later works obviously did not think that it was essential that they draw attention to their knowledge of previous utopias. With the notable exception of W. D. Howells in the *Altrurian Romances,* very few of them did so. More important, none of the American utopias that preceded *Looking Backward* had a wide readership. Therefore, it would be difficult to argue that the early American works significantly affected the nineteenth-century readers' ability to recognize and give meaning to a work such as *Looking Backward.*

Travel/adventure stories that introduced readers to alternative lifestyles were, on the other hand, significant pre-texts for future readers of utopias, especially popular works such as Defoe's *Robinson Crusoe* (1719), which was still in great demand in late nineteenth-century American libraries (Mabie 509), and Melville's best seller *Typee* (1846). Cooper's *The Crater* (1847), which appeared a year after *Typee,* is an excellent example of a transitional work that incorporates the conventions of a shipwreck narrative and the history of an ill-fated utopian community. As noted previously, even after the publication of *Looking Backward,* there were many utopias, including Howells's *Altrurian Romances,* that were set on distant islands, continents, and planets or within the earth.

A few scholars have explored the relationships between late nineteenth-century American utopian fiction and the popular forms of eighteenth- and nineteenth-century fiction variously labeled "sentimental," "domestic,"

"women's," and "women's exploratory" fiction.[11] These relationships deserve more attention; hence my decision to devote the next chapter to the
domestication of utopia. Here I will only note that the elements of domestic fiction incorporated into late nineteenth-century utopias made the latter more recognizable, especially to women readers, who dominated the
domestic fiction reading audience. Virgil Lokke has even speculated that
women readers attracted to the Edith Leete–Julian West romance and the
domestic environs of *Looking Backward* may have been inspired to urge
their husbands to seek reform. Thus, men could be "led . . . through the
bedroom door into utopia" (142). Of course, the membership rolls of the
Bellamy and Nationalist Clubs suggest that a significant number of women
bypassed the bedroom and went directly to the reform meeting. The train
of cause and effect linking domestic fiction, utopian fiction, women readers, and their husbands would be, to say the least, hard to trace. It is, however, practically self-evident that the intellectual and emotional lessons
learned by female and male readers from the settings, plots, characters, issues, and appeals of domestic fiction and sentimental reform novels such
as *Uncle Tom's Cabin* prepared them to perceive the Leetes' home, West's
separation from his nineteenth-century lover, Edith Leete's nurturing love
for him, and his guilt about not helping those who suffered in the nineteenth century as moving invitations intended to evoke the "right feelings,"
to borrow Stowe's words. In the next chapter I examine the advantages and
drawbacks of this marriage of the domestic and the utopian.

Without this marriage I doubt that readers would have transformed
*Looking Backward* into an influential literary-social phenomenon. That
transformation also depended upon the fundamentals of book publishing and literacy and upon attitudes about the power of books. Historians
of book publishing, literacy, and the reading public emphasize the importance of nineteenth-century economic and technological development, urbanization, and the common school system that together created
a steady and affordable supply of books and a strong demand for reading
materials. The expansion of the railroad system, the invention of the steam-
powered printing press, the "economic manufacture of paper from wood
pulp," and improvements in eyeglasses and home lighting all helped to increase the supply of reading materials and the number of readers (Howe
521, Zboray 3–16, Kaestle 167). In *Literacy in the United States* (1991), Carl
Kaestle estimates that "there was a three fold increase in the number of

books being published between 1880 and 1900" (282), and for the later half of this period publishers were more apt to print or reprint more American authors than they had in the past, because the 1891 international copyright law prohibited the pirating of popular European works and gave protection to American books (282). Bellamy obviously benefited from this law and from all the other developments in book publication and distribution.

Another obvious development that prepared American readers for *Looking Backward* was increased literacy. Kaestle indicates that by the late nineteenth century the common school system had prepared more Americans to read the increasing numbers of newspapers, magazines, and books. He admits that literacy data for the nineteenth century are crude. The figures are based primarily on signature records and census self-reporting beginning in 1840. He also notes that by 1880 literacy was "broadly based" rather than "highly developed"; more of family budgets went to newspapers than to books (xv; 163–66). Furthermore, "broadly based" did not extend to all segments of the population. In 1880, 70 percent of the nonwhites responding to the census classified themselves as illiterate (125). Still, for the white adult male and female population, the available figures are impressive. By 1880 only 9.4 percent of them classified themselves as illiterate (125).

Despite the scarcity of data and the obvious need to qualify comments about the extent and depth of American literacy during the late nineteenth century, Kaestle can point to "the decreasing prices [of newspapers, magazines, and books], escalating circulation figures, and rising educational levels" as strong evidence that more Americans than ever before were reading better and reading more (202–03). In a comment particularly relevant to the preparation of readers for utopian literature, Kaestle also observes that "print matter was more important in some ways in 1880 than it is today, because travel was less common [i.e., people tended to read about rather than go to other places] and there were no [serious challenges from] electronic media" (278).

As I'm certain Kaestle would admit, the lack of competing entertainment and information media and the impressive developments in print production, distribution, and literacy do not fully explain the elevated position of reading books during the late nineteenth century in America. We must also consider nineteenth-century attitudes about the functions of reading books, especially their transformative powers.

In *A Fictive People* (1993) Ronald J. Zboray offers a provocative theory about the development of the transformative powers of books during the first half of the nineteenth century. Rapid economic development and the accompanying opportunities for upward mobility often separated family members from one another and from childhood hometowns. According to Zboray, the separations made it difficult for many Americans to establish a sense of identity and community grounded in personal contacts and a sense of place. As the availability of books increased, Zboray argues, "readers increasingly sought common experience in literature" (xxi). "The symbolic community of the printed word replaced or compromised much direct personal contact" (xx).

After the Civil War there was increasing hope that this symbolic community would offer Americans a sense of unity. As Robert H. Wiebe in *The Search for Order, 1877–1920* (1967) and other historians have concluded, the perceived need for order and unity, especially among the middle and upper middle classes, increased as the Civil War, and the previously discussed economic, social, and cultural turmoil of the late nineteenth century, further aggravated feelings of dislocation and confusion. It is not hard to understand why these Americans would find comfort and hope in literary utopias that invited vicarious experiences in a unified and just alternative America.[12]

In *Alternative America* (1983) John L. Thomas suggests a complementary viewpoint about the increased significance of "the symbolic community of the printed word" and about why the "belief in the power of print was almost unlimited in Victorian America" (Sicherman 142). In the late nineteenth century he identifies a crucial "community of moral discourse" (91), a concept not unlike Stanley Fish's "interpretive communities," Tony Bennett's "reading formations," and Elizabeth Long's "social frames." This community had a strong faith in the power of books to shape lives that was expressed in nonfiction, prescriptive writing—"child-rearing manuals, books on household management, etiquette books, even joke books to tell people how to be funny" (Howe, "American Victorianism" 527)—and in fiction, notably popular sentimental reform novels covering issues ranging from slavery (*Uncle Tom's Cabin*, 1852) to treatment of Indians (*Ramona*, 1884) to temperance (*Ten Nights in a Barroom*, 1854). Barbara Sicherman notes that some critics and reviewers even "maintained that the novel had replaced the sermon as the principle shaper of character" (143). Henry

Demarest Lloyd, a leader in the community of moral discourse and author of *Wealth against Commonwealth* (1894), particularly emphasized the power of fiction. "It's not the stern and accurate thinkers who wield humanity directly, but the philosophers who can weave truth into a moving fiction or story." These were the people who could "move mankind and make history" (qt. in Thomas, *Alternative America* 216).

Lloyd's impressions are, at least indirectly, supported by a very interesting and extensive survey of library withdrawals throughout the country during the early 1890s. The survey was conducted by Hamilton W. Mabie, the "literary editor of *Outlook,* whose inspirational messages on ideals and literature comforted hundreds of audiences up and down the country" (Thorp 819). With the data collected, Mabie concluded that "fiction is, on the whole, the most representative kind of literature, that is, that appeals to the greatest number of readers and the distribution that covers the widest area" (511). Of course, sales figures could also be cited to support Mabie's claim.[13]

Considering the general faith in the power of didactic fiction and the library withdrawal and sales figures, it should not be surprising that American readers could see a work such as *Looking Backward* as a powerful guide to thought and action in the present and future. Nor is it surprising that the reviewers (both celebrants and detractors) of *Looking Backward* discussed in chapter 6 assumed that America could be altered by readers inspired by literary utopias, or that, as previously noted, at least twenty-two authors of utopias written between 1888 and 1900 incorporated into their fictional narratives descriptions of books, including utopian fiction, that inspired reformers (Roemer, *America as Utopia* 321). In *Equality,* Dr. Leete even tells West that the popularity of reform literature published just before The Change practically explains the timing of the transformation of America (336).

Beyond the general attitudes about the power of didactic books, especially fictions, the community of moral discourse was also characterized by a certain "style of inquiry and a mode of analysis" (Thomas, *Alternative America* 55). The style could be recognized in the manifesto sections of the utopias as an adaptation of the "oral conventions of the pulpit, the lecture platform, and the stage" (Lokke 141). As the long sermon by Rev. Barton in *Looking Backward* indicates, this rhetorical style was firmly grounded in the parables and imagery of the Bible, which was for American Christian readers the primary example of book power.[14] Seen through this network of religious rhetoric, the presentation of problems and solutions became a form of "moral inquiry" and visionary prophecy (Thomas, *Alternative America* 56). Hence, Bellamy's American readers were well prepared to give powerful meanings to Dr. Leete's characterizations of social problems as Evil and to Rev. Barton's claim that, although the "material" progress represented by their utopia could be compared to the progress made in past epochs of history, "history offers no precedent, however far back we may cast our eye" for the "moral aspect" of their progress (275).

The foregoing attempt to define significant factors that created an interpretive community prepared to recognize, give meaning to, and even act out utopian fiction is limited and at times speculative. But the overview should help us to comprehend the forces that enabled late nineteenth-century readers to perceive literary utopias as meaningful personal and social guides. Furthermore, four of the basic assumptions that underlie many of the claims in this chapter are relevant to understanding processes that transform other types of literature into cultural forces.

First of all, presenting a text from the past as the culmination of perceptual origins that prepared readers to interpret it robs that text of its status as a fixed object containing inherent meanings intended by the author and accessible to "correct" readings by modern scholars. The emphasis on perceptual origins and their effects on readers does not, however, render the author invisible and the text totally malleable. The concept of perceptual origins assumes that certain authors—who are themselves members of "prepared" reading audiences—are capable of inviting readers to construct particular meanings by presenting them with networks of characters, episodes, settings, and other signs that, because of their readers' preparation, will direct them toward anticipated intellectual, emotional, and, in the case of utopian fiction, behavioral responses.

A second important assumption is that an analysis of perceptual origins should not necessarily be limited to the time period that defines the generation that made the text popular and influential. We do not have to go back to the first human attempts to interpret cave drawings every time we hunt for a text's perceptual origins. But too narrow a time scope can lead to narrow views of how readers create meaning. Post–Civil War events did influence how readers interpreted *Looking Backward*. But there have been other disruptive eras in American history, notably the Great Depression years, when similar historical events did not prepare great numbers of American readers to find significant meanings in utopian fiction. In other words, in spite of the great impact of the panics, strikes, and other wrenching circumstances of the late nineteenth century, without the existence of other perceptual origins (including some that were centuries old and others, like sentimental romance interpretive conventions, that seemed to have little to do with current events), Bellamy's utopia would have been an invisible nowhere that had no place in the purview of the American reader.

The third assumption is closely related to the second. An appropriate "ethnography of reading" must consider the probable influences of many different types of perceptual origins: those as broad as millennial expectations and Victorian value systems and as specific as conventional interpretations of a heroine's diction or a decline in the cost of books. Avoiding such diversity may lead to the articulation of consistent arguments that are easy to communicate to the members of a specific academic discipline, but an overly narrow focus can also greatly limit our understanding of the rich and complex network of influences that shape interpretive communities of readers.

The other assumption is practically self-evident: the central question to be asked of every potential influence is, "How might this influence prepare readers to recognize, to pay attention to, and to give meaning to the text?" This general question spawns numerous specific questions related to the text being examined. For instance, if a utopian fiction articulates its critiques through contrasts, are there discoverable circumstances that sensitize readers to seeing meanings in contrasts? If the utopia is meant to be a practical blueprint for the future, what helps readers to perceive utopias as feasible prescriptions? If the text evokes guilt, what reading conventions make this evocation acceptable and significant? These and similar questions were assumed to be important in the foregoing discussions of historical, technological, attitudinal, intellectual, religious, and literary origins of late nineteenth-century reader responses to utopian fiction.

In the following chapter I will continue to examine the forces that prepared readers to see utopia, by focusing on the role of popular eighteenth- and nineteenth-century domestic and domestic reform fiction. The intent of this focus is not to suggest that—among the many important perceptual origins—books such as *Wide, Wide, World* and *Uncle Tom's Cabin* were the key agents shaping the reception to late nineteenth-century utopian literature. My concentration represents, instead, an attempt to highlight a significant perceptual origin that has received less attention than other historical, economic, and cultural forces. The domestic placing of utopia deserves special attention. The associations between domestic and utopian fiction enabled many American readers to perceive Bellamy's other-worldly fantasy as a homespun tale.

# Four

## The Literary Domestication of Utopia
### *There's No Looking Backward without Uncle Tom and Uncle True*

The publication of *Looking Backward* in 1888 overshadowed the appearance in the same year of another work of fiction by Bellamy, "A Love Story Reversed." Another little-known fact: in the early 1890s, Hamilton Mabie's extensive survey of American public libraries, mentioned in chapter 3, revealed that among the most popular fictions, *Looking Backward* and Susan B. Warner's *The Wide, Wide World* (1850) were borrowed with precisely the same frequency (509). In and of themselves these two coincidences may not be significant. But they do help to remind us that during the heyday of utopian fiction in America both authors and readers were still captivated by domestic fictions.[1]

To understand fully why so many readers responded so strongly to *Looking Backward,* we must, as I briefly indicated in the last chapter, acknowledge the central importance of the domestic and sentimental fictions that prepared nineteenth-century readers to perceive utopian literature as accessible and important.[2] An awareness of this intertextual process will help us to appreciate "the special conventions and procedures of interpretation that enable readers to move from the linguistic meaning of sentences to the literary [and in this case, social] meaning[s] of works" (Culler, "Prolegomena" 49). Or to borrow Peter Rabinowitz's terms, acknowledging the importance of domestic fiction as a prereading experience for an encounter with *Looking Backward* is to acknowledge a striking example of the "rule of configuration": knowing relevant conventions and reading protocols can help readers to develop expectations, an awareness of narrative patterns, and meanings as they read (*Before Reading* 44).

In this chapter I will focus on several crucial intersections between *Looking Backward* and popular eighteenth- and nineteenth-century domestic fictions: (1) the narrative structure, particularly the use of the separated-lovers plot and episodes designed to evoke grief and guilt; (2) the domestic locales, notably the dining room and bedrooms and the home library; (3) the angelic heroine—Edith Leete is the obvious embodiment of this familiar and nurturing figure; and (4) an androgynous narrative voice that combines expected masculine poses with striking resemblances to the voices of anxious female heroines and didactic female narrators. All four intertextual intersections invited nineteenth-century readers familiar with domestic fictions to experience what Susan Feagin has called "affective flexibilities" that allowed readers to empathize with Edith and West by "simulating" their "mental processes" (Feagin 17, 83–112).

A few clarifications and qualifications will help to define my claims and foci. First, this is not a "sources and influence" analysis. Rather than suggesting specific parallels between *Looking Backward* and domestic novels by women that Bellamy knew, I'm more interested in establishing the importance of several types of well-known conventions in domestic fiction that would help Bellamy's contemporaries to become "competent" readers—competent in the sense that they could experience *Looking Backward* as a meaningful and moving text, even, to borrow Jane Tompkins's term, as a powerful cultural "agent."[3]

Second, in my allusions to conventions, I will emphasize three types of domestic novels: the pre-1820 seduction-separation tale defined by the popular eighteenth-century novelist Susanna Rowson as a story involving impassioned lovers, seduction, extended separation, intrigues, surprising discoveries, and happy reunions (Petter 27); the "woman's" fiction, described by Nina Baym as flourishing between 1820 and 1870, that narrates the trials, separations, and triumphs of a little child, as in Maria Cummins's *The Lamplighter* (1854), or a young "pampered heiress" suddenly deprived of support but who eventually triumphs over adversity (Baym, *Woman's Fiction* 35); and the domestic reform novel, such as *Uncle Tom's Cabin,* that combines, in didactic and melodramatic presentations, specific private and broad public issues such as temperance and abolition. Variations of conventions in these fictions appear frequently in *Looking Backward*. Many of Bellamy's original readers would be thoroughly familiar with them and could use this competence in their attempts to comprehend Dr. Leete's Boston of A.D. 2000.

Third, *Looking Backward* was certainly not the first example of an intersection between sentimental and utopian fiction. Barbara Quissell discusses earlier examples of sentimental temperance and abolitionist reform novels and a few sentimental utopian fictions. Bellamy has even been accused of borrowing from one of these works (John Macnie's *The Diothas* [1883]), which includes a sentimental, nineteenth-century descendant named Edith.[4]

Fourth, my emphasis on domestic conventions should not obscure the fact that, as argued in chapters 1 and 3, the competence of Bellamy's readers was also defined by their ability to recognize the conventions of many other forms of literary and nonliterary, written and oral discourses, including the Bible (especially parables, prophesies, visions, and revelations), tracts, dialogues, declarations, literary utopias, travel accounts, sermons, speeches, and lectures.

Understanding the importance of the domestic literary conventions recognized by readers in *Looking Backward* may suggest new ways to understand not only utopian fiction but also the iconoclastic, prescriptive, and idealistic functions of eighteenth- and nineteenth-century domestic fictions. At the very least my approach to *Looking Backward* should help us to see that the power of domestic fiction not only lasted beyond the 1870s, but also survived the transplantation to another fictional genre—survived, indeed thrived, and helped to reshape that genre in ways that prepared modern readers to appreciate the emphasis placed on feelings and personal relationships in many of the best utopian fictions written by Ursula K. Le Guin, Marge Piercy, Samuel Delany, Dorris Lessing, and Kim Stanley Robinson more than a century after the publication of *Looking Backward*, "A Love Story Revisited," and *Wide, Wide World*.

## Narrative Structure: Separations and Tears for the Dead

*Looking Backward* abounds in well-known plot formulas, especially the scenarios of utopian fiction (e.g., the strange journey, the confused entry, the socialization via guide and guide's daughter, and the "return"—in this case an imagined return) and of the domestic novel, especially the pre-1820 emphasis on separated lovers reunited after various intrigues and surprising discoveries and the post-1820 drama of an heiress's sudden separation from emotional supports and familiar surroundings. In *Looking Backward* there are three types of interrelated separation plots. In the opening chapters, the wealthy Julian West (who inherited his riches) and his fiancée, Edith Bartlett, must delay their wedding. West can't properly house his love. He does not want his "dainty bride" to live in his "elegant" and "old-fashioned" family mansion because the neighborhood has been changed by an "invasion [of] tenement houses and manufactories." The building of his new home in a less contaminated part of town has been delayed by a strike (104–05). These frustrations dwindle in magnitude when compared to the barriers posed by West's miraculous 113-year sleep, which permanently separates him from Miss Bartlett and, because he is an anachronism from an evil era, impedes his courtship of Edith Leete. His hyperbolic response to this situation recalls the despair of the separated lovers who populated domestic novels: he portrays his fate as one of "utter forlornness, such as no other lover, however unhappy, could have felt" (287).

The "happy accident" that dissolves these apparently impenetrable obstacles is a variation of what Alexander Cowie has called the sentimental "long-lost relative" motif (423): Edith Leete is Edith Bartlett's great-granddaughter. "Quite in the manner of a nineteenth-century sentimental heroine, Edith Leete had fallen in love with the Julian West of her great-grandmother's letters" and vowed that she would never wed until she found his equal (Towers 60). Again, in the tradition of domestic fiction, the crucial discovery is withheld until the concluding episodes; in this case the pretext for the delay is the Leetes' fear that a premature revelation might be too much of a shock for someone as bewildered as their time-traveling guest. But once the revelation is made, all barriers seem to vanish. Edith Leete is free to love the Julian of the nineteenth-century personal letters and in the flesh (with proper Victorian restraint, of course), and West can love and marry his two Ediths. Edith does not have to worry about the dilemmas of misinformed choices in love or the threat of cruel parents or guardians that plagued so many sentimental heroines (Davidson, *Revolution* 123, 139). West is clearly the right choice, and the Leetes bless their (re)union. Indeed, for West the Leete family performs the same functions as the kind "surrogate kin" who nurture the suddenly deprived heroines of domestic novels (Baym, *Woman's Fiction* 38). Even West's initial housing problem is solved. He is obviously welcome to stay with the Leetes, whose land coincidentally covers the spot where West's old mansion once stood. The two Wests, two Ediths, two lovers, and two homes are now one.

For many readers today, Bellamy's love story may seem ridiculously contrived—an embarrassing obstacle to an appreciation of his social criticisms and models for the future. But for those nineteenth-century readers who expected, even desired, such narrative tensions and resolutions, Bellamy's variations of familiar domestic plots would facilitate entry into his estranging world of socialism and high technology. Lee Cullen Khanna has argued convincingly that the withheld information in several of the intrigues of *Looking Backward* can still entice modern readers into playing the utopian "game" and engage them in acts of textual and self-discovery ("Reader" 70, 75, 77–79), an opinion supported by my survey of more than seven hundred readers that revealed the continued appeal of Edith Leete and her love story (see especially my discussions of responses to images of women in chapter 9). Furthermore, the love story reinforces much of Bellamy's social criticism and utopian model (Dowst 95, 99). The separated/(re)united-lovers motif especially contributes to the delineation of West's conversion from a nineteenth-century aristocratic perspective to a utopian worldview. West's initial account of nineteenth-century obstacles—invaded neighborhoods and striking workers—portrays West as the victim and the tenement dwellers and the workers as the victimizers. Near the end of the narrative, when (in an ingenious inversion of the sleeper-returns motif) West dreams of his return to the Boston of 1887, his perceptions are reversed. He is the victimizer; they are the victims. In other words, the separation-reunion plot conventions augment the utopist's penchant for iconoclastic contrasts that invite readers to question their concepts of reality. The melodramatic discovery of Edith Leete's identity and the blossoming of love between her and West also helped Bellamy to delineate the nature of his model of a better future. For readers accustomed to domestic romances, the depiction of a powerful love that could quickly obliterate the psychological and cultural barriers between West and Edith Leete could signify the possibility of a good place where love can triumph over artificial and cruel separations, a place where, to quote Dr. Leete, "there are nothing but matches of pure love" (269).

The intersections of Bellamy's domestic and utopian plots do, however, create significant and disturbing inconsistencies. Other than the Edith Leete–Julian West relationship, the only demonstration the narrator offers of the end product of a social structure free of true-love-thwarting obstacles is not particularly loving. John L. Thomas has noted that the "family life at the Leetes is . . . disengaged. Father, mother, and daughter move through each other's lives without collision and almost without incident" (*Alternative America* 255); and, he should add, with very few open expressions of love. Perhaps the utopian conventions that dictated the calm, reserved, and logical demeanor of the guide, or Bellamy's tendency toward paternalism, or his concept of impersonal love (as defined in his essay "Religion of Solidarity," with its emphasis on a selfless identification with humanity) help to explain the contradictions between claims of "love galore" (205) in utopia and the example of Leete's household. Whatever the explanations, the contrasts between the impassioned story of the separated lovers and the rather separate lives of the Leete family deprive readers of the opportunity to see, within Bellamy's narrative, how the free and fair passions of utopian youth can function and develop in mature utopian family life.

It would be unfair to Bellamy to suggest that his use of domestic narrative structures was limited to the separated-lovers plot. Overtones of death, sorrow, and guilt, familiar to readers of women's fictions, were also crucial elements of key episodes in *Looking Backward*. In her provocative interpretation of *Uncle Tom's Cabin*, Jane Tompkins stresses the importance of little Eva's death as an episode that tapped into the nineteenth-century readers' deep religious beliefs about the "power of the dead or dying to redeem the unregenerate," especially if the victim is "pure and powerless" (127–28; see also Baym, *Woman's Fiction* 15–16). Not only was this a significant motif in "popular fiction and religious literature" (Tompkins 128), death and guilt-evoking episodes were, as mentioned in chapter 3, also reflections of what Daniel Walker Howe has called the "great age of prescriptive writing," which included novels that "legitimated themselves by the morals they taught" ("American Victorianism" 527); what Thomas refers to as a "community of moral discourse," which articulated a moralistic and eschatological vision of reform (*Alternative America* 57); and what Barbara Quissell defines as a "rhetoric designed to direct the reader's emotional responses" ("Sentimental" 33) and to persuade them to alter their attitudes (Dowst 8, 12).

Julian West is certainly not a reincarnation of blessed little Eva. The closing scenes of *Looking Backward* do, nonetheless, empower him with the voice of the redeeming dead who is both pure and powerless. In his nightmare return to the lavish dining table at the Bartlett's home, he learns painfully the limits of his ability to communicate utopian ideas to the unregenerate (Pfaelzer, "Immanence" 64). After his horrifying dream, he awakens in his bedroom in the Leetes' twenty-first-century home with "the morning sun shining through the open window" (310). This reawakening into the twenty-first century demonstrates how an author can attract attention to an episode by setting up expectations—in this case expectations for a sleeper-awakes episode—that are reversed and thus "create [a] surprise" that draws attention to the episode (Rabinowitz, *Before Reading* 111).

Readers are therefore invited to pay special attention to West's reawakening into the year 2000. He is tremendously relieved and symbolically purified by sunlight and tears. And he is soon by his beloved's side. But this is not the blissful happy ending portrayed in most of the Bellamy scholarship. It is closer to the sentimental novel's tearful "might-have-been" formula identified by Herbert Ross Brown (173). As noted in chapter 3, West is "pierced" with "pain" and "self-reproach." His life had been wasted in sinful "indifference to the wretchedness" around him. He had no "right" to utopia. In this guilt-ridden and tear-drenched state of self-hatred and before his final act of throwing himself in the dust before Edith, he delivers the previously quoted cathartic apostrophe addressed to himself (but obviously intended to move Bellamy's first readers): "'Better for you, better for you,'" a voice within me rang, "'had this evil dream been the reality, and this fair reality the dream, better your part pleading for crucified humanity with a scoffing generation, than here, drinking of wells you digged not'" (310–11). Like many sentimental heroines and some sentimental heroes, West had been purged by trials and tears. He is now purified. He is also powerless; or to borrow Jonathan Auerbach's apt term, he is "impotent" (41). He could not change the minds of his former contemporaries in his dream; he can not return "in reality" to try again; and his role in his new "present" is one of a marginalized anachronism whose authority lies in performing his role as a relic of the past that demonstrated how much better things are in the Leetes' world.

West's powerlessness was one of Bellamy's powers. Like Stowe, Bellamy could use West's "death," purity, and powerlessness, not, as Auerbach suggests, to invite readers to "embrace their collective impotence" (41), but to make his readers "feel right" (*Uncle Tom's Cabin* 2: 317). W. D. Howells even argued that Bellamy's greatest strength was his "power to make the reader feel [the fictional experience] like something he has known himself" ("Editor's Study" 254). This "feeling" is an experience akin to Susan Feagin's concept of "simulation" (94) or perhaps even closer to Georges Poulet's notion of astonished consciousness: "I am a consciousness astonished by an existence which is not mine, but which I experience as though it were mine" (48). No doubt, Bellamy believed that the ideal readers of the conclusion of his narrative would be astonished at how well they could feel and know West's disturbing guilt as their own. Of course, the crucial difference was that, as the postscript proclaims, the readers could do something, since, unlike West, they were living in the nineteenth century and had power to transform disturbing guilt and confusion into actions that would change society in the future. Viewed from this interpretive perspective the conclusion of *Looking Backward* has the potential to function as a "dialectical" text, as defined by Stanley Fish: "The purpose of its style is not to affirm the received and approved but to induce an experience of deliberate intellectual uncertainty in the reader, urging and instructing him towards a self-denying visionary acquiescence or 'conversion' beyond language" (qt. in Freund 98).

In *Looking Backward,* as in many domestic novels, domestic reform novels, and other literary utopias, the plot is not resolved within the text, despite all the happy and the sad endings. In these novels, readers were often directly or indirectly invited, even implored and provoked, to read their worlds as continuations of the narratives and, empowered with the right feelings, to articulate their readings in acts as private as helping orphans or warning young women about untrustworthy men, or as public as joining temperance or abolitionist groups. In the case of *Looking Backward,* textual invitations to feel hope, horror, guilt, and anger could be worked out in Nationalist Clubs or other forms of social action. The original power of *Looking Backward* depended to a great degree on this concept of narratives that had to be completed with feelings and actions outside the text.

Bellamy would most certainly agree with Robert Scholes that reading is incomplete "unless and until [the text] is absorbed and transformed in the thoughts and deeds of the readers (*Protocols,* x).

## Domestic Settings: Utopia as Home Sweet Home

Bellamy located most of the invitations to readers to feel and act outside the text within his descriptions of events and discussions inside the Leetes' home. This homeyness was deeply rooted in Bellamy's own life. According to his great-grandson, Michael Bellamy, Bellamy really never left home, and he preferred it that way (ch. 1, 3, 36).[5] He was particularly aware of his home environment as he composed *Looking Backward*. Bellamy's father died in 1886. The son wrote *Looking Backward* sitting in his father's chair, in his father's study, surrounded by his father's books—including Dickens, one of his father's favorites (ch. 2, pt. 3, 3; ch. 3, pt. 1, 5). *Looking Backward* was a homegrown utopia.

Contemporary readers noticed this. Howells even praised Bellamy's ability "to start to heaven from home" ("Editor's Study" 256), and the book was included in the "Home Sweet Home" publication series, which must have gratified Bellamy. The intersections with the post-1820 and reform domestic novels are obvious. The "happy home"—in contrast to the cruel homes experienced by many of the heroines and slaves—was a utopian goal, an earthly metaphor for the Kingdom of God, and a familiar and reassuring locale for nineteenth-century readers. Domestic reform had even been used by the novelists (Stowe, for instance) as a metaphor for social reform (Brown, "Getting in the Kitchen"). Furthermore, like the familiar separation narrative, the domestic settings helped readers, especially women readers, orient Bellamy's alternative America within networks of known assumptions and expectations. Hence it is not surprising that most of the American women who wrote utopian fiction during the late nineteenth and early twentieth centuries also anchored their utopian visions in the home. As Darby Lewes emphasizes, women protagonists in these utopias "embrace home as a center of female power: the kitchen and nursery are places of nurture and generation; the parlor and bedroom, sites of intellectual and physical communion" (73).

R. Jackson Wilson and Arthur Lipow have argued convincingly, however, that the homeyness of *Looking Backward* and other late nineteenth- and early twentieth-century utopias deprives readers of demonstrations of how Nationalism would affect the daily lives of the members of the industrial army. Wilson points out that on those rare occasions when West strays from his guide's home, the amount of description is inversely proportionate to the distance from domestic activities. We see quite a bit of a public eating hall, a bit less of a retail store, much less of a wholesale store and a library, and nothing of schools, businesses, or factories (xii–xiii). Possibly we could defend Bellamy by reminding Wilson that West's narrative covers only the first week of his visit to utopia. He was still in shock and needed to stay near a home base. But this is a rather lame defense. If the government operations and factories of utopia are as clean and orderly as Leete claims, then a brief peek at a production line under the good doctor's guidance and his daughter Edith's nurturing eye should not pose much of a threat to West's health. Furthermore, the increased emphasis placed on nondomestic settings (e.g., outdoor farm work) in *Equality* (298–303), the sequel to *Looking Backward,* suggests that Bellamy eventually realized the importance of indicating in some detail the influence of Nationalism on the daily lives of workers outside their homes. But before we write off the domestic focus of *Looking Backward* as an example of embarrassing contamination by sentimental literary conventions or as a reflection of Bellamy's middle-class perspective, we should consider specifically how Bellamy used domestic settings and the impacts of his homes on his contemporary and even modern readers.

As mentioned previously, West's nineteenth-century attitudes about neighborhoods and home construction create a domestic backdrop against which readers can measure his changing perspectives on victims and victimizers in industrial society. Three of the dining scenes also help to dramatize West's and society's progress. (Dining episodes were common in domestic novels [Cowie 416]. Readers even wrote to Warner for recipes from *Wide, Wide World* [Papashvily 7].) In the first scene, West has been invited to "dine with the family of [his] betrothed" on May 13, 1887. He tells us nothing about the food, the serving people, the cook, the table setting, or the dinner attire. Instead he focuses on the after-dinner conversation. West dominates the talk; he "lavishe[s]" "objurgations" against the "workingmen," especially the "strikers." He recalls that he "had abundant sympathy about [him]"; all his listeners agree with him (103–04).

In chapters 13 and 14, West describes a very different type of dining experience. In A.D. 2000, the Leetes take him to the Elephant, the general dining-house of their ward. The Leetes consider this place "a part of their house." As is the case with other families, they have "a room set apart" for them where they eat their evening meal, the two "minor meals of the day" being prepared in their private home. They can order their dinners from a huge variety of excellent but inexpensive food prepared in the hall's "public kitchens." A young waiter serves the Leetes and West. He, like the other waiters, is in a temporary "unclassified grade" of the industrial army, a grade that requires all entering members of the labor force to do "all sorts of miscellaneous occupations not requiring skill." Dr. Leete himself had served as a waiter. The after-dinner tour of the hall dazzles West. He sees the building as an enormous "pleasure-house and social rendezvous" open to everyone. As might be expected, the conversation during and after this meal is quite different from the talk during the meal 113 years earlier. We hear about the efficiency and excellence of the public kitchens, the reduced workload for women, the equality of labor and "solidarity of humanity," and the implications of the contrasts between the "simplicity of our private home life" and the "splendor" of a public life that is "ornate and luxurious beyond anything the world ever knew before" (188; 194–96). The contrasts between the 1887 and 2000 meals are striking, and at least one scholar has argued that such contrasts had an important impact on Bellamy's readers. Dolores Hayden relates the domestic scenes in *Looking Backward* to "the pervasive popular concern with domestic reform" during the late nineteenth century (136). She claims that a "broad audience became sympathetic to socialized domestic work for entire urban populations, an audience which had not existed before Bellamy" (149).

The third dining scene presents a stark contrast to the previous two. In chapter 28, West's horrifying nightmare return to the Boston of 1887 culminates in an invitation to "join [the Bartletts] at table." He now notices many details that he had taken for granted earlier: the Bartletts have a "magnificent" private home with "carved stone steps"; the women are "sumptuously dressed" and wear "the jewels of queens"; the table glitters "with plate and costly china" and displays "costly viands" and "rich wines." The conversation and group dynamics change drastically. West's altered perceptions compel him to preach to the diners about their role in the creation of the poverty, manifest in the nearby homes and factories, and to predict wonderful changes if they and their government would but see humanity as he does. Instead of giving West unanimous sympathy, his listen-

ers become mortified, scandalized, and furious. At the first meal everything West said was appropriate and meaningful to his audience. Now all
his words are infuriating and ultimately "meaningless" to them. Finally,
Mr. Bartlett commands the assembled husbands to throw West out of his
house (306–09).

Taken together these three contrasting dining scenes make strong statements about nineteenth-century ways of organizing labor and interpersonal relations. The contrasts also dramatize Bellamy's emphasis on radical alterations of perception systems as prerequisites for social change.
One obvious advantage of expressing this message in a domestic meal
setting is that the familiarity of dining situations could lead to repeated
reinforcement of Bellamy's ideas. I'm not claiming that every time one of
Bellamy's readers sat down to lunch, he or she would be flooded with feelings and thoughts about labor, interpersonal relations, and the necessity
of perceptual changes. But the very familiarity of the act of dining would
make the lessons that Bellamy professed more accessible during the reading process and more reenforceable after the reading experience than if he
had chosen to teach his lessons using scenes and actions more removed
from his readers' daily lives.

Similar statements could be made about Bellamy's home library and
bedroom scenes. These domestic settings are the backdrops for two of the
most important conversion events in the book. True, West's anxious two-
hour walk alone in Boston soon after his arrival brings out many symptoms
that indicate the early stages of his conversion (142–43). But the crucial
changes occur under the Leetes' roof and under the nurturing influence of
Edith Leete.

As noted in my preface, in an attempt "to make [West] feel at home,"
Edith Leete takes him to a "cosy apartment," the home library. Before leav-
ing, she points out many of his "friends," his favorite authors, including one
of Bellamy's favorites, Dickens (188). Like many of the conceptualized
and real female readers described by contributors to Elizabeth Flynn and
Patrocinio Schweickart's *Gender and Reading* (1986), West submerges himself in Dickens's narrative, collapsing the boundaries between text and
world and, in the process, voicing strong personal and emotional responses. As he reads Dickens and juxtaposes what he reads against what
he has seen in A.D. 2000, he even experiences his first major shift in perceptions. "Every paragraph, every phrase, brought up some new aspect of

the world-transformation which had taken place" (190). He also expresses his first clearly articulated feelings of guilt: he "so little deserved" this new world that he had not "toiled" to create (190).[6] These perceptual and emotional changes foreshadow the devastating and liberating shifts he experiences in his bedroom during his nightmare return and as he awakes from that dream and seeks and finds Edith Leete.

A "cosy" home library, a bedroom, and public and private dining rooms certainly lack the grandeur of the expansive prairies, gloomy forests, grand rivers, and majestic oceans that represent the sacred spaces available for masculine transcendental leaps in American literature. But as Helen Waite Papashvily and Jane Tompkins have pointed out, the solitary hero's transcendent experience in the great outdoors was not the only model of personal transformation available to nineteenth-century readers (Papashvily 6; Tompkins 170). The domestic environments of West's conversion bear out their argument. Considering the nature of Bellamy's intended audience (middle- and upper-middle-class readers), he made appropriate setting choices. Experiences such as dining, reading a moving book at home, or having a nightmare in one's bedroom were types of experiences that were very familiar to these readers. At least they were much more common to them than whaling voyages, life among the Mohegans, or raft trips down the Mississippi. By contrasting the relative unfamiliarity of Melville's, Cooper's, and Twain's settings with the relative familiarity of Bellamy's settings, I am not suggesting that West's changes in perception are more profound or more moving than Ishmael's, Natty Bumpo's, or Huck's. But I am suggesting that if a nineteenth-century author intended to write a book that would motivate middle-class readers to change their self-images and their society, it made sense to draw upon the types of settings familiar to readers of domestic fictions—settings that could easily be read into their own lives, where they could begin to translate the fictional narrative into real-world action or at least into altered perceptions of their environment.

## Sentimental Heroines: Anachronistic Angels

One element of Bellamy's domestic environment that was especially familiar to his readers was Edith Leete. The daughter of the guide in utopian literature represented an obvious invitation for nineteenth-century utopists to people their strange and potentially unsettling landscapes with reassuring sentimental heroines, "transplanted Victorian 'belle-ideal[s]'"

(Lewes 35). Bellamy accepted the invitation. Especially for his early readers, Edith Leete became a major element in a process variously labeled by structuralist reader-response critics as "recuperation, naturalization, motivation, *vraisemblabisation*" (Culler, *Structuralist Poetics* 137). This process invites readers to domesticate "into 'naturalness' the strangeness which defies and resists understanding" (Freund 82).

For many nineteenth-century readers Edith Leete was a natural at naturalizing the strange. She "embodied all the admirable traits given to the sentimental heroine" (Quissell, "Sentimental" 25), particularly the attractive pre-1820 heroine: "[She] was in the first blush of womanhood, was the most beautiful girl I had ever seen. Her face was as bewitching as deep blue eyes, delicately tinted complexion and perfect features could make it" (118). At crucial moments this "most beautiful girl" can "drop her eyes with a charming blush" (207) and flash a "quaint smile" (256), and of course, like a good pining female, she cries. Her roles include being an "indefatigable shopper" (155) who loves "pretty clothes" (161) and a patient advisor who offers West advice about retail stores, music, dining, and literature—all proper women's topics. Of course, her most important role is the nurturing mother figure—a figure who, like Alice Humphrey in *Wide, Wide World* and Emily Graham in *Lamplighter*, can soothe and advise troubled souls. Michael Bellamy even calls Edith Leete a "parent/therapist" specializing in a "talking cure" (ch. 2, pt. 3, 2; ch. 8, pt. 1, 33). She reassures West with her endless reserves of "sympathy," one of her favorite words (Pfaelzer, *Utopian Novel* 37), and a word that carried strong religious authority. The nineteenth-century concept of sympathy had as its ultimate model God's sympathy for the terrestrial sphere (White 85–86). Edith Leete's sympathy has inspired critics to compare her to the Virgin Mary and even Christ (Stupple 74–78; Suvin, *Metamorphoses* 174). It is debatable as to whether her pedestal should tower that high, but it is clear that it would be easy for nineteenth-century readers to perceive her as an emblem of what Tompkins has identified as "the story of salvation through motherly love" (125). Furthermore, her beauty, her mannerisms, and her nurturing powers make her a primary example of the role of utopian women as "icons for men's inspiration, flagellants for masculine ambition, and prizes awarded to the most successful of the men" (Tichi 25; also *Looking Backward* 267; 271–72).

It is not difficult to understand why West fell in love with such a woman and why she could ease readers' entries into utopia. As Jean Pfaelzer observes, West's love of Edith Leete represents his naturalization as a citizen of utopia ("Immanence" 59). And since West is an obvious point of identification for readers, Edith Leete may help them to be vicariously naturalized also. Naomi Jacobs elaborates convincingly on this process of identification with utopian heroines: "The love of a utopian woman assuages the visitor's sense of estrangement, resolves his emotional struggles, and makes him feel he belongs in this world so much more perfect than he himself can be. To the extent that the reader identifies wholly with the protagonist, the reader will share those struggles and their ultimate resolution" (79).

No doubt, Edith Leete was an inspiring combination of sentimental heroine, nurturing savior, and utopian icon, capable of consoling West and many nineteenth-century readers as they encountered Bellamy's alternative America. But as Jacobs also notes, some female readers might not identify with the love story the way male readers would (79). Moreover, some of the very qualities that make her an ideal nineteenth-century sympathizing woman also make her an unconvincing demonstration of the new woman Dr. Leete describes in chapter 25. In *Looking Backward* we see her care for West, but we never see or hear about her job in the industrial army. By contrast, as Quissell and Baym have noted, many of the heroines in domestic novels worked (Quissell, "Sentimental" 90–92; Baym, *Woman's Fiction* 28). As Patrick Parrinder has noted, Edith also does not fulfill her duty to improve the human race. Women were supposed to select the best men of their time as mates. Certainly West falls below those standards ("Eugenics" 6). Even the two nonsentimental qualities Kenneth Dowst praises (96) and West often mentions—Edith's frankness and directness—are not always demonstrated. At a critical point in the separation-(re)union narrative, just after West has finally admitted his love for her, she is as coy and indirect as a helpless sentimental heroine in a seduction novel. She blushes, her eyes lower; she sighs, smiles quaintly, and says, "Are you sure it is not you who are blind?," which is her indirect way of saying that she loves him too (289). Edith's mother, an "exceptionally fine looking and well preserved" woman (118), saves her embarrassed daughter by taking West aside and explaining Edith's love and identity (290). Edith's performance in this scene confirms Susan Lynch Foster's warning about combining the sentimental and the utopian: "The mixture of sentimental and radical ingredients tends to induce ideological indigestion" (49).

It is ironic that the behavior of Bellamy's "utopian" heroine of 1888 is so different from his "love story" heroine of 1888. Maud Elliott, in "A Love Story Reversed," is painfully shy, blushes on every page, and cries on every other. Nevertheless, she has the courage to state to a man, with honesty and directness, "I care for you very much," long before he has any romantic feelings for her (30). The mature relationship that grows out of this courtship reversal expresses Bellamy's approval of frank-speaking women and female initiative. Bellamy evidently believed that in the familiar nineteenth-century domestic setting of a love story he could successfully dramatize a feminine directness and a type of interpersonal relationship different from proper Victorian standards, whereas in his utopian domestic world he conceived of his heroine primarily as a stabilizing, rather than a liberating, agent.

Despite the reassurances Edith Leete must have given Bellamy's first readers, her individual "performance," as contrasted to Dr. Leete's general descriptions of women's characteristics and occupations, undercuts the "relation between character and environment" (Pfaelzer, *Utopian Novel* 35). Her favorite minister, Rev. Barton, may orate eloquently about the wonderful effects of transplanting the sickly rosebush of humanity from the swamp of the nineteenth century to the "sweet warm, dry earth" of the twenty-first century (283–84), but Edith Leete's example suggests that Bellamy's variety of sentimental rose is a rose, is a rose, is a rose, no matter where it is planted. Indeed, one might argue that Edith represents a much less subversive form of criticism and a less idealist model then her mid-nineteenth-century sentimental ancestors, who—because of their victimization and triumphs—were at least indirect signifiers of both the suffering and potential of women. During the 1890s, even Bellamy seemed to admit this. In "Woman in the Year 2000" (1891) he called for "self-elected and useful work for women" (3), and in *Equality* (1897) Edith serves as a worker on a high-tech farm (44).

And yet, the old-fashioned angel who nurtures West through his crises helped Bellamy to create one of the most forward-looking elements of *Looking Backward,* an androgynous narrative voice. Certainly the sights of the new Boston and the revelations coming from Dr. Leete's masculine voice changed West. But he was also powerfully affected by Edith Leete. Mary Kelley argues that one of the most important functions of the nurturing female figure in domestic fiction is the "feminization of the male":

"Led by the angel of mercy, man's self-concern gives way to concern for others, . . . and the novel or story concludes with the overwhelmed male bathing his mate in bathetic praise, and the woman, deluged in tears, consenting to continue as his mentor" ("Sentimental" 443). Kelley is describing the rare "ideal man" as reformed by a heroine in domestic fiction, but her portrait also illuminates the nature of Edith Leete's effect on West and the conventions that would speak so clearly to nineteenth-century readers of the final scene of *Looking Backward* as West bows down to his sympathetic lover.

## An Androgynous Voice from "Nowhere": Julia(n) West

One of the most significant changes Bellamy made in his conception of *Looking Backward* was his decision to alter the narrative viewpoint from a general "twentieth-century" perspective to the first-person voice of a nineteenth-century "resuscitated man" ("How I Wrote" 2). As was the case with most nineteenth-century domestic fiction, a personal voice, which often makes direct appeals to the reader, controls the entire narrative, including the preface and the footnotes. (The obvious exception is the postscript, signed "Edward Bellamy," that was added to the second edition.)

Barbara Quissell has noted the similarity between the direct addresses and appeals of the female narrators and authors of domestic novels and the "Dear Reader" addresses of utopian fiction ("Sentimental" 19–23), and several scholars have specifically examined the nature and importance of West's direct addresses in *Looking Backward* (Dowst 63–75, esp. 72–75, Khanna, "Reader" 75, Roemer, "Contexts and Texts," 216–19, Ruppert 63–64). Pfaelzer has detected differences between West's emotional voice in the love scenes and his "dry" and passive voice during the guide-visitor episodes (*Utopian Novel* 30), and there are several fascinating analyses of West's emotionalism and nervous disorders.[7] An awareness of West's acquisition of stereotypical feminine traits that are strikingly similar to the mannerisms of female narrators and heroines in domestic novels is, in my opinion, also crucial to our understanding of the appeal of *Looking Backward*.

The narrator's name and certain masculine stereotypical qualities characterize West before he arrives in utopia. Michael Bellamy points out that Bellamy was an ardent student of military history, and the name Julian was associated with Roman generals (ch. 6, pt. 1, 5–6). "West" evokes the vigor of exploring frontier territories and the notion of Manifest Destiny.[8] West's initial demeanor seems conventionally masculine. Tom H. Towers accurately describes the West of 1887 as an "American gentleman" who, despite his agitation about the construction of his new house, is "sober, upright, and responsible" (53). After his arrival in utopia, we can still detect familiar male connotations, and it is certainly understandable why, in *Narrating Utopia* (1999), Chris Ferns would place *Looking Backward* within the long tradition of masculine utopias. West's long sessions with Dr. Leete take on the aura of "men of the world" rituals. Typically, when the time came for an important man-to-man talk, "the ladies retired" (121). Presumably, women are not appropriate dramatis personae for such weighty scenes. (In contrast, women sometimes discussed "politics, law, philosophy, and history" in domestic fiction [Davidson, *Revolution* 123].) In *Looking Backward* the men's stage is set with "our wine and cigars" (243). Dr. Leete takes on the role of the wise paternal guide, while West acts the part of the naive, curious, and impressionable, though rarely emotional, male student/foil. He becomes a substitute for the son Leete never had. The sessions are concentrated facts-of-life lessons delivered in a secure domestic setting and designed to enable the newborn yet fully grown son to cope with the manly characteristics of the outside world of A.D. 2000.

In the separation-(re)union episodes the narrative voice has a much more lively and anguished personality, one that manifests numerous stereotypical female reactions familiar to readers of domestic fiction. Soon after his arrival, he feels an "extraordinary mixture of emotions," which is certainly understandable for someone who has just experienced a 113-year sleep (114). The intensity and duration of these emotions go far beyond the typical range of confusion called for by the conventions of pre-twentieth-century utopian fiction. Admittedly, some of his behavior has stereotypical masculine overtones (e.g., he grinds his teeth, and once he flees the domestic setting and roams the streets of Boston alone). Most of West's outbursts, however, more closely resemble the hysterics of mistreated sentimental heroines separated from their lovers or the lamentations of destitute orphans and suddenly impoverished and uprooted "pampered heiresses" of the mid-nineteenth century. He shouts, he pants, he cries, he faints and gets dizzy spells, recalling the helplessness of the "swooning heroine" (Cowie 418). In chapter 8, his awakening disorientation leads to a frenzied collapse that rivals the performances of a Charlotte Temple, a Gerty in *Lamplighter*, or an Ellen Montgomery in *Wide, Wide World*: "Leaping from bed, I stood in the middle of the room clasping my temples with all my might between my hands to keep them from bursting. Then I fell prone on the couch, and, burying my face in the pillow, lay without motion" (141). Later in the same chapter we find him throwing himself "into a chair"—an act, incidentally, aptly performed by the dismayed Maud in Bellamy's "A Love Story Reversed" (31). He covers his "burning eyeballs with [his] hands to shut out the horror of the strangeness. [His] mental confusion [is] so intense as to produce actual nausea" (143).

Stereotyped male heroes might get upset once in a while, but they should not collapse into pillows and chairs. That is a stereotypical "woman's work." Moreover, they should not admit to queasy stomachs or to other nervous disorders. Towers has demonstrated effectively that one particular nervous disorder, insomnia, is nevertheless a central element of West's character ("Insomnia of West"). West's insomnia has obvious psychological (guilt) and thematic (utopia as peaceful sleep) importance. It is also significant because it combines with West's feelings of ignorance about A.D. 2000 and his other emotional and physical problems to render him almost as dependent as the victimized heroine of a seduction romance or the impoverished heroine in the early chapters of a domestic novel. That one of the people on whom he depends is a male doctor even evokes the connotations of the stereotyped relationships between supposedly hysterical women and supposedly wise male medics addressed in many studies of Victorian women (e.g., Haller and Haller, and Smith-Rosenberg).

West's sudden awakening in A.D. 2000 and the disorienting effects of what he sees in Boston and hears from Dr. Leete are the primary "causes" of his hysteria. Still, Edith Leete plays a tremendously important role in West's development by, in effect, giving him permission to feel and express strong emotions of despair. Instead of ignoring his plight or hinting that in crisis situations real men should keep a stiff upper lip, she gives him endless waves of sympathy. She allows him to cry, indeed loves him for crying. Of course, such feminine behavior must not occur outside the domestic retreat. Edith is very upset by West's one public outburst of hysteria, when for two hours he roams the streets of Boston. West, like a good and pining female heroine, should restrict such displays to settings of domestic isolation often associated with women (e.g., in home libraries reading and in bedrooms dreaming) or to situations of domestic companionship with a nurturing woman.

Nonetheless, in one significant way, West lets his female side go public. His career crisis and its resolution reflect female stereotypes, as well as actual situations confronted by nineteenth-century women. Wilson relates West's career difficulties to Bellamy's own struggles to place himself in the changing world of late nineteenth-century America (xviii–xx). He also concludes that West's decision to become the author of a "romantic narrative" (*Looking Backward* 94) reveals a "retrospective" element of *Looking Backward,* since authors in A.D. 2000 gain their living in the old-fashioned way (i.e., competition for readers) instead of working in the ranks of the industrial army (xxxiii). Another way to interpret West's career crisis and decision to write a romance is to imagine that he was speaking for or to many of his women readers who were aware of the numerous old and new occupational opportunities of their era but, because of sexual discrimination and because they had been denied the appropriate training or were "overeducated" for the "proper" domestic and public positions, had great difficulty fitting into the "new" occupational world of the late nineteenth century. When the confused gentle man, Julian West, expresses concern about finding a place in his new world ("What can I possibly do? . . . I never earned a dollar in my life" [210]), he could be speaking for many helpless heroines and frustrated nineteenth-century women readers.

Other than teaching, which West also does (*Looking Backward* 93), writing fiction was one public occupation sometimes available to women and to fictional heroines such as Augusta Evans's Edna in *St. Elmo* (1867). In *Private Woman, Public Stage: Literary Domesticity in Nineteenth-Century America* (1984), Mary Kelley examines the successes and anxieties of twelve women authors, including Warner, Cummins, Evans, and Stowe. The similarities between West and these "literary domestics" should not be pushed too far, but some commonalties are significant. West, like the women authors, often used the conventions of domestic fiction to engage his readers intellectually, morally, and emotionally. Two of Kelley's general observations about the position of her authors and the dual nature of their works reveal crucial characteristics of West's anxieties and the book he writes: "They found themselves in a world they did not know and that did not know them" (xi). They "reported their own phenomenon and became un-

witting witnesses to both the public event and their own private experiences" (viii). West is a homebody. It will take him a long time to know his
new world and to be understood. And his attempts to convince his twenty-
first-century readers of the grand public achievements of their age led him
to reveal many details of his private experiences in that age.

The point of characterizing West as a "literary domestic" and of emphasizing his feminization is not to turn Julian into a Julia West or to claim
that he was the first important "female man" of American letters. Domestic fiction had already familiarized American readers with positive images of nurturing and emotional males. Charlotte Temple's father is as nurturing as her mother; John Humphrey is a nurturing surrogate brother for
Ellen in *Wide, Wide World*; and Uncle True (Trueman Flint) is a sympathetic "mother" to the orphan Gerty in *Lamplighter*. And, of course, there
are Stowe's kind-hearted heroes: Augustine St. Clare, whose "marked sen-
sitiveness of character, [made him] more akin to the softness of woman
than the ordinary hardness of his own sex" (1: 221), and the victimized, nurturing, sobbing, passive, and forgiving Uncle Tom. Furthermore, American
readers would have to wait almost three decades before encountering a
male utopian narrator who could articulate the benefits of combining masculine and feminine characteristics (Vandyck Jennings in Charlotte Perkins Gilman's *Herland*, 1915) and almost a century to discover more fully
androgynous characters in utopian fiction in the works of Le Guin, Lessing, Piercy, Russ, Delany, Robinson, and several other compelling writers of
the last three decades. Acknowledging the androgynous character of one
of the most famous utopian narrators does, nevertheless, help us to understand why *Looking Backward* was so recognizable and meaningful to
Bellamy's readers.

Especially his women readers. If they could not identify with the two
Ediths or Mrs. Leete, they might borrow Judith Fetterley's question and
ask, "Where in this story is the female reader to locate herself?" (9). West's
career and related crises may have helped these readers to find a place in
Bellamy's no place. Therefore, it is not surprising that important woman
leaders, including Gilman, were attracted to *Looking Backward*, or that
both the Women's Christian Temperance Union and the National Council
of Women endorsed *Looking Backward*, that the *Ladies Home Journal*
distributed it at a reduced price (Pfaelzer, *Utopian Novel* 48), and that the
few women reviewers-interviewers uniformly liked *Looking Backward* (see

chapter 6). Nor is it surprising that so many women read *Looking Backward* (Lokke 124, 142) and, as previously noted, joined Bellamy Clubs.

More evidence of *Looking Backward's* appeal to women appears in a particularly revealing response to Bellamy's utopia by Frances E. Willard, one of the few women reviewers-interviewers and an important leader in temperance, education, and women's movements. Like many of the readers described in Michael Steig's *Stories of Reading* (1989), Willard believed that to understand and appreciate a book, she had to make "a conceptualization of an author" (Steig 24), in this case a feminine image. In a letter sent to her friend Lillian Whiting, who worked for Ticknor (the original publisher of *Looking Backward*), she wrote, "Some of us think that Edward Bellamy must be Edwardina—i.e., we believe a big-hearted, big-brained woman wrote the book. Won't you please find out?" (qt. in Bowman, *Year 2000* 120 ). Even after she met the "real" Bellamy and interviewed him in 1889, she persisted in feminizing him. Near the end of her interview she concluded, "It seems to me you are your mother's baby" (542).

Dr. Leete's discussion of women in utopia in chapter 25 no doubt attracted some women readers. I would argue, however, that the androgynous nature of the narrator, along with the familiar separation-(re)union narrative, the domestic settings, and the sentimental heroine, were equally, if not more, important factors in influencing women, who, we should recall, constituted the majority of the fiction readers during the nineteenth century (Tompkins 124).

## Familiar Estrangement: Looking Backward and Forward

Again and again, knowledge of conventions of sentimental and domestic fiction invited Bellamy's nineteenth-century readers to perceive as familiar and meaningful certain narrative structures, emotion- and guilt-evoking episodes, domestic settings, and the stereotypical female traits of Edith Leete and the narrator, Julian West. It was crucial that Bellamy establish this rapport with his readers if he hoped to "convert the experience of reading into the experience of conversion" (Morson 94). He did not want to share the fate of West in his nightmare return when his listeners perceived his exhortations as being estranged to the point of meaninglessness. And yet, *Looking Backward* had the power to unsettle readers, to force them to consider new ways of perceiving the familiar, because Bellamy combined reassuring elements both with strong criticisms of the American status quo and with a model of a society that represented a radical alternative to the readers' culture.

Nevertheless, the narrative structure, domestic settings, heroine, and narrative voice also reveal how Bellamy's use of conventions of domestic fiction could undermine his criticisms and model. Indeed, for many modern readers, especially academics, his adaptations of domestic conventions may render his utopia more anachronistic, even more conservative, than eighteenth- and nineteenth-century domestic fiction. Today, the separation-(re)union plot can seem contrived and contradictory, and episodes that celebrate variations of the death of the "pure and powerless" or other Christian motifs may be "virtually impossible for us to believe" (Oates 423). The domestic environment does obscure the potential effects of changes in economic, social, and family systems on the daily lives of workers. Most importantly, the notion that in Bellamy's utopia the sentimental heroine has finally found a suitor and parents who will not victimize her, a home life apparently free of anguish, and opportunities to prove her independence suggests the elimination of the overt and covert expressions of frustration and triumph that instilled late eighteenth- and nineteenth-century American domestic fiction with significant subversive and prescriptive elements.

Bellamy's use of "sentimental" conventions to domesticate utopia was, nonetheless, forward-looking. The episodes in *Looking Backward* that concentrate on West's intense internal struggles, on the emotional relationship between West and Edith Leete, and on Edith's feminization of West anticipate the intimate illustrations drawn by "Elise" for the 1941 edition of *Looking Backward* and, more importantly, anticipate the sophisticated and dominant focus on internal development and interpersonal relationships found in the powerful feminist utopias of the 1970s and 1980s. West's introspections are rather primitive compared to the ruminations of Margaret Atwood's nameless handmaid in *The Handmaid's Tale* (1986). West and Edith are certainly crude ancestors of Le Guin's Shevek and Takver in *The Dispossessed* (1974), Piercy's Connie and Luciente in *Woman on the Edge of Time* (1976), and Lessing's Al-Ith and Ben Ata in *The Marriages between Zones Three, Four, and Five* (1980). Furthermore, Hawthorne's *Blithedale Romance* (1852) and Carol Farley Kessler's anthology of early American utopias written by women, *Daring to Dream* (1995), attest to the fact that earlier American eutopias and dystopias by men and women had explored internal struggles and interpersonal relationships.

Still, the fact that *Looking Backward*—the most popular and influential American utopian work—incorporated examinations of intense personal struggles and complex interpersonal relationships helped to prepare authors and readers of later generations for more sophisticated projections of introspection and personal relations in utopia. Viewed from this perspective, it not only seems plausible to claim that there would be no *Looking Backward* without the domestic novels, but that the handmaids, Sheveks, Connies, and Al-Iths of late twentieth-century feminist utopian landscapes should also trace their ancestry and much of their emotional impact back to the Charlottes, Uncle Toms, and Gerties of eighteenth- and nineteenth-century domestic fiction and to a Julian who was just one consonant away from being a woman.

# Part Three

*From Constructs to a
Historically Documented (First) Reader*

# Getting Nowhere beyond Stasis
*Reading as Exposé, Textual Implication, and Life Story*

# Five

Defending the static qualities of utopia may be more challenging than defending utopian domesticity and sentimentality. Indeed, stasis is the perpetual whipping boy of utopia. From an anti-utopian viewpoint contemporary feminist utopists would banish us to an androgynous treadmill, Skinner would turn us all into unchangeable salivating machines, Wells would technocraticize us eternally, Morris would fossilize us in a medieval village guild, Bellamy would turn us into industrialized army ants, More would lock us up in a monastery, and Plato would test our mettle and forever mold us into one of several fixed alloys. Darko Suvin sums up the modern abhorrence of utopian stasis by proclaiming that "utopia as a static goal has been dead since the 19th Century, even if its putrefying cadaver poisoned the 20th" ("Utopianism" 182).

I admit overstating the case. Not all critics of utopias are muckrakers (or "stuckrakers") preoccupied with exposing elements in literary utopias that tend toward changeless states. But many of them are. This pattern may in part be explained by their literary training, their relative economic stability, and/or their self-perceptions as innovative thinkers that incline them to perceive spontaneity and dynamism as more interesting and important than stability and security. They, as well as many proponents of the value of utopian literature, assume a preferred reading protocol for utopias. Their "ideal" reader is one who can see beyond "superficial" literary and rhetorical "surfaces" and expose the "true" utopian ideas. Like Louise Rosenblatt's "efferent" readers, they are adept at "selecting out and analytically abstracting the information or ideas . . . that will remain when the reading is over" (*Literature* 38). This process is similar to the one Habermas describes in his portrait of the utopian social thinker Ernst Bloch— "within the ideological shell Bloch discovers the utopian core" (qt. in Levitas, *Concept of Utopia* 90). This exposé approach to reading utopias is still very useful to the study of utopian literature. It can sensitize us to many of the contradictions in utopian narratives between their revolutionary, or at least evolutionary, claims and their sometimes dull portraits of stagnant societies.

The exposé method can also help us to define and organize the huge body of utopias by enabling us to categorize them, for instance, as socialist, capitalist, anarchist, ecofeminist, or to categorize and arrange them on recognizable spectrums: For example, in terms of opportunities for personal development, a typical spectrum based on extracted information about individual freedom might begin (on the static side) with works such as Plato's *Republic* and Thomas More's *Utopia,* continue with nineteenth- and twentieth-century works such as Bellamy's *Looking Backward* and B. F. Skinner's *Walden Two,* and conclude with twentieth-century works that stress dynamism: H. G. Wells's *A Modern Utopia* (1905), Ursula Le Guin's *The Dispossessed* (1974) and *Always Coming Home* (1985), Marge Piercy's *Woman on the Edge of Time* (1976), Doris Lessing's *Marriages between Zones Three, Four, and Five* (1981), Samuel Delany's *Triton* (1976), and Kim Stanley Robinson's *Pacific Edge* (1990) and Mars trilogy.

Considering the usefulness of exposing utopian cores, it is not surprising that many of the studies of utopian literature, even during the last two decades, have formulated claims about static and dynamic qualities based, to some degree, on constructions of extrapolated models of better cultures (e.g., Rooney; and especially Bowman 1986, and Lipow). A more recent case in point is the Bellamy section of Thomas Peyser's *Utopia and Cosmopolis* (1998). Peyser focuses on several paradigmatic episodes particularly in *Looking Backward* and *Equality,* including West's ability to sample the products of the world in a department store and his ability to visit vicariously cities around the world by viewing an "electroscope." Peyser uses these significant examples to argue that the core of Bellamy's vision was a fixed Americanized consumer utopia that made the products, cultures, and experiences of the globe "available for manipulation and ordering"; all "otherness" is commodified in this "culture to end all cultures" (25, 39, 54).

Despite their obvious advantages, there are serious flaws inherent in stasis hunts grounded in the discovery of utopian cores. The reductive tendencies of this type of content analysis become especially obvious when we examine the type of contemporary literary utopia Fredric Jameson has described as "auto-referential" utopias—a form of discourse that perpetually interrogates its own capacity to exist, that is, to narrate utopian possibilities ("Progress" 156). Imagine reducing the interactions between Lessing's Zones Three, Four, and Five or the implications of Le Guin's "The Ones Who Walk Away from Omelas" to lists of economic and political "content" denoting stasis or dynamism. Of course, similar reservations could be expressed about much older works: imagine reducing the ambiguities and ambivalence of More's *Utopia* to such lists. It seems natural, therefore, that some of the most interesting studies of modern utopias deemphasize reductive content analyses and that several students of utopia have moved toward a type of reader-response criticism that calls into question the usefulness of extrapolating fixed socioeconomic content models from utopian texts produced in any era.[1]

Still, it would be foolish, in my opinion, to move so far away from content analyses and utopian core constructions that the study of stasis and dynamism in utopian literature is limited to implied-reader textual analyses of "non-content" material such as conventions, style, narrative voice, and structure or to studies of the documented responses of actual readers. Because of the didactic, often prescriptive, nature of and the strong nonfictional elements in much utopian literature, it is evident that the responses of both implied and actual readers are strongly influenced by their own extrapolations of the content that to them is most relevant to the construction of a model of a better culture. My discussions of late nineteenth-century reviewers in chapter 6 and of late twentieth-century readers in chapters 7 through 9 demonstrate this. Furthermore, implied-reader and actual-reader studies also involve types of content analyses and extrapolated models, though the definitions of "content" and "model" may be very different from their equivalents in conventional content analyses.

One appropriate response to the obvious drawbacks of stasis-dynamism studies based on exposés of utopian cores would be a method that utilizes content analyses, implied-reader textual analyses, and examinations of the documented responses of actual readers. Each of these angles of perception articulates significant and different ways of defining stasis and dynamism in utopian literature. The first stresses the importance of certain types of content traditionally associated with utopian models of better cultures (e.g., statements or implications about alternative political, economic, social, religious, cultural, and psychological models). The second deemphasizes these types of content and emphasizes the possibilities suggested by reading conventions, styles, and structures that can invite readers to imagine degrees of stasis and dynamism. The third examines evidence indicating how and why actual readers have accepted or rejected the socioeconomic and stylistic invitations of utopian texts. The "results" of this three-dimensional method will not be as easy to categorize as conclusions based on conventional content models, nor as compellingly unified as text-based constructions of ideal or implied readers, nor as consistently grounded in extra-textual documentation as biographical or historical studies of actual readers. But as I attempt to demonstrate in the following examination of *Looking Backward,* the method may help us to move beyond overly reductive studies and toward an appreciation of the complexity of grasping the meanings of stasis and dynamism in utopian literature.

## Content Analysis / Model Construction

The nature of the cultural model readers extract from a content analysis will, of course, depend upon how they define "content." If they are primarily interested in economic systems, they will be prone to "see" economic principles and proposals and to construct a model that emphasizes economics. If their interests focus on gender relationships, gender issues will dominate their model. Since the focus of this chapter is stasis/dynamism, the inclination I bring to *Looking Backward* might best be defined by two related questions: Is there potential or desire for change in the society described by Dr. Leete and witnessed by Julian West? Is there potential for individual development/freedom within the described and witnessed society?

Both Julian West and Dr. Leete state that there is much room for changing the society of A.D. 2000. The preface reveals that both the readers and writers at the beginning of the twenty-first century are progress-oriented. The author of the preface (West, who is now a historian) characterizes the readers of A.D. 2000 as being accustomed "to improvements in their conditions" (93). The writers of the day are so fascinated with the possibilities of "progress that shall be made, ever onward and upward" that he feels compelled to balance this bias toward future change with historical comparisons that emphasize the progress made during the past century (94). At several points during the narrative that follows the preface, Leete's celebrations of progress confirm West's characterization of the readers and writers. For instance, in chapter 1, he specifically associates the restricted horizon of nineteenth-century thought with the belief in a cyclical theory of history instead of with the current "idea of indefinite progress in a right line" (102). He returns to this theme in chapter 15 when she links his culture's astounding renaissance in engineering, science, and the arts to the realization that the "race" had risen to "a new plane of existence with an illimitable vista of progress" (199). In the second edition of *Looking Backward,* the one that began the book's rise to popularity, Bellamy's own authorial voice supports West and Leete when, in the postscript, he bases his claims for the possibility of rapid change in the nineteenth century on "principles of evolution" that make believable the "next stage" of society's development (312).

Nonetheless, most of Leete's and West's observations delineate a stable, even static, model of social organization. From the first sentence of the preface, in which West associates the utopian culture with "completeness" (93), to the postscript, in which the author's voice associates his model with the "ideal society" and "an ultimate realization of a form of society" (311, 313), the impression given is that Leete's society is a finished product, not a part of an evolutionary process. Many of the key descriptions of this utopian stasis are presented in the form of negations, that is, indications of what is not in utopia. This means of defining utopia should have been quite familiar to Bellamy's readers. As Terence Martin has noted, the "national habit" of defining "paradise by negation" was well established by the mid-nineteenth century in America (2–3). Leete's statements of negation leading to stasis culminate at the conclusion of chapter 19 in response to West's questions about the lack of state legislatures, the infrequent meetings of Congress, indeed the disinterest in legislation of any kind:

> *"We have no legislation," replied Dr. Leete, "that is, next to none. It is rarely that Congress, even when it meets, considers any new laws of consequence, and then it only has powers to commend them to the following*

*Congress, lest anything be done hastily. If you will consider for a moment,*
*Mr. West, you will see that we have nothing to make laws about. The*
*fundamental principles upon which our society is founded settle for all*
*time the strifes and misunderstandings which in your day called for leg-*
*islation." (230)*

If Leete's descriptions of social organization offer little support for his
claims about limitless change, perhaps his comments about opportunities for individual development suggest dynamic possibilities on a personal
level. Indeed, within the systems of family structure, free educational
institutions, and the industrial army (with its provision of substantial and
equal support for all), there are possibilities for personal growth. These
systems provide the basic physiological, safety, belongingness, esteem, and
self-actualization "needs" (to borrow Abraham Maslow's terminology) that
enable individual development. Primarily in chapters 7 and 9 Leete reveals
that parents watch for and encourage budding interests and talents.
Teachers reinforce this attention with excellent classes and frequent field
trips that allow children to see adults using their talents on the job (133–
34). After the three years of mandatory menial service in the industrial
army (ages twenty-one through twenty-four), the members of this organization can select jobs requiring no specialized training or opt for up to six
more years of specialized education/training (137–38). Leete admits that all
professions are not equally popular and that all workers do not initially get
their first choice of work assignment. But he claims that the sliding scale
of work hours (less for distasteful jobs, more for popular ones) and other
mechanisms adjust the job market. Furthermore, provisions are made for
individuals who, for personal reasons, want to change professions (137).

This bright picture of opportunities for personal development is tar-
nished (especially for modern readers) when Leete reveals that the choice
for jobs for women is restricted (263), that in the female branch of the industrial army only wives and mothers can attain the highest ranks (266),
and that anyone who is able to serve in the industrial army and who rejects
this "absolutely natural and reasonable" requirement of service "is sen-
tenced to solitary imprisonment on bread and water till he consents" to
serve (175). In his or her position outside the static concept of social organization, such a person practically ceases to exist. Leete explains:

*"Our entire social order is so wholly based upon and deduced from [service in the industrial army] that if it were conceivable that a man could escape it, he would be left with no possible way to provide for his existence. He would have excluded himself from the world, cut himself off from his kind, in a word, committed suicide." (132)*

We should recall, however, that for those willing to serve in the industrial army, there are opportunities for personal development outside of its organization. During pregnancy and child-rearing years, women are excused from service and still receive their full credit allotment. Hence, most mothers serve five to fifteen years instead of twenty-four (263). (There is no indication that fathers can exercise this option.) For women and men there are also other options. Creative individuals, especially writers and artists, can use part of their credit allotment to produce their works. If these are good enough to convince enough people to buy them (popularity is the key criterion), they can live on their creative efforts (200–01). (Leete claims that the highly educated citizenry will support only works of excellence.) Another option is early retirement—as early as thirty-three years of age. If, for personal reasons, an individual wishes to retire early, he or she may do so and obtain an honorary discharge and a lifetime credit of 50 percent of the usual annual allotment (204).

As David Bleich has argued in "Eros and Bellamy," the regular retirement age (forty-five, with rare emergency callbacks to fifty-five) indicates clearly that Bellamy's concept of personal development went far beyond the context of the industrial army. For half their lives, Leete's fellow citizens can devote themselves to "personal idiosyncrasies and special tastes" and experience the "full enjoyment of [their] birthright" (222). To Leete this means a period when he can pursue intellectual and spiritual "enjoyments," which "alone mean life" (221). Bleich observes that this attitude is much closer to Herbert Marcuse's concept of dynamic personal development than it is to a static view of development based on the Protestant work ethic (447–49).

How useful is the foregoing model of Bellamy's utopia? My interest in stasis/dynamism inclined me to a definition of "content" that highlighted Leete's and West's comments about progress, social organization, and personal development. From these selected statements, I constructed a mixed model comparable to models extracted from other utopian texts. On a general socioeconomic level, Bellamy's utopia seems almost as static as Plato's or More's. On the level of personal development, however, there is room for dynamic development both within and outside the industrial army—not to the degree we find in works such as Lessing's *Marriages* or Delany's *Triton,* but certainly to a larger degree than in many classic and nineteenth-century utopias. The model can also serve as a corrective to interpretations of *Looking Backward* that stress the static and authoritarian elements (e.g., Arthur Lipow's *Authoritarian Socialism*) or the dynamic characteristics of the book (e.g., Bleich's "Eros and Bellamy"). Most significantly, the model can become a touchstone for the type of studies, so brilliantly done by John L. Thomas ("Introduction"; *Alternative America*), that speculate about the relationships between utopian authors' ambivalence about change and the forces that shaped their personal lives and historical eras. My mixed model could, therefore, serve as an initial step toward an analysis of how Bellamy attempted to incorporate dynamism into his utopia without unsettling his readers (and himself) with visions so changeable that they offered little reassurance during an era of bewildering change.

## Textual Analysis / Implied Reader Construction

As useful as "content" models can be, they are, as previously noted, based upon a very limited concept of a utopian text (i.e., the only important elements are the proposals and models) and upon a false assumption about the act of reading (i.e., "content" can be extracted from the text, shaped into a fixed model, and then used as a valid representation of the whole text). Reader-response theory offers a broader perspective of the text, one that includes elements not directly related to explicit or implicit statements about proposals and model cultures.[2] This critical orientation is particularly useful to the study of stasis and dynamism because it can help us to understand how a text can invite readers to perceive dynamic elements in supposedly static texts and vice versa. To be more specific, instead of perceiving *Looking Backward* as a text whose valid representation is a static social structure that allows some degree of dynamic personal development, the text can be perceived in terms of networks of invitations (some disruptive, some reassuring) that imply a reader who can interpret (or decode) invitations to see static and dynamic possibilities that might not be discovered in typical attempts to discover fixed utopian models.

Directly or indirectly, Robert J. Cornet, Lee Cullen Khanna ("Reader"), Jean Pfaelzer *(Utopian Novel)*, Peter Ruppert, and I ("Contexts and Texts") have examined various aspects of the reader implied by the text of *Looking Backward*. I will limit my discussion to networks of invitations related to the two interrelated roles of the narrator, Julian West: West as the historian/author who can stand back from his awakening experience and compose a book addressed to twenty-first-century readers (the "narratee," to borrow Gerald Prince's term); and West as a surrogate reader—an estranged visitor immersed in his responses to and questions about an unexpected and bewildering visit to utopia. The historian/author is most obvious in direct addresses to readers; the estranged visitor is especially evident in question-and-answer sessions and during moments of solitary crisis or liberation that challenge his nineteenth-century concepts of the potential for change.

As the author of a historical romance, Julian West is fond of using direct address to his twenty-first-century readers that invites both nineteenth-century and modern readers to question conventional, static notions about their cultures. Given the fictive circumstances of West's position, "Dear Reader" addresses seem natural. West arrived in utopia on September 10, 2000, and, according to the dated preface, completed his book approximately three months later. Though he is to some degree removed from the traumas of his first week in utopia (which he describes in his romance), he is still very new in town and very self-conscious. This dynamic, in-between stance may well be an invitation to read West's entire narrative as a therapeutic act. The writing of a narrative that celebrates the wonderful fruits of the transition to utopia becomes a way of appeasing the guilt I discussed in the previous chapter.

After the preface, West begins his direct addresses by apologizing for the implausibility of his existence in the year 2000 and for the strangeness of the era of his birth (95–102). This pose reverses the conventional returned visitor-reader relationship of utopian literature. In More's *Utopia* Hythloday tries to convince his narratee that Utopia exists. In contrast, West tries to convince utopians that the nineteenth century existed. This reversal implies two types of invitations. First, West's initial comments about the nineteenth century would invite nineteenth-century readers to feel superior to West's twenty-first-century narratee, who seems so ignorant about the nineteenth century. Using her concept of distancing, Robyn

R. Warhol would probably consider West to be a distancing narrator at this point (29), since the twenty-first-century narratee, though not precisely defined, is clearly separated from nineteenth-century readers. But just as the nineteenth-century readers are beginning to relax in their confidence about their knowledge, West begins asking disturbing rhetorical questions about living off the work of others and the selfishness of his era. Next, in the first chapter of *Looking Backward,* the coach analogy further estranges nineteenth-century readers by using a familiar image to present an unfamiliar picture of the nineteenth century. Suddenly, these readers have lost their sense of superiority. Like the once privileged coach riders, they enjoyed a brief period of security before tumbling into the muck of insecurity. This is, however, a constructive insecurity. Before the ideal readers of Bellamy's text can reconstruct new ideas about the future, they must deconstruct their notions of the past and present.

This implied process of necessary deconstruction is more powerfully expressed in episodes that capture West's other primary narrative role: the estranged visitor in moments of crisis. West's anxiety about his double identity, his dual perception of Edith Leete, and his nightmare return to 1887 offer fascinating examples of this type of episode and have received attention from nineteenth-century reviewers and twentieth-century scholars.[3] Three other episodes, placed strategically at the beginning, middle, and end of *Looking Backward* also constitute significant invitations to empathize with West, to feel his confusion and guilt, and to want to resolve that guilt in the world West left behind. This narrative role is much closer to Warhol's concept of the engaging narrator (29). West becomes a curious and anxious audience for Dr. Leete's explicit messages and for Leete's culture's implicit messages. The roles of narrator, narratee, and actual reader begin to overlap. In this situation West becomes a surrogate for the actual reader, even a model for an ideal reader of Bellamy's utopia.

In the third chapter of *Looking Backward,* the paragraph describing West's (and the reader's) initial view of the new Boston offers a paradigm for the way the three episodes superimpose images of the past and future to jar static perceptions of both (115). The first five sentences present a bird's-eye view of the "great city," which is practically unbelievable to West. Then comes a transitional sentence as his eyes drift toward the horizon. In the last two sentences he sees the Charles River and Boston Harbor. These familiar sights enable West to believe that he has journeyed to A.D. 2000.

The overlay of the new city on the old landscape also instantaneously transforms West's view of the nineteenth and twentieth centuries by demonstrating what his present (Leete's past) could become.

In the previous chapter I stressed the importance of West's reading experiences in the Leetes' domestic library. As Ruppert and I have argued, familiar landmarks—Dickens and Tennyson, especially Dickens—can transform static images of past and future.[4] West provides vague hints about the new literary landscape represented by the author Berrian. By contrast he offers an intimate account of his own response to Dickens, an account that invited nineteenth-century readers to see Dickens's portraits of the poor in a new way, from the perspective of an estranged twenty-first-century reader. In part this invitation is effective because it is expressed in terms that would be familiar to nineteenth-century Protestant readers. West's portrayal of his reading experience evokes two familiar elements of a religious conversion: Jonathan Edwards's emphasis on new perceptions and Edward Taylor's stress on grace as being absolutely undeserved. Because he now understands more about the poverty of the past and the potential of the future, it is as if West, and by implication the reader, were reading Dickens for the first time and using him to understand the future, not the present or past. To once again quote the key passages: "Every paragraph, every phrase, brought up some new aspect of the world-transformation. . . . I gradually obtained a more clear and coherent idea of the prodigious spectacle." He knows, however, that he does not deserve such illumination. He is awed by "a deepening wonder" that someone "who so little deserved it" had been suddenly graced with this "new world" (190).[5]

If West's initial view of Boston hints at the possibility of changed perceptions, and if his response to Dickens demonstrates progress toward that goal, then the nightmare (ch. 28) represents a complete conversion. As I indicated in chapter 4, during his dream West's new perceptions of the past and his sense of guilt are so deeply felt that his viewpoint is incomprehensible to the wealthy Bartletts and their friends, who know only one, very static way to view their world. The obvious invitation of the text is that readers should not be like the Bartletts. They should have the courage to change their perceptions. Critics have commented on the power of the dream sequence (Lewis, "Utopian Dream" 199). As I stressed in my discussion of sentimental conventions, the nightmare's invitation is re-emphasized, even augmented, after West awakes. At first he feels relief. But almost immediately he is pierced by guilt. He is tormented by a voice that calls him to return to the past when he could have been part of the transformation (310–11).

True, West has Edith Leete, his domestic angel, to console him. But their reunion does not represent the attainment of stasis. West is still an anguished, estranged visitor. The clear implication is that, as I suggested earlier, this narrative has no resolution within the text. It must be resolved by readers competent enough to discover the networks of often disturbing invitations, to transform their views of the present and future, and then to alter the static views of their contemporaries so that progress toward a new type of society can begin.

## Documented Readings

Textual analyses that enable us to speculate about implied readings certainly broaden our concepts of stasis and dynamism. Bellamy's text is no longer limited to being a static social model that incorporates opportunities for some degree of personal development. It can be perceived as a network of possible interactions between text and reader that bars narrative stasis and compels feelings, thoughts, and even actions outside the text. Nevertheless, if we want to consider stasis and dynamism from the perspective of specific, documented reactions as opposed to implied possibilities, we need to examine how actual readers responded to *Looking Backward*. Admittedly, this process still involves speculation and reconstruction. We often have to depend upon fragmentary documentation (e.g., letters, diary entries), potentially misleading evidence (e.g., the reviews examined in chapter 6), or the responses of readers far removed from Bellamy's historical circumstances (e.g., the responses of the 733 readers discussed in chapters 7 through 9). These sources do, nonetheless, suggest how actual readers have responded and will respond to the text's invitations.

The first "real" reader of *Looking Backward* was Edward Bellamy. He was an important reader and rereader who sent and received, reinterpreted, and resent and reinterpreted his text. We can use standard biographies (Morgan; Bowman 1958, 1962; Lipow; and Thomas), Bellamy's essays about composing *Looking Backward,* his revisions of the first edition, his articles in the *Nationalist* and the *New Nation,* and his final work, *Equality* (1897) to indicate some of his major responses to *Looking Backward.* These responses suggest an intriguing process of opening and closing the text— making it dynamic and static—that was not fully revealed in the content model or implied-reader analyses. This process offers striking support for Robert Scholes's provocative claim that the "person who reads a text is never the person who wrote it—even if they are the 'same' person" (50).

The first published evidence of this process appeared in the revisions for the Houghton Mifflin edition of *Looking Backward,* but many crucial responses to the text occurred earlier, as Bellamy indicates in his first essay about composing the book ("How I Came to Write" 1889). This es- say portrays an author who had no "affiliations" with "industrial or social reformers." He was intent upon writing an open-ended "literary fantasy, a fairy tale of social felicity" (22). Suddenly while writing, this author re- sponded strongly to one element of the fantasy, the industrial army, as a realistic rather than a fantastic notion. This new perception transformed a "merely" "rhetorical analogy" into a "prototype" for industrial and social organization (23) and simultaneously began the dynamic opening of the text to applications to the "real" world and a closing of the text to fantasies that might divert attention away from Bellamy's new reading of what had suddenly become a core element in his concept of utopia: "A great deal of merely fanciful matter concerning the manners, customs, social and polit- ical institutions, mechanical contrivances, and so forth of the people of the thirtieth century . . . was cut out for fear of diverting the attention of readers from the main theme" ("How and Why" 24). For similar reasons Bellamy changed the setting from North Carolina in A.D. 3000 to Boston in A.D. 2000.

This process of closing and opening the text continued before *Looking Backward* became popular, as Bellamy responded to the first edition with numerous revisions. (These are noted in Thomas's excellent 1967 scholarly edition.) Even minor revisions reflect Bellamy's attempt to make his text seem closer to reality. For example, he changed the date of the preface from December 28, 2000, to December 26, 2000. The twenty-sixth was the birth date of Julian West and of Bellamy's son Paul. The change sig- naled a closer bond between author and narrator and framed the text with the implication that his fiction would be reality for his children: the second edition thus opens with a private allusion to his son's day of birth, and the postscript closes with a public promise that "our children" will "see" the world West visited (313).

Major changes in the Houghton edition suggest that Bellamy hoped to create a text that would be more accessible than the first edition to middle-class readers and more open to dynamic moves from text to world. For example, in the crucial twelfth chapter, in which Leete finally reveals the workings of the industrial army, Bellamy made several extensive revisions (171–73). Some of the changes indicate Bellamy's desire to facilitate reader engagement by cleaning up such awkward lines as, "usually the coarser kinds to this all recruits during their first three years belong" (173n). Other changes indicate a desire to eliminate suggestions of the types of class divisions that might confuse, anger, or threaten middle-class American readers. Bellamy's narrator made it clear that "all recruits," not just the "coarser kinds," belonged to the unclassified grade of common laborers during their first three years of service in the industrial army (171, 173n). In these same pages, in an obvious attempt to convince educated readers that he had considered the practical aspects of work motivation, Bellamy added numerous details about the industrial army's grading system, incentives, and emblems, whose iron, silver, and gilt composition echoed Plato's divisions of humanity.

Stanley Fish has noted how "statements of purpose" in an authorial voice can be used to "establish an expectation on the part of the reader" ("Literature" 89). The postscript (311–13) added to the Houghton edition clearly directs readers, not only toward expectations for practical applications, but also toward perceiving Bellamy's futuristic fiction as nonfictional history. As I indicate in chapter 6, the postscript was in part a response to a professional reader, a reviewer for the *Boston Transcript*, who questioned Bellamy's timeline. Using his authorial voice, Bellamy specifically defined *Looking Backward* as a "forecast" of "industrial and social development" in a real place, America, at a real time, approximately fifty years in the future. To support this interpretation, he refers to historical precedents: radical transformations that had already occurred in short periods of time in America, Italy, and Germany. In other words, Bellamy was saying that his type of "history" text was just as practical and real as descriptions of past events. He just happened to be looking the other (future) way. Of course, this opening up of practical and historical readings of his model society also tended to close off readings that perceived Bellamy's fictional world of A.D. 2000 as a "thought experiment," as an invitation to indulge in fantasies, or as dynamic notions of good places other than Bellamy's concept of utopia.

During the decade following the revising of *Looking Backward,* Bellamy continued to make public rereadings; for example, the 1890 Ward, Lock edition of *Looking Backward* included his response to critics that he originally wrote for the March 1890 issue of the *North American Review.* This response and other essays and interviews continued the trend away from contemplative, imaginative invitations and toward historical comparisons and practical applications. In Bellamy's interview with Frances Willard in 1889, he was already speaking in terms of "a practical working plan" (542). His second essay about composing *Looking Backward* ("How I Wrote" 1894) was written after the popularity of his revised text had transformed his life. He was no longer a retiring author of local journalism and psychological fantasies. He had become actively involved in reform politics. This change is reflected in his altered reconstruction of the composition process originally described in the 1889 essay. Instead of emphasizing his lack of contact with social reform and the surprising transformations of the text, he stressed his long-standing interest in social and economic problems and his intent to solve these problems. (Though he did not mention it specifically, his experience as a journalist and reviewer for the *Springfield Penny News* and the *Springfield Daily Union* had indeed exposed him to a variety of social thinkers.)[6] He thus gave the impression that even before he sat down at his writing desk, he planned to offer a believable parallel history and practical solutions to real problems. One prescriptive implication of this rereading is that Bellamy now imagined his ideal readers as approaching their reading desks with heightened sensitivities to literal and practical applications and diminished sensitivities to fantastic readings.

As Bellamy biographers from Arthur Morgan to Franklin Rosemont have indicated, Bellamy's essays in the *Nationalist,* the *New Nation,* and other magazines during the late 1880s and the 1890s further emphasized the practical possibilities of *Looking Backward* and demonstrated Bellamy's willingness to establish connections between his concept of utopia and concepts shared by Populists, feminists, labor leaders, socialists, and even anarchists (Rosemont 158–200). These later writings suggest a reading-interpreting process similar to the one described by David Bleich in

*Subjective Criticism* (1978). After a solitary reading, a person may discuss his or her reading with others. During this exchange, each reader may modify his or her interpretations and either achieve a new individual perception or concur with the group's consensus reading. Similarly, Bellamy entered into interpretive "negotiations" (Bleich's term) as he changed from being a rather solitary reader, writer, and editor to becoming a very public writer, editor, and speaker who was reviewed in an impressive number of journals (see chapter 6) and recognized as an important reform leader.

These negotiations changed his perceptions of certain aspects of his text. Most significantly, he began to see certain static and negative connotations to the military overtones of the industrial army. In part he was responding to General Francis A. Walker's February 1890 *Atlantic Monthly* essay criticizing his use of military concepts. Bellamy deemphasized the necessity of a literal reading of the military aspects of the industrial "army" analogy that had, during the composition process, been the catalyst that altered his view of the entire text, transforming it from a fantasy into a prophecy. His emphasis on equality and on opening the text to literal applications did not decline, however. If anything, his break with the theory-oriented *Nationalist* and his founding of the more activist *New Nation* signaled an increased emphasis on application and a transformation of his definition of what a "text" was. When he began composing *Looking Backward,* utopia was an open-ended book formed in fantasy and crafted with literary tools. As he wrote and spoke during the 1890s, Bellamy conceived of himself as having moved beyond literary nowheres. Now the world was his text, and reading it meant dynamic interactions with municipal and state governments and the creation of political parties.

The culmination (in published form) of Bellamy's openings and closings of *Looking Backward* was *Equality,* which appeared in 1897. *Equality* was written with a sense of urgency sparked by Bellamy's suspicion that this sequel to *Looking Backward* might represent his last opportunity to present a rereading to the public. (He was dying of tuberculosis as he wrote the book.) Certainly there are fundamental elements of this final rereading that demonstrate the strong consistencies in Bellamy's re-creations of his initial ideas about the utopia he envisioned in *Looking Backward*: to name just a few—the very strong emphasis on economic equality, the religious appeals, the celebration of human solidarity, and the use of the fictional settings and characters from *Looking Backward.*

Bellamy's preface (vii–x) to *Equality* does, nevertheless, signal several basic changes. First of all, the preface is spoken in an authorial voice signaling a deemphasis of the fictional pose. (As noted earlier, Julian West "wrote" the preface to *Looking Backward*.) The preface of *Equality* also signals a belittling of Bellamy's phenomenal best seller. The preface opens by introducing *Looking Backward* as a "small book" significant for its omissions: "What was left out of it has loomed up as so much more important than what it contained that I have been constrained to write another book" (vii). Bellamy's plot summary of *Looking Backward* is also revealing. In an attempt to (re)orient readers to the narrative circumstances, the authorial voice focuses on West's means of departure from the late nineteenth century, his arrival in the future, his contacts with Dr. Leete and Edith, his conversion to a new worldview, his nightmare, and his return from the nightmare to A.D. 2000. The authorial voice does mention West's "hopeless loneliness" before his romance with Edith blossomed, and he also notes the nightmare. Nevertheless, it is clear that the author of *Equality* is intent on offering a misreading of the ending of *Looking Backward* that obscures the trauma that accompanies a transition to an altered worldview. The final sentences of the preface make the agonies of West's post-awakening emotions appear to be so transient that they practically disappear:

> *Then it was that in an agony of weeping, he awoke, this time awaking really, not falsely, and found himself in his bed in Dr. Leete's house, with the morning sun of the twentieth century shining into his eyes. Looking from the window of his room, he saw Edith in the garden gathering flowers for the breakfast table, and hastened to descend to her and relate his experience. At this point we will leave him to continue the narrative for himself. (x)*

In the opening dialogue of West's narrative Edith Leete does refer to the possibility of "'what good [West] might have done'" had he remained in the nineteenth century (1), but West's tone of guilt and despair—a crucial element in maintaining his narrative roles as an estranged interloper and a surrogate for the reader—has all but disappeared.

In the rest of *Equality* Bellamy modified many of his earlier views and in the process limited the potential interpretations and audiences of his text. The modified views include his image of the ideal woman, Edith Leete. As discussed in chapter 4, in *Looking Backward,* despite her frankness, Edith

Leete could be read as a rather predictable (even static) romantic heroine. In *Equality* she is an agricultural worker on a high-tech farm. We see much less of her sentimental side and more of her "new" career-woman role. It is clear that this Edith is a product of "negotiated" readings, especially the criticism Bellamy received about the original Edith and his increased sensitivity to the "Woman Question." Bellamy also revised his notion of the importance of the details of historical process by including more information about the political, educational, religious, and labor movement activities that led to utopia. These elements were becoming blueprints for action rather than allegories that invited "thought experiments" and "right" feelings. His rhetoric, especially the increase in his use of such words as "revolutionary," also changed the historical perspective and tone of his utopia.

Most of the changes imply that opening up the dynamic imaginative possibilities of utopia (for both writer and reader) is not as important as opening the utopia originally presented in *Looking Backward* to specific dynamic interactions between West's fictional world and the readers' "real" world. The changes further suggest that for Bellamy in the mid-1890s, engaging middle-class readers—competent to interpret domestic fiction and other utopian literary conventions and willing to engage in speculation but fearful of disruptive changes—was not as important as engaging an audience willing to take many practical, including political, actions to ensure that their altered perceptions (originating in a utopian reading experience) would be translated into experiential acts designed to transform the world into a utopian text.

Of course, even before the publication of *Looking Backward,* Bellamy's utopian text invited practical and activist readings. We have documented proof of that. One reader, Edward Bellamy, read the draft of the "mere literary fantasy"—the "cloud-palace for an ideal humanity" ("How and Why" 22)—and discovered potential applications to his world. The point is that as Bellamy mused about, composed, read, revised, reinterpreted, and negotiated his utopia, he gradually closed off some and opened up other readings. In terms of multiple literary and speculative possibilities, he made his text much more static. This process began with the changed setting and the elimination of numerous fanciful speculations about utopian culture in an unpublished "romantic narrative" (preface, LB 94) and ended with a published rewriting/rereading that minimized the differences between fiction and nonfiction, speculation and application. Using the concepts developed in *The Boundaries of Genre,* Gary Saul Morson might conclude that Bellamy transformed a "threshold art" reading experience that exhibited "two exclusive sets of conventions" (fictional and nonfictional) into a one-dimensional reading experience of practical application (48). By contrast, from Bellamy's viewpoint, the process represented an exciting, almost frighteningly dynamic opening-up experience that began with the surprising discovery of a "new" meaning for an analogy in his partially completed manuscript, an experience which, one could argue, he dramatized in West's surprising rediscovery of Dickens. This process of discovery continued with each revision, reinterpretation, and negotiation until it completely revolutionized Bellamy's concept of literature and reading: literature became a pretext for action, the text became the world, the reader acted as world shaper in a dramatic, open-ended drama.

Dramatic evidence of this expansive process comes from an eyewitness report a few months before Bellamy's death. R. E. Bisbee, a "friend and neighbor" (Morgan, *Edward Bellamy* 419), asked Bellamy if *Equality* represented his last word on "human progress":

> *"Oh, no. . . . It is only the beginning. When we get there we shall find a whole infinity beyond." These were his last words to me. He had opened the door to let me out when I asked the question. His hand was still on the knob when he answered. There he stood, that little pale man, within eight months of his death, with a far-away look in his eyes which I shall never forget, as he repeated—"A whole infinity beyond." (420)*

If we could invite Bellamy back (forward?) from different stages of his life and ask him to respond to this chapter, what would he say? No doubt, during his final years, he would prefer the content analysis–model construction method, though he would probably recommend implementing rather than contemplating extracted models, and he would be annoyed at my emphasis on the static qualities of Leete's society. To him this model had become a dynamic force that reshaped his life, inspired hundreds of thousands of readers to feel, think, and act, and had influenced the development of several cities, states, and political parties, including the Populists and Democrats. "Static" does not describe those experiences or his final contemplations of "infinity beyond." On the other hand, if he responded to this chapter early in the 1880s when he was first musing about

his literary fantasy, he might have been sympathetic to the concept of stasis and dynamism indicated by textual analyses that defined implied readers who were as intrigued by Julian West's emotions and psyche—and the
disturbing questions they posed—as they were by invitations to contem-
plate the workings of the industrial army. If, however, Bellamy could return
with simultaneous and full recall of all his responses to his utopia experienced during the 1880s and 1890s, he would probably say that, despite their
usefulness and internal consistency, neither the content extrapolation nor
the implied-reader methods could adequately account for the many responses and concepts of stasis and dynamics evidenced by the documented reactions of one reader, Edward Bellamy. He might then argue
(and I would agree) that the best way to get beyond reductive notions of
stasis and dynamism in *Looking Backward,* or any other literary utopia,
would be to use at least all three perspectives in an attempt to imagine
readers who could experience a literary utopia as a discovered model and
as a network of invitations and as a life experience that transforms the
world into a potentially utopian text.

# Part Four

*Real Utopian Readers from
the Turns of Two Centuries*

# Reviewers Placing Nowhere

The *New York Times* reviewed *Looking Backward* early (27 February 1888) and favorably. The anonymous reviewer concluded that the "whole business is elaborately well worked out, and Utopia neatly described" ("Recent Books" 3). The writer also (mis)informed his readers that in Bellamy's future Boston every man begins his career as a waiter; there is absolutely no cooking in the home; the amount of income/credit an individual receives depends on how many hours he or she works; and that the entire utopia "has only been [West's] dream" ("Recent Books" 3).

One group of professional readers of *Looking Backward*—book reviewers—might be expected to fulfill the recommendations of the previous chapter by discovering/exposing fixed utopian models, by suggesting how the text implied various types of readers, and by linking the book to its first reader, Edward Bellamy. Unfortunately, as the *Times* review demonstrates, these readers were often less-than-ideal guides. The results of tight deadlines and restricted space allotments can be misleading observations drawn from hasty or even incomplete readings. (The *Times* reviewer evidently skipped the last pages of West's reawakening.) Poor writing abounds. We also can't assume that the reviews are accurate reflections of their readers' opinions. As Nina Baym notes in *Novels, Readers, and Reviewers* (1984), "a review does not necessarily represent the notions of anybody except its author, and even numbers of congruent reviewers may express only the opinions of a particular group of interested people" (18).

And these reviewers and "interested people" were, moreover, often swayed by strong ideological biases. In *Knights of Labor* (6 February 1890), Carlos Martyn railed against the "hateful system of competition" (n.p.); in his union's publication the *Locomotive Fireman's Journal,* Eugene Debs praised the "possibility, or rather many possibilities" for workers in Bellamy's utopia (qt. in Rosemont 163); writing in *Révolte* (Paris), the anarchist Peter Kropotkin criticized Bellamy's authoritarianism (Rosemont 182); Henry George, in his *Standard* review (31 August 1889), presented Bellamy's utopia primarily as a step toward his own single-tax paradise; and E. Douglas Fawcett's *Theosophist* review (June 1890) categorically defined the "ill-read and complacent bourgeoisie," the "sleekly opportunistic capitalist," the "orthodox political economist," the "individualist," and the "anarchist" as woefully incompetent readers of *Looking Backward* (475).

Another obvious limitation of nineteenth-century American reviews noted by Baym is the discouraging scarcity of women reviewers, despite the fact that, according to Alberto Manguel, "the first full-time book reviewer in America" was a woman, Margaret Fuller (*History* 167). Baym focused on the first half of the nineteenth century. Unfortunately there had not been much improvement by the end of the century; my sample includes only three women reviewers. Nor was there evidence of racial diversity. Among the "signed" reviewers, I discovered no "minority" writers. No wonder thorough examinations of gender and race were absent from the reviews.

As flawed as many of the reviews may be, they are an essential part of a reader-response study of utopian literature. As James L. Machor stresses, nineteenth-century reviews in America were "the primary vehicle for the dissemination and assimilation of ideas about the relation between fiction and readers" (64). Certainly, Bellamy's reviews were the most widely distributed public responses to *Looking Backward.* As I mentioned in chapter 2, there were numerous book-length fictional eutopias, anti-utopias, and dystopias that directly or indirectly responded to Bellamy, and these books represent important public readings, as several scholars have noted.[1] But with the exception of a few titles, notably Twain's *Connecticut Yankee* (1889), Ignatius Donnelly's *Caesar's Column* (1890), and Charles M. Sheldon's *In His Steps* (1897)—none of which responded directly to *Look-*

*ing Backward*—the vast majority of the various types of late nineteenth-century utopian literature had very small reading audiences compared to the readerships of periodicals such as the *New York Times*, the *New York Tribune*, the *Standard, Ladies' Home Journal, Atlantic, Harper's*, the *Saturday Review*, and many of the other newspapers and magazines that published reviews of *Looking Backward*. In *Literacy in the United States* (1991) Carl F. Kaestle emphasizes that there were impressive increases in the circulation of all forms of print matter during the late nineteenth century, but magazines and newspapers made especially impressive gains. There was a ten-cent-magazine "revolution" and "almost every family bought newspapers, whereas a smaller elite bought books" (170, 280). *Looking Backward* would have gone on to be a remarkable literary and social phenomenon without the publication of the book-length responses. But without the reviews, *Looking Backward* might well have remained an ignored, "scrofulous-looking and mangy" first edition (to borrow Twain's terms), incapable of performing its cultural work (Budd 76). It also seems especially appropriate to consider the reviews, since, as a *Critic* (29 June 1889) reviewer reminds us, Bellamy himself was a "book-reviewer on the *Springfield Union*" (Young 323) and later for the *New Nation*, and, as mentioned previously, his important postscript to the second edition was inspired by a review ("The Millennium of Socialism") that appeared in the *Boston Evening Transcript* (30 March 1888).

We can even learn important cultural and ideological lessons from the shortcomings of the reviews. The implicit and explicit statements of bias can help us to appreciate the powerful role of ideologies in reviewers' constructions of utopian and nonutopian texts. The lack of gender and racial diversity of the reviewers and the corresponding lack of extended discussion of women and race highlight the central role played by the experiential reality a reviewer brings to the reviewing process. The scarcity of comments about women readers and the scarcity of women reviewers of *Looking Backward* also demonstrate the important role of genre-gender stereotyping. James L. Machor and others have observed that one of the primary goals of nineteenth-century reviewers was to "instruct women" about appropriate responses to fiction (xv). The rarity of such instruction in the Bellamy reviews suggests that the reviewers thought that women were inappropriate readers for utopian literature. Just as revealing as this possibility is the fact that during approximately the same years that reviewers evaluated Bellamy's utopia, the first edition (1890) of Emily Dickinson's poems appeared and was reviewed extensively. Less than 4 percent of Bellamy's reviewers were women; according to Willis Buckingham, 40 percent of Dickinson's reviewers were women (Machor 164–65). The implication seems clear. Magazine and newspaper editors and publishers thought it was entirely proper for women to read and review poetry (especially when the poet was a woman) but not utopian literature. Apparently they assumed that women should behave like Edith Leete and leave the room when men discussed economic and social issues. The inaccuracy of that view is highlighted by the previously mentioned substantial number of women who not only stayed in the room but became leaders in the Nationalist movement.

Other significant advantages of using the reviews to examine how a particular type of professional reader gave meaning to *Looking Backward* are the number and diversity of the reviews. My eighty-three *Looking Backward* reviews—drawn primarily from Toby Widdicombe's excellent annotated bibliographies, "Edward Bellamy's Utopian Vision" and *Edward Bellamy: An Annotated Bibliography of Secondary Criticism* (1988)—were published in many different types of periodicals that reached diversified reading communities. Some were well-known mainstream periodicals in America (e.g., *Harper's, Atlantic, Lippincott's, Literary World*), in Great Britain *(Saturday Review)*, in France *(Revue des deux mondes)*, and in New Zealand *(Monthly Review)*. Reviews also appeared in reform, labor, socialist, and anarchist magazines (e.g., in the United States, *Liberty, The People, Lend a Hand, Locomotive Fireman's Journal,* and *Knights of Labor;* in Britain, *To-Day;* in France, *La société nouvelle*); in domestic magazines (e.g., *Good Housekeeping, Household Guest,* and *Cottage Hearth*); in regional journals (e.g., *Overland Monthly*); and in religious journals (e.g., *The Month* [British], *Unitarian Review, Theosophist,* and *Presbyterian and Reformed Review*). Important national and regional newspapers carried reviews (e.g., *New York Times, New York Tribune, Standard,* and *Times Democrat*).

Another kind of diversity was the degree of authority the reviewers' names brought to the reviews. Several of the reviewers were nationally or internationally recognized, including William Morris, William Dean Howells, Henry George, Peter Kropotkin, and at least two prominent New Zealanders—William Pember Reeves, a minister of education and later minister of labor, and John Ballance, the future prime minister. Their by-lines enhanced the authority of their opinions. Others had more localized reputations defined by specific reform activities, profession, or region: for example, Frances Willard (temperance, education, women's rights reform), Francis A. Walker (military reputation), Sylvester Baxter (popularizer of American socialism), Adam Shortt (professor at Queen's University in Kingston, Ontario), and H. P. Peebles (president of the Los Angeles Nationalist Club). These reviewers' biographical notes or explicit references to their positions were clearly intended to enhance their positions as authoritative evaluators. Most of the reviewers could not depend on biographical authority. They were lesser- or un-knowns who had to depend on their insights and rhetorical skills.

There is variety in length and form of the reviews. The length of the commentaries ranged from a two-sentence "note" in the *Author* (15 November 1889) to Michael Maher's two-part, thirty-five-page "A Socialist's Dream" in the British Catholic magazine the *Month* (January, February 1891). Most of the commentary in my sample comes in the form of a review of one or a group of books. But I followed Widdicombe's example by not excluding obituaries (most notably Howells's *Atlantic* eulogy [August 1889]), biographical sketches, letters, interviews, and a couple "What's doing in Boston?" pieces (e.g., Young, 29 June 1889).

The mix of favorable and unfavorable evaluations, the publication dates, and the international coverage attained by *Looking Backward* again indicate the variety of the review responses. (For more comprehensive overviews of international reviews, see Bowman's *Bellamy Abroad,* Sargent's bibliographies of New Zealand and Canada, and Toth's "Transatlantic Dialogue.") In my sample there were 43 positive, 27 negative, and 13 mixed reviews. I decided not to include the hundreds of evaluations of issues relating to *Looking Backward* in the *Nationalist, New Nation,* and other Bellamy and Nationalist publications. Their inclusion would radically alter the "count" of positive and negative responses, creating the misleading impression that practically all the published reviews were positive.

Most of the reviews in the sample (66 of 83) appeared in 1888, 1889, and 1890. Important reviews did, however, continue to appear in every year (except 1893 and 1896) at least through 1898, when Bellamy's death inspired at a minimum of six (re)evaluations of his work, especially *Looking*

*Backward.* This decade of reviewing enables us to perceive patterns or at least to raise significant questions that might not be noticed or asked when studying a typical two- or three-year reviewing cycle. For example, we witness the changing "visual" and social reviewing contexts established by editors and reviewers. The early reviews sometimes lumped discussion of *Looking Backward* in with comments on other books in "recent fiction" columns; the later reviews gave the novel separate treatment. The early reviews tended to focus on the book and general social, literary, and biographical contexts. Later reviews often placed *Looking Backward* in the contexts of its particular and astounding popularity and the reform parties and attitudes it inspired. The shift in contexts signaled basic changes in the perceived functions of Bellamy's utopia.

A decade of reviews appearing in several countries raises other important issues. For example, how significant is it that almost all of the important very early reviews appearing in 1888 in America were extremely positive and that they appeared in widely distributed periodicals: 5 February (Whiting, *Times Democrat*), 5 February ("New Utopia," *New York Tribune*), 27 February ("Recent Books," *New York Times*), 17 March ("A Look Ahead," *Literary World*)? In England the first two reviews, which appeared a bit later and in respected publications, were negative—both 24 March 1888, *Saturday Review* ("Novels") and *Academy* (Wallace). Throughout the decade the American reviews were more positive than the British. The early reviews may have set national patterns.

There were also differing social and literary attitudes shaping the international perceptions of *Looking Backward.* In a comparative study of selected American and New Zealand reviews, Francis Shor argues that the existence of government-directed utilities and the faith the "liberal collectivists" had in the national state of New Zealand helped to increase the influence of positive reviews and the implementation of Bellamy-like ideas on a national level ("Ideological Matrix" 39, 46–47). Attitudes about literary criteria also played an important role in shaping reviewers' responses. During the antebellum period, for instance, Baym noted a significant difference between reviewing in America and Britain: "Overall, the [American] reviewers were both less severe in their judgments and much less savage and lofty in their rhetoric" (*Novels* 20). Steven Mailloux's comparative analysis of the American and British receptions of *Moby-Dick* supports Baym's view. For the more "professional" British reviewers, who tended to have a "thorough knowledge of traditional literary conventions," accepted aesthetic standards became prescriptive interpretive strategies used to expose literary shortcomings (174–77). Baym's and Mailloux's conclusions certainly apply to comparative examinations of late nineteenth-century reviews of utopian literature. Whereas most of the American reviewers seemed to accept, even advocate, the didactic functions of popular fiction, the early *Academy* and the two *Saturday Review* reviewers from England argued that *Looking Backward* was not entertaining enough and bemoaned Bellamy's drift away from the "clever" *Dr. Heidenhoff's Process* (1880) in pursuit of a "deplorable fantasy" genre that depicted nonexistent societies (Wallace 203, and *Saturday Review* ["Novels" 27 April 1889] 508). The impressive variety of magazines and newspapers that published the reviews (and their diverse audiences), the varying levels of authorial authority and differing ideologies, national reviewing conventions, and historical perspectives make the reviews of *Looking Backward* fascinating indices to contemporary responses to Bellamy's utopia, and often to utopian literature in general and to late nineteenth-century American culture. Despite this diversity, there was a dominant and consistent trend expressed in the Bellamy reviews that reflects a significant change between early and late nineteenth-century roles of reviewers. Before midcentury, the cost of book publication and distribution limited the number of books that individuals and libraries could purchase. Reviews, which frequently included long excerpts, often "substituted for the book" (Baym, *Novels* 19, 21). By the late nineteenth-century, when books were much more available, the book review became less of a substitute and more of a guide. Reviewers advised whether or not to purchase a book and offered advice about reading strategies (Machor 70). Moral guidance became an especially important "part of the reviewer's job" (Baym, *Novels* 21, 160–61, 173).

Advice about reading strategies and moral guidance achieved special prominence in the reviews of *Looking Backward*. Reviewers from differing ideological and cultural viewpoints often agreed that preparing readers for a book like *Looking Backward* demanded special acts of placing and controlling. Utopias had to be placed because readers might be unfamiliar with the utopian reading experience. They needed special guidance—and control. The reviewers typically perceived *Looking Backward* as having the power to alter their readers' society in fundamental ways; Bellamy's literary utopia was perceived as a striking example of the book power I discussed in chapter 3. Reviewers who opposed Bellamy's vision of the future hoped to dissipate the book's power by exposing its flawed utopian core.

Bellamy supporters hoped to control readers' doubts about utopian literature in general and Bellamy's vision in particular so that they could appreciate (i.e., reach a "valid" reading of) *Looking Backward.*

The reviewers depended primarily on four strategies of placement and
control. First, they adopted a synecdochic approach to the discovery-
exposé interpretive strategy. Reviewers controlled *Looking Backward* by
reducing it to particular episodes "in" the text defined as interpretive
metaphors or paradigms that revealed the utopia's core ideas and values.
Second, they juxtaposed their constructions of the utopian core against reality "outside" the text, including the growth of socialism, as a means of
evaluating Bellamy's ideas. Third, they used various historical perspectives
to place and judge Bellamy. These historical contexts could be as broad as
national and global economic and social trends, or as specific as *Looking
Backward*'s publishing, distribution, and reception history, or as private as
the history of Bellamy's life and family. Fourth, the reviewers attempted to
place and control the reading experience by constructing models of readers and reading processes.

I will examine each of the four strategies, concluding with a focus on the
fourth, the construction of models of readers of utopias—a neglected and
important topic in utopian studies. Much of this chapter will be synthesis,
description, and quotation; I will frequently define the strategies by allowing representative reviewers to speak for themselves. To give senses of the
publication and time contexts, I have included indication of the periodical
and date, especially the first time I mention a review.

The reviewers' strategies, in particular the constructions of models of
readers, elevated the role of the reviewers. From their perspectives, they
became heroic social and cultural mediators who either protected readers
from or enabled them to use the power of *Looking Backward.* Examining this process offers insights into the ethics and ideologies of late
nineteenth-century reviewing, into the concept of "book power" discussed
in chapter 3, and, of course, into the processes of giving meanings to
utopias, processes that can be compared to the strategies used by the late
twentieth-century readers analyzed in chapters 7 through 9.

## Placing by Synecdoche

A typical review of *Looking Backward* included a brief plot summary, mention of primary targets (inequality was frequently indicated), and glimpses

of Bellamy's solutions (most notably the nationalization of production, the industrial army, the career system, and the equal sharing of the national product). (One of the best summaries is in part 1 of Michael Maher's January 1892 *Month* review [1–10].) Since their space was usually severely limited, the reviewers could not discuss what they summarized in great detail. Instead, they followed the familiar reviewing convention of selecting a character, episode, or issue that would function as a "representative" guide for understanding the rest of the text. In effect the reviewers were following Peter Rabinowitz's "rule of notice" by highlighting parts of the text that often became the "scaffolding" upon which they built their interpretations (*Before Reading* 53). They especially focused attention on Edith Leete, the Rev. Mr. Barton's sermon, and two key narrative frames—the stagecoach parable and the concluding nightmare/awakening. How the reviewers interpreted Edith and the other three episodes reveals much about how they constructed strategies they hoped would govern the public's reading experiences.

Considering the importance of Bellamy's use of domestic and sentimental fiction conventions, it is not surprising that the reviewers paid attention to Edith Leete, and it seems logical to assume that their discussion of her would lead to discussion of Bellamy's "new woman." Indeed, a few reviewers did use Edith as a touchstone for brief comments on women. The *Christian Union* ("Looking Backward" 17 May 1888) reviewer portrayed Edith as "quite in keeping with the industrial conditions around her" (617), and one of the few women reviewers, Lilian Whiting, used Edith's shopping tour to emphasize the practicality and efficiency of Bellamy's system and its women (11). But most of the reviewers who discussed Edith used her as a means of revealing the hybrid nature of the genre: the love story/utopia. Michael Maher's view was typical: Edith Leete was part of the "requisite love element" designed to break up the monotony of narrator/guide dialogues (2). The general approval of the reviewers for the love story also suggests that, at least within this professional readers' community, Edith's inclusion was a successful means of achieving the "domestic" familiarization I discussed in chapter 4.

Nevertheless, the glaring absence of reviews that depict Edith Leete as a signifier of changes in women's roles also highlights the wide gap between the nature of *Looking Backward*'s only individualized portrait of a utopian woman and the generalized portraits, a gap stressed by many twentieth-century scholars. The few reviewers who did focus some attention on "women's issues" typically did not use Edith as a catalyst for their discussion. Whether they attacked Bellamy's new women as dangerous representations of threats to "maternity" and violations of "laws of nature" (Goldwin Smith 612–13) or praised them, as Francis Willard did, as representations of "independence" from men (540), they based their interpretations on Bellamy's general portraits of women, not on the particular woman West learns to love.

Pulpit oratory was a familiar part of many of Bellamy's readers' lives; hence, Rev. Barton's sermon, like Edith Leete's portrait, should have functioned as a powerful familiarizing element that outlined the belief system supporting Bellamy's utopia. One of the most thoughtful reviewers, Maher, does identify the sermon as "one of the most striking chapters" in the book (10). Nonetheless, using arguments remarkably similar to those used by readers in my late twentieth-century sample, Maher and most of the other reviewers who commented on Barton had two strong reservations about the sermon: it deemphasized primary dependence on spirituality and God, and its delivery system undermined communal religious experience. In "The Ethics of Nationalism," Geraldine Meyrick saw the goodness in Barton's emphasis on "morality and justice" and the "brotherhood of man." But for her, Barton's sermon was a false friend that located its faith in changes in "materialistic" social and physical environments instead of a faith in God (566–67). Maher identified another element of false friendship, or rather false fellowship. Addressing his primarily Catholic readers of the *Month,* he criticized Bellamy's distribution and consumption system. Instead of an immediate and communal experience, Rev. Barton's sermon is distanced and private. To quote Dr. Leete, most preaching is "delivered in acoustically prepared chambers, connected by wire with subscribers' houses" (273). For West, Barton is "an invisible person in the room" (274); disembodied words heard in a private space. Maher objects: "To the Catholic, the conception of theological doctrine being administered to subscribers like gas through tubes . . . will scarcely be satisfying" (183).

Reviewers' responses to the framing episodes of the stagecoach and the nightmare/awakening were much more positive. Although the "prodigious coach" analogy is simple and brief (96–98), it represents an ingenious use of analogy. Analogies are typically used to render the unfamiliar understandable. In a narrative sense, the coach analogy helps West's fictional readers in A.D. 2000 to grasp the distant and unfamiliar nineteenth century. For Bellamy's first "real" readers, including the reviewers, the analogy uses a familiar object (a coach) to transform their (familiar) reality into an accessible drama of injustice and chaos. Reviewers who supported Bellamy's viewpoints often pointed to the coach analogy as a powerful means of enabling readers to perceive the inequalities of their society (for example, see Fawcett, "Looking Backward"; and "The New Utopia"). Even reviewers who disagreed with Bellamy's emphasis on socialism acknowledged the power of the coach analogy to reach readers and change their perceptions. In his *Harper's* "Editor's Study" (June 1888), Howells draws attention to (and quotes) the coach analogy as an example of an "alluring allegory" that can trick readers into "gulp[ing]" down socialism by convincing them that their society represents "the reverse" of equality (154–55).

A few of the reviewers disliked the closing nightmare-awakening episode (Maher thought it disrupted a realistic narrative [2]); most enjoyed it immensely. The most perceptive reviewers used the nightmare-awakening episode as the best example of the affective powers of *Looking Backward*. The coach analogy invited a cognitive grasp of inequality; the nightmare/awakening invited the emotional engagement necessary to move readers to feel guilt and to change perceptions and actions so that the real world could more closely resemble Bellamy's vision of equality, efficiency, and justice. In his laudatory *Atlantic* obituary (August 1898), Howells pointed to the closing as a striking example of how Bellamy could make readers feel the imaginary, transforming it into a "veritable experience" (254). The descriptions, the sudden narrative twists, and West's responses invite readers to feel "that moment of anguish at the close, when Julian West trembles with the nightmare fear that he has been only dreaming of the just and equal future, before he truly wakes and finds that it is real" (254). For the *Christian Union* ("Looking Backward" 17 May 1888) reviewer, this anguish that Bellamy's ideal readers feel moves them to create their own dreams of "the new social order" and to wonder what they can do for others (618).

## Juxtaposition and Extrapolation: Placing Utopia against Reality

Howells's and the *Christian Union* reviewer's responses to the nightmare/awakening point toward a fundamental assumption about nineteenth-century reading held by almost all the reviewers: reading certain types of books, including sentimental reform and utopian fiction, could move readers beyond engagement with particular characters, analogies, and episodes to engagement with the "real" world. Like the ideal teachers in Louise Rosenblatt's *Literature as Exploration* (1938, 1995), the reviewers advocated reading literature as a "lived through" experience that tested the text against their perception of the realities and possibilities of their world, including their concepts of human nature. Like Rosenblatt's ideal readers, the reviewers also assumed that reading could change a person's life (174).

At the very least, the reviewers argued, the utopian reading experience could alter perceptions of "reality." This assumption about the relationships connecting the text, readers, and reality was implicitly and sometimes explicitly used to justify evaluations of *Looking Backward* that tested Bellamy's utopian model by placing it against the reviewers' portraits of what they liked about their reality, against despicable tendencies they perceived in the present that would be enlarged in Bellamy's utopia, and against what they believed were inherent characteristics of human history and human nature that were violated by Dr. Leete's world of A.D. 2000. These reviewers were, in effect, engaging in what Frank Kermode calls "experimental assent." Readers compare the text to their reality. If the comparisons seem "operationally effective," they accept the text. If not, they reject it (qt. in Rabinowitz, *Before Reading* 95).

The reviewers who relied primarily on this form of interpretive evaluation were highly critical of *Looking Backward,* though some of Bellamy's supporters qualified their enthusiasm with these presumed doses of reality and also supported Bellamy by proclaiming that his utopia represented a hopeful alternative to some of the worst realities of the present, notably inequality and poverty. In this section I will focus on the critics, since the "reality check" was frequently their central argument.

Some of the comparisons to despicable trends were quite specific, for instance, complaints about replacing family amateur performance with piped-in professional entertainment (Higgs 237). More prevalent were concerns about the potential for increases in specific trends toward materialism/secularism, militarism, and bureaucracy. The former position has already been suggested by the criticism of Barton's sermon. As I noted in chapter 5, General Francis A. Walker voiced the strongest opposition to the militarism implicit in the industrial army (*Atlantic* [February 1890]). Bellamy was "moon-struck with a fancy for the military organization" (256). Even "Mr. M'Cready," who wrote for the single-tax newspaper *The Standard* (2 June 1888) and sympathized with Bellamy, worried about encouraging trends toward increased bureaucracy—Bellamy's utopia promised "a frightful number of government book keepers," "infinite convolutions of tape," "tons upon tons of daily reports," and "armies of lightning calculators" (8).

Although there were numerous other particular comparisons to specific realities and potentialities, the major critical arguments focused on two broad areas—(1) potential threats to individuality accompanied by an increase in the monotony of life and (2) Bellamy's misguided notions of historical process and human nature. Both forms of criticism typically came framed with categorical definitions of *Looking Backward* as a "state socialist" utopia, a labeling sometimes announced in the review's title: "*Looking Backward* and the Socialist Movement" (Fawcett); "*Looking Backward*: A Socialistic Dream" (Christian Union); "A Socialist's Dream" (*Maher*); "The Millennium of Socialism" (*Boston Evening Transcript*); "Socialist Millennium" (*Lyttelton Times* [New Zealand]) (Shor, "Ideological Matrix" 40). For most of the reviewers, socialism was a reality they did not want to encourage in the future. *Looking Backward* could foster that growth. Reality tests had to be imposed on Bellamy's utopia to ensure that his book would not contribute to the evolution of an undesirable reality.

A common line of attack was the argument that Bellamy's socialistic utopia would undercut individuality and promote monotony and dullness. In his long *Forum* review (October 1889), W. T. Harris declared that Americans were currently enjoying a high form of individuality, the result of hundreds of years of social evolution (205–06). The society Bellamy envisioned would "throw away all that the race has gained for eighteen hundred years" (208). Higgs matched Harris's doomsday hyperbole, claiming that Bellamy's "leveling process" would destroy individuality—the source of "all wise and noble things" (236). Even some of Bellamy's supporters—who countered these proclamations with criticism of the cruel excesses of competitive individualism—occasionally voiced reservations. In the 7 April 1888 *Pilot* celebration of what Bellamy's utopia would do for the "working class," the reviewer voiced concern that "paternalism run mad" could stifle individuality ("New Utopia" 1).

Bellamy's critics, especially the foreign reviewers, asserted that Nationalism would replace individuality and variety with dullness and monotony. "TOO DULL FOR ENDURANCE" was the subtitle used for a discussion of M. Bentzon's French review in the *Review of Reviews* [London] ("French Opinion," November 1890). The reviewer quoted Bentzon, who was especially concerned with the homogenization, democratization, and industrialization of the arts:

> "The golden age promised to the hopes of the human race attracts us very little. To summarize it in a word, it is too industrial; it must end inevitably—the very doubtful taste of the public being the sole criterion in questions of art and literature—in the triumph of cheap bronze chromo-lithographs and newspaper novels. " (457)

The most important reality check trend used by Bellamy's critics (and by many of the modern readers discussed in chapter 9) questioned his concepts of historical process and human nature. Promoters of *Looking Backward* often admitted "how improbable, even impossible" the changes Bellamy envisioned seemed. But, like the early *New York Tribune* ("New Utopia" 5 February 1888) reviewer, they thought that the "modern evolution" described by Dr. Leete seemed "natural and practicable" (10). The critical reviewers disagreed strongly; Bellamy had not provided enough realistic details about the method of change, had not anticipated the hostile response to change, had not allowed enough time for change, and, most significantly, had a false notion of human nature.

In one of the most important reviews—important because it inspired the postscript to the second edition of *Looking Backward*—the *Boston Evening Transcript* (30 March 1888) reviewer praised much of Bellamy's utopia but seriously doubted his timetable. The reviewer notes that according to Bellamy's preface, the new order is about a hundred years old (actually the narrator of the preface indicates "less than a century old" [93]). He further notes that if Dr. Leete is approximately sixty years old and has no recollection of the times of inequality, then the radical changes must have occurred very suddenly, during the "thirteen years" after 1887, the date indicated in the book's title (6). There would be a brief period of less than two decades to establish the new order. The swiftness of the change falls far short of "common sense requirements" (6).[2] The first *Atlantic* (June 1888) reviewer implied a similar criticism when he wishes West had found a U.S. history book covering 1887–1937 in Leete's library ("Recent American" 845).

Human nature defines human timelines. For Dr. Leete the reality of his world was that the changes required no alterations in human nature; the appropriate environments would quickly bring out the innate goodness in people. Bellamy's critics responded to this optimism with a view of human nature expressed by anti-utopians for centuries: Leete's concept of human nature could not be verified outside the text of *Looking Backward* because Dr. Leete's comments about what motivated people and the extent to which humans could change violated their concepts of human nature. Adam Shortt (Canadian) and Michael Maher (British) articulated representative positions: honor, distinction, devotion, "duty to the state," and "desire to excel in service" were insufficient "incentive[s] to labor" and insufficient agents of basic attitudinal and behavioral change (Maher 14; Shortt 275). Emile de Laveleye, who admired many of Bellamy's ideas, concurred: the spur of honor could not transform "man's heart" (April 1890, 445).

The transformation was so difficult because humans were basically selfish. John Ballance, the future prime minister of New Zealand, presented an interesting form of this argument. He believed that human nature had improved, that "selfishness ha[d] diminished," as evidenced by the more humane treatment of victims of war and by increased reform activities. But he also believed that at this stage in history reformers led by inspiring acts by individuals were more effective than visions based on large-scale collaborative efforts that assumed humans were ready for dramatic changes:

> . . . *when we consider the nature of the [human] elements which have to be moulded,* . . . *and the far-reaching nature of the organizations which will have to supply the material wants of dense populations, the hope cannot be fostered that thrice 100 years will mark the dawn of the age when men will see,—*
> *"This kindly earth lapt in universal law." (219)*

More typical was a neutral stance depicting selfishness and individuality as a natural survival response to the conditions of human existence; a force that thrives on challenge, even adversity, and builds great civilizations. Utilizing late nineteenth-century social Darwinism and racism, General Walker became the most vociferous anti-Bellamy advocate of this position. With a universalist's sweep he proclaimed that "from the origin of mankind to the present time, the main spur to exertion has been want." He added that it would be "little short of downright madness to assume that disinterested motives can be altogether trusted to take the place of selfish motives in human society" (255). To demonstrate his theory, General Walker noted that people who have not been forced to struggle, such as the Polynesians, will "never become noble races" and that selflessness and equality are found only among "savages" who are uniformly "poor, squalid wretches" (255, 258, 259). At least General Walker's position, to which Bellamy responded in the March 1890 issue of *North Atlantic Review,* indicated that humans were malleable; they responded to different social and physical environments. Maher was more pessimistic. In the *Month,* a previously mentioned British magazine for Catholic readers, he argued that to expect selfish human nature to change was an "utterly baseless illusion." Humans had been "crippled by the fall" (pt. 1, 18; pt. 2, 184).

Although the skeptical and hostile reviewers' focus on their perceptions of human nature was the crucial element in their reality check strategy, their arguments rarely went beyond the standard late nineteenth-century positions voiced in the dialogue between social and reform Darwinists. One significant exception was the position of Canadian professor Shortt, whose review appeared in the *Presbyterian and Reformed Review* (2.6, 1891). Anticipating twentieth-century concepts of human nature and of utopia that emphasize desire and needs hierarchies, Shortt asserted that human desires are insatiable, because the fulfillment of one desire fosters another. The status quo of human existence is a dynamic and infinite series of gaps between the real and the desired. Shortt argued that the most important and insatiable desires are not materialistic. They are the "thirst for power" and the "passions of love and hatred" over "ideas, religious, political and social" (280). This assumption is the foundation of Shortt's two-pronged criticism of Bellamy. First, Bellamy placed too much emphasis on fulfilling material needs. Second, if Bellamy's utopia did succeed and all people's basic material needs were fulfilled and they enjoyed half their lives in "retirement," then the resulting liberation of religious, social, and political passions could "overwhelm society" (280). Freed of their worries about necessities, citizens would indulge in their most powerful personal political, religious, and social desires, creating dystopian chaos.

## Public and Private Historical Placement

Anti-Bellamy reviewers often held his utopia up against reality and found it wanting. Many of Bellamy's supporters (and several of his detractors) looked in another direction—backward—in attempts to give historical explanations for and authority to the text. A typical strategy presented *Looking Backward* as a logical offspring of or answer to historical trends. In "*Looking Backward* and the Socialist Movement," E. Douglas Fawcett perceived Bellamy's utopia as part of the global evolution of socialism originating in Plato's thought and in the nineteenth century, taking root especially in Germany but also in Italy, France, England, and the United States (*Theosophist,* June 1890, 475). William Morris speculated that without the interest in socialism *Looking Backward* would have attracted "very little" notice (287). Another common and related tactic portrayed the book and its popularity as logical responses to an unusual historical moment. The "inequality" (Harris 202), the "plutocratic despotism" (Heinemann 191), the numerous strikes (Goldwin Smith 600), the poverty, the general uncertainty (Shuttleworth 655–56) created pressing needs for a book like *Looking Backward.* Bellamy's advocates and critics agreed that this historical moment gave the book tremendous power. In his *Hartford Seminary Record* (May 1898) review Alexander R. Merriam added that the historical situation had created major transformations of the nature and functions of utopian thought. Anticipating Elisabeth Hansot's interpretation of utopian literature in *Perfection and Progress* (1974), Merriam argued that unlike the "classic" utopias, the new utopias professed an "earnestness and immediateness" that "means business now." Utopia became "an immediate fact of history" rather than a speculative exercise (225).

Two other means of historical placement define *Looking Backward* on a much smaller scale than the evolution of socialism and the reflection of powerful social and economic forces. And yet locating the book within the contexts of its publishing and distribution history and its author's life history constituted crucial strategies for establishing the authority and power of Bellamy's utopia.

As early as April 1889, a British reviewer for the *Saturday Review* noted seventeen editions as a reflection of *Looking Backward*'s "popularity in America" ("Novels" 509); a few months later, in July, *Lippincott's Monthly* cited a twentieth edition as evidence that the book had "the power within it to catch people by the throat" ("Book Talk" 136). In his "Boston Letter" section of the *Critic,* Alexander Young kept a running sales count, informing his readers in June that *Looking Backward* was moving at the rate of 2,000 copies a week (322), and in December was averaging 2,000 a day, with one day reaching 4,300—quite impressive for a book that "scarcely sold during the first year of its publication" (289). By March 1890, the *Nationalist,* a convenient source of sales figures for reviewers, indicated sales of 310,000 (MacNair 7), and *Looking Backward* was routinely compared to *Uncle Tom's Cabin* in terms of sales and social impact. During the 1890s reviewers sometimes drew attention to international sales and translations as proof of Bellamy's global reach. The obituary writer for the *Twentieth Century: A Weekly Radical Magazine* ("Our Weekly" 28 May 1898) claimed that the "Emperor of Germany bought ten thousand copies and distributed them among the students in Germany" (14). Bellamy's critics used the wide distribution of *Looking Backward* to justify their contentions about the dangerous power of the book and about the necessity to expose its flaws; supporters used the sales, editions, and translations as proof of the widespread "dissatisfaction" with the "hateful system of competition" (Martyn, n.p.) and the appeal of its solutions.

Long before Foucault popularized the term *authorial functions* or Michael Steig emphasized how conceptualizations of the author could shape readers' responses, reviewers had used selected information about the private history of authors to add authority to their interpretations of texts. Reviewers of utopias find this tactic especially useful. They often assume that readers suspect the veracity or even the sanity of the unfamiliar and speculative imaginary worlds described by visiting narrators and guides. If a reviewer can convince a reader that "behind" the voices of the narrator and guide there spoke a trustworthy and qualified "author," then the reviewer might succeed in undermining some of that reader's skepticism. The pro-Bellamy reviewers tended to focus on his family history and his intellectual and writing preparation to establish a trustworthy authorial presence.

"Good stock" became a key phrase in validating Bellamy's family history. In his biographical sketches of Bellamy that appeared in both the *Critic* and *Book News,* Alexander Young portrayed Bellamy as coming "from good intellectual stock, being a direct descendant of the eminent theologian of the Revolutionary period, Dr. Joseph Bellamy, the Connecticut divine who was an intimate friend of Jonathan Edwards and the preceptor of Aaron Burr; while his maternal grandfather was Rev. Benjamin Putnam, one of the earliest Baptist clergymen of Chicopee Falls" (*Book News,* November 1889, 68).

A writer for *Current Literature* ("General Gossip," March 1890) described Bellamy's father as "a gentle and kind old Baptist clergyman" (185), and noted that Bellamy himself was a fine husband and father with a "charming wife and bright-eyed little boy of some five summers, and also his four-year old little girl" (185). Frances Willard was obviously a biased reviewer/interviewer. In "her presidential address to the W.C.T.U. [Women's Christian Temperance Union] in 1888, she urged members to read *Looking Backward*" (Strauss 86). Hence, it is not surprising that she offered a favorable family portrait: "Of good New England stock; son of a Baptist minister. . . ."; and his wife was from a Women's Christian Temperance Union family (539, 542). Willard focused especially on Bellamy's daughter, associating her presence with his sympathy for women's financial independence: "I believe a man must have a daughter of his own before he really learns how to sympathize with women in their difficult relations to life" (540).

Willard and Sylvester Baxter's views of Bellamy's intellectual and writing preparation were typical. Bellamy was "a student of Union College; . . . a graduate of law, but not working at it much; a journalist and author both born and made" (Willard 539). According to Baxter, Bellamy was "foremost of the younger American writers" and "Hawthorne's spiritual heir" (93, 94), an opinion Howells reinforced in his *Atlantic* obituary when he asserted that only Hawthorne surpassed Bellamy in "romantic imagination" (256). Bellamy's journalistic work on the *Springfield Union* prepared him to discuss social and economic issues; his "thirty or forty stories" in leading magazines (*Atlantic, Scribner's, Century*) and his novels (especially *Dr. Heidenhoff's Process*) had clearly demonstrated his narrative and imaginative skills (Baxter 92–94; Young, *Book News* 68).

Although most of the biographical information mentioned by reviewers was used to establish a trustworthy and qualified authorial presence "behind" the text, some of Bellamy's critics used his private history to question the literary merit and intellectual sophistication of *Looking Backward*. British reviewers were not averse to using the ingenuity of Bellamy's earlier psychological fantasies against him. The bluntest example of this approach appears in the first *Saturday Review* review ("Novels" 24 March 1888), in which *Dr. Heidenhoff's Process* is praised as a "clever book," and *Looking Backward* is written off as a "stupid" and "wonderfully dull book" (356, 357). Other critics admitted to *Looking Backward*'s literary merits but questioned the appropriateness of a "literary man" performing the role of a social critic. In an essay for the *Quarterly Journal of Economics* (October 1889) and in a *Literary World* review (25 May 1889), Nicholas P. Gilman and an anonymous reviewer deemed Bellamy a respected "man of letters" and a "practical master of literary effect," but they doubted that he had the necessary knowledge of economics and the requisite research skills to propose valid social reforms or to lead a serious reform movement (Gilman 66; "Philanthropic Fiction" 176). For these reviewers *Looking Backward* was a misleading and potentially dangerous combination: an appealing reading experience that had its origins in an unqualified authorial presence.

## Constructing Readers for *Looking Backward*

For most of the reviewers, creating models of ideal, typical, and incompetent implied and real readers was just as, or more, important than identifying authorial authority, historical, ideological, and "reality check" contexts, and synecdochical episodes. Long before twentieth-century scholars such as Everett MacNair, Arthur Lipow, Peter Ruppert, Lee Cullen Khanna, Francis Shor, and I began studying Bellamy's real and implied readers, even before his supporters wrote about his readers in the *Nationalist,* the *New Nation,* and other magazines inspired by Bellamy's utopia, reviewers were proclaiming which types of readers would, should, might, wouldn't, and couldn't respond appropriately to a book like *Looking Backward.*

One of the first steps in this process, indeed one of the most important mediative tasks for the reviewers, was to indicate the nature of the text to which the readers were responding. They assumed that readers had to know what they were getting into if they were to respond properly, and what they were getting into was both unusual and powerful. Typically the reviewers defined the text using specific intertextual comparisons and broad genre contexts that identified the nature and functions of a utopian text. The specific comparisons and genre contexts defined by the reviewers established foundations for their models of readers.

The specific comparisons to Irving's, Hawthorne's, and Dickens's fiction and to Henry George's popular treatise *Progress and Poverty* (1879) emphasized *Looking Backward*'s imaginative qualities, its exposé and reform appeals, and its ability to popularize ideas and shape public opinion. The most common comparison to a popular novel—*Uncle Tom's Cabin*—again attests to the significant connections between utopia and sentimental reform fiction. In part this choice reflected a perceived similarity in content. The *Pilot* reviewer ("The New Utopia," 7 April 1888) proclaimed *Looking Backward* "the *Uncle Tom's Cabin* of the industrial slavery of today" (1). Just as important was the potentiality (early reviews) or the actuality (reviews after mid-1889) of appealing to hundreds of thousands of readers (as Stowe had done) to alter their perceptions of the present and future and to use these altered perceptions as guides to the construction of new, more egalitarian societies.

By making the specific comparisons, the reviewers' primary argument was not that being a "competent" reader of Bellamy meant being a reader fully aware of the intertextual relationships between *Looking Backward* and the other texts. The reviewers were primarily concerned with using the comparative texts as defining markers, shorthand paradigms, that demonstrated how *Looking Backward*'s power was rooted in combinations of imaginative flights; emotional, ethical, and realistic exposés; and socioeconomic proposals. They implied that readers needed to be aware of these combinations and, as the evocation of Uncle Tom emphasized, that the *Looking Backward* reading experience had the potential to alter personal lives and entire societies.

Most of the reviewers went beyond comparisons to specific books to place *Looking Backward* within broad genre or multigenre contexts. Their comments frequently implied genre hierarchies and appropriate reading processes. Like the intellectual and cultural leaders I discussed in chapter 3, they were often suspicious of fiction as a medium of serious thought. J. A. M., the reviewer for the *Knox College Monthly and Presbyterian Magazine* (no. 4, 1889), countered this position by noting that Bishop Vincent gave a "strong recommendation" for *Looking Backward* (209). J. A. M. was the only reviewer to seek dispensation from a bishop to discuss fiction. More typically, reviewers depicted the fictional elements of the book as necessary though "slight" sugar coatings to the important ideas expressed (for example, Morris, "Looking Backward" 287).

This strategy—a close relative of the exposé of a utopian core discussed in chapter 5—became the basis for advice about reading techniques of separation and discovery. In the British magazine *Academy* (27 April 1889), William Sharp proclaimed that Bellamy's "real aim" was to examine "the most exigent problems of our day" and to "trace the evolution of social life within the twentieth century" (284). Although other reviewers avoided essentialist terms such as "real aim," the clear message was that competent readers were similar to the discoverers/exposers examined in chapter 5. They could separate the fictional from the intellectual-ethical portions of the text and privilege the latter, which Morris called the "serious essay" (287). This essay was typically defined with nonfictional labels, including "political economy," "social and political science," "sociological tendencies," even "philosophy," according to the *New York Tribune* reviewer ("New Utopia" 5 February 1888: 10).

Besides training readers to distinguish between the surface and the core of a literary utopia, the reviewers also hoped to help their readers to distinguish between fiction that was "ordinary" (a label used by the *Tribune* and other reviewers) and fiction that was serious and responsible. It is not surprising that they often turned to utopian literature as the most appropriate serious fictional genre designation for *Looking Backward*. Thus a century before Robert Elliott's *Shapes of Utopia*, Gary Saul Morson's *Boundaries of Genre*, and Chris Ferns's *Narrating Utopia* appeared, many of these reviewers argued that literary utopias were "designed to be interpreted in the tradition of previous utopian literary works" (Morson 74). Typically, reviewers made brief associations between respected utopias and *Looking Backward*. The early reviews mentioned Plato and Sir Thomas More frequently; later reviewers included works such as Morris's *News from Nowhere* and Howells's *Altrurian Romances* that were, in part, responses to Bellamy. A few reviewers, notably Alexander R. Merriam (*Hartford Seminar Record,* May 1898) and E. Douglas Fawcett (*Theosophist,* June 1890), even offered extended overviews of utopian literature.

As was the case with the comparisons to specific texts, most of the reviewers were not suggesting that a specific reading background (e.g., utopian literature) was a prerequisite for understanding *Looking Backward*. (The notable exceptions were reviewers who claimed that Bellamy plagiarized from literary utopias—John Macnie's *The Diothas* [1883] or Mary E. Lane's *Mizora* [1889, serialized in 1880–1881].)[3] Placing Bellamy within the tradition of Plato and More did, nonetheless, give *Looking Backward* a historical identity that, for Bellamy's supporters, helped to familiarize the text and give it authority and, for his critics, helped to justify assertions about dull or dangerous literature. In either case the reviewer became a crucial mediator who instructed readers by placing *Looking*

*Backward* within a network of recognizable titles, genre connotations, hierarchies, and reading processes that would enable them to grasp Bellamy's "real aims" and potential impact. The reviewers were activists. They were hoping to do more than construct models of readers; they hoped to create competent readers of this literary utopia. These readers would approach the reading experience armed with some knowledge of the hybrid nature of the text and with a charge to surpass the efforts of "mere tale-devourers" (Freeman 297) by using their ability to identify and separate the fictional elements from the "central points" (Shortt 273) and then to examine these points by constructing and evaluating "in the reader[s'] mind[s]" the "contrasts" suggested by the text ("Recent American Fiction" 845).

The reviewers went beyond descriptions and implications of the intertextual and genre contexts to speculate about the nature of those readers' minds as they were shaped by ideology, profession, class, and geography. The *Current Literature* ("General Gossip" March 1890) reviewer singled out Bellamy's Nationalism movement as offering the best recruit, the "enthusiastic Nationalistic neophyte" (185); in a mixed review, E. Douglas Fawcett chose those willing to consider socialism seriously and wrote off the "sleekly optimistic capitalist" who was not willing (475). Considering his anticipated audience of Presbyterian readers, it is not surprising that J. A. M. presented ministers as the ideal readers (211). It is also not surprising that the reviewers for the *Knights of Labor* (Carlos Martyn) and *Pilot* ("The New Utopia") focused on laborers. For Morris and Howells the British and American middle classes were the appropriate audience. A "Housekeeper" in the Home Correspondence department of *Good Housekeeping* critiqued Bellamy by taking a negative approach to defining (out of existence) Bellamy's readers. The rich would not be interested, because they had servants; middle-class wives do not need help and would resent the interference in their "independent" private lives; and the poor were too weak-minded and "stubborn" to comprehend Bellamy's theories. Besides, poor women would be too "idle" without housework, since they have no other "interests" (214).

Morris and Howells maintained opposing positions on the ideal place for a Bellamy reader. Morris argued that *Looking Backward* empowered the urban industrial middle class. For them work was a curse. Urban centralization and technology had made this curse tolerable. The greater degrees of centralization and technological development that Bellamy's vision offered confirmed, even empowered, their misguided views of life and work ("Looking Backward" 288–89). Howells's American perspective was quite different. City dwellers had seen enough of technological development. They were tired of and oppressed by it. Rural Americans had not seen enough technological improvements to desire or fear them. Villagers, on the other hand, had "seen something of them," enough to "desire them" but not to fear them ("Edward Bellamy" 254–55). For Howells's small-town readers, Bellamy's utopia offered the promise of pleasure beyond the tolerable.

Most of the reviewers avoided overly restrictive ideological, professional, class, or geographical definitions of Bellamy's potentially competent or incompetent readers. Instead they preferred general terms such as the "average" reader (Howells, "Edward Bellamy" 254). Merriam made this point by placing Bellamy's readers in the context of centuries of readers of utopias. More's *Utopia* (first published in Latin) and other "classic" utopias demanded "select readers" in a society where all readers were only a tiny fraction of the population. Furthermore, the visions portrayed in pre-nineteenth-century utopias were often so removed from the readers' realities that it could be difficult even for "select readers" to conceive of the utopias as anything other than thought experiments. Comprehending *Looking Backward,* on the other hand, did not demand a great deal of specialized knowledge, and the industrial and technological developments of the nineteenth century had placed many elements of Bellamy's utopia within the realm of possibility (225).

Despite all the explicit and implicit arguments about "average" readers these were select averages—readers who had special characteristics that made them both vulnerable and powerful. As indicated above, they were vulnerable enough to need reminders about (or a beginner's lesson in) how to read utopian combinations of fiction and nonfiction. The "average" reader also lacked sophisticated knowledge about and the mental capacity to comprehend fully their historical moment and the complex theories designed to improve life. They could enter into the complexities of social and economic discussions and of socialism only if the "serious essay" came wrapped in familiar fictions and if the "central points" were simple.

Reviewers depicted the simplification process with various degrees of praise and condescension for readers. Clark W. Bryan, a reviewer for *Good*

*Housekeeping* (21 December 1889), complimented readers and Bellamy by suggesting that *Looking Backward* "lifted" the discussion of socialism out of the realms of complex economic issues and statistics to a level of "broader human sympathy" (96). M. Bentzon's compliments were a bit more condescending. For him, Bellamy was "'a very ingenious vulgarizer of ideas'" ("French Opinion" 457). The anonymous British reviewer who commented upon this Frenchman's review gave a positive, if somewhat deterministic, spin to this view of simplification: "ideas must be vulgarized before the vulgar can become ideal" ("French Opinion" 457). Howells presented this process in a much less condescending manner, linking it to the blend of materialism and faith that for him was the essence of the American "average": "Our average is practical as well as mystical; it is first the dust of earth, and then it is a living soul; it likes great questions simply and familiarly presented, before it puts faith in them and makes its faith a life. It likes to start to heaven from home, and in all of this Bellamy was of it, voluntarily or involuntarily" ("Edward Bellamy" 256).

The reviewer for *Twentieth Century* ("Our Weekly News-Letter" 28 May 1898) celebrated the faith that grew from the simplicity of *Looking Backward,* by proclaiming Bellamy's book the "Bible of the Socialists" (14). Using similar comparisons, General Walker and William Morris were distressed that the book had become "the Koran of a new faith" and the "socialistic bible of reconstruction" (Walker 257; Morris, "Looking Backward" 289).

The reviewers' depictions of simplification and the results of the simplification process suggest an important aspect of the vulnerability and power of average American (British and French) readers. They were dependent on ingenious popularizers like Dickens, Stowe, and Bellamy; they would be unable to grasp the great issues and reforms of the times without their humanizing fictions. Yet once they had grasped what they could grasp, they experienced "great" ideas and intellectual debates as articles of faith that could motivate and empower them to change their perceptions and their worlds. For the *Twentieth Century* reviewer this was something to celebrate. For General Walker and Morris it was to be feared.

The reviewers defined another manifestation of the combination of vulnerability and power in their comments about the readers' thoughtfulness, concern, and dissatisfaction. The primary reason that Bellamy's "average" readers were superior to "mere tale-devourers" was that they were "thoughtful readers" who were concerned about "the great evils of our times" ("Nationalism and Modern Romance" 57). As the *Nation* (29 March 1888) reviewer observed, their concern and dissatisfaction drove these readers to look for books that offered "a pleasing tinge of optimism," a way out of the morass, "a glowing prophecy and a gospel of peace" ("Recent Novels" 266). Anticipating Jameson's emphasis on the power of literary utopias to "open the space into which [a utopian synthesis] is to be imagined" (qt. in Fitting, "Concept of Utopia" 15), Henry George represented the conjunction of historical moment, readers' longing, and utopian text as a reform process initiated by "breaking up [the readers'] minds," so that there would be openings for new thoughts (1). George could not accept Bellamy's "wild impossibilities of state socialism," but he hoped that the readers' minds liberated by *Looking Backward* would become more open to single-tax reforms (1). Bellamy's critics depicted these broken-up minds quite differently. Morris, for instance, worried about concerned but unsophisticated readers, whose longing for hopeful prophecies inclined them to turn misleading simplifications of socialism into articles of faith (289).

A basic assumption underlay many of the comments about the readers' responses to simplification of complex ideas and the concern, dissatisfaction, and longing of the readers. It was that the most important readers of *Looking Backward,* like the readers of Stowe's *Uncle Tom's Cabin,* were capable of being deeply moved by a reading experience. Howells, and many other reviewers, believed that the emotional responses of readers could in part be understood by defining the text as a powerful stimulus that drew forth reactions triggered by an empathetic correspondence between text and reader. As Howells put it, "somehow, whether [Bellamy] knew or not, he unerringly felt how the average man would feel" (254). But the reviewers' explanations of emotional response typically were not one-way dramas between text-as-stimulus and reader as passive respondent. In order to establish the type of text-reader correspondence suggested by Howells's assertion, the readers had to approach *Looking Backward* with knowledge, attitudes, and beliefs that, as I argued in chapters 3 and 4, would allow them to perceive elements of the text as the stuff of correspondence.

For most of the reviewers the concerns about the "great evils of our times," the dissatisfaction about suffering and insecurity, and the longing for hopeful (and simplified) solutions explained why these readers were ready to "correspond" actively with Bellamy's text even before they read the enticing opening line of the preface, spoken from "the closing year of the twentieth century" (93). One perceptive reviewer went beyond these logical personal and social explanations to outline a fundamental attribute of human nature that inclined all readers toward strong responses to utopian speculation. I previously mentioned Adam Shortt's concept of human desire. In his *Presbyterian and Reformed Review* essay (no. 6, 1891), he offers a theory of human desire that anticipates Ernst Bloch's and Ruth Levitas's concepts of utopia (with a touch of Platonism), as well as needs-hierarchy models of human nature similar to Abraham Maslow's. Shortt offers the following model of human nature in an attempt to explain what motivates people to respond, not only to texts, but to all forms of stimuli:

> *The primary incentive to action is the presence of natural cravings and desires. Of the meaning of these and of the means to satisfy them man is at first ignorant. He is born in a condition of incompleteness, but with many capacities for development. . . . This incompleteness and the divine unrest which compels man to seek completeness are the ultimate grounds of life and action as humans. The primary characteristic of man as a progressive being lies in his consciousness of needs and his capacity to combine these in a rational end or ideal. This ideal then becomes the standard of his life and the personal measure of his success or failure. The ideal is, of course, capable of constant development, for it grows with his needs and takes its character at any given time from the most important of these. . . . The whole of life is thus summed up in the struggle to make the desirable real.* (274)

Again we see a combination of power and vulnerability. These readers are capable of synthesizing their needs and projecting them as ideals; the ideals they create are dynamic; and they can use the ideals as inspirations for improvement. Nevertheless, as Shortt writes later in the review, the insatiable drive to fill the gaps between reality and projected ideals can lure readers into hasty acceptance of false routes between incompleteness and completeness. This is especially the case with average readers who lack sophisticated knowledge about complex social and economic issues: "the popular interest in [Bellamy's] scheme shows a great blank in the popular mind as regards the knowledge of social first principles" (281).

## Placing Utopian Readers and Reviewers in an Industrialized, Democratic Society

Despite the obvious weaknesses of the reviews of *Looking Backward,* especially the lack of extended comment on women and race, they offer insightful and widely read interpretations of Bellamy's utopia and of the readers who transformed his text from a poor-selling first edition into an international phenomenon. They anticipated the focus on particular episodes that continue to attract attention. They explicitly or implicitly portrayed *Looking Backward* as a modern paradigm of utopian literature that signaled a shift away from thought experiments intended for select audiences to idealistic, simplified blueprints that must be verified or exposed by comparisons to "reality"—in particular, the "real" characteristics of human nature. The reviewers also realized that Bellamy's text and his readers were historical and social constructions. Forces as broad as inequality, as documentable as announcements about sales figures, and as domestic as the impact of Bellamy's daughter on his view of women contributed to the authority of the text and its enormous circulation.

The depictions of the modern reader of utopias and, by implication, the role of reviewers of serious and powerful fiction were, arguably, the most original contributions of Bellamy's reviewers. According to the reviewers, readers of *Looking Backward* did not need a great deal of specialized literary and socioeconomic knowledge to understand and be moved by Bellamy's clear, simple, and logical (favored modifiers used by Leete and West) visions of the present and future. They did, nevertheless, need to be aware of the way Bellamy used familiar fictional elements as invitations to considering issues frequently associated with serious nonfiction. The reviewers' comparisons to popular social reform novels like *Uncle Tom's Cabin* and to genres like utopian literature could provide this necessary education. Just as or more important than reading skills were the concern, dissatisfaction, and desires the readers brought to the text. Depending on the reviewer's perspective, these prereading attitudes inclined readers to accept Bellamy's accurate, practical, and exciting critiques and visions or to embrace false and dangerous notions of the present and future. In both cases readers could be moved deeply enough by guilt, dissatisfaction, and hope and in enough numbers to effect significant changes in the world outside of Bellamy's utopian text.

The models of powerful yet vulnerable readers say much about the reviewers' notions of their roles and the roles of "serious" books and readers in modern industrial and democratic societies. As I discussed in chapter 3, during the mid- and late nineteenth century, a huge reading audience was created by fundamental changes in technology and distribution networks combined with a public education system that fostered mass literacy. This audience was not "distracted" by the many audio, visual, and virtual forms of media available to readers today. Serious and moving books could reach hundreds of thousands of readers and, as in the case of *Uncle Tom's Cabin*, even contribute to changing the course of history. Especially after mid-1889, but even before the book's popularity and the rise of Bellamy Clubs and the Nationalist Party, most reviewers presented *Looking Backward* and its readers in these history-altering terms. The reviewers perceived themselves as being much more than literary or cultural gatekeepers. They were the gatekeepers of social change, who mediated between the most powerful (non-oral) medium of expression and the readers created by industrialized, democratic nations.

This may sound a bit grandiose for readers whose deadlines might prohibit them from even finishing the books they mediated. Furthermore, only a minority of the reviewers (most of them critical of Bellamy) openly articulated the urgency that this grandiose role implied. Still, Professor Shortt's explanation of his primary motive is revealing:

> *Dismal and pessimistic as it must seem to those who find such a charm in the simplicity and thoroughness of Mr. Bellamy's scheme, I am nevertheless compelled to maintain that the very attractiveness of his scheme, its charming simplicity, its miraculous harmony of all the elements, the smoothness of operation and the universal effectiveness of the whole system, are the surest indications of its utter failure as a working plan for social and industrial life.* (272, *emphasis added*)

Shortt, like William Morris and others critical of Bellamy, saw charm and danger. More sympathetic reviewers, like Howells, admitted that *Looking Backward* could trick readers into "gulp[ing]" socialism ("Editor's Study" 154). Even enthusiastic supporters felt compelled to advise readers of the hybrid form of the text. In diverse ways the reviewers expressed their ambivalence about late nineteenth-century book power. The mighty collaboration between numerous readers and a readily available and moving "serious" book could, for better or worse, change the course of modern society.

These powerful–vulnerable readers were in desperate need of compelled and compelling advisers to help them distinguish between true and false utopias.

As inflated as this notion of the reviewer's role may be, it is not without historical justification. Considering the cultural attitudes and technological-educational realities that made books such powerful agents of change during the late nineteenth century and the wide readership of many of the publications in which the reviews appeared, it could be argued that *Looking Backward*'s reviewers represent the zenith of the role of book reviewers as mediators of utopia. These mediations combined the roles of authors, translators, educators, and fellow readers in attempts to prescribe how to interpret and use the potential powers of Bellamy's utopia. They deserve an important place in the history of utopian audiences.

We certainly have dramatic proof that the interpretive stances and actions of one very important reader were powerfully affected by one of these utopian mediators. The *Boston Evening Transcript* reviewer's attack on the timetable described by Dr. Leete inspired Bellamy's rereading of his text as he transformed it into the realistic blueprint described in the postscript to the first popular edition of the book, the second edition. This act of rereading or re-viewing gave permission to thousands of readers to downplay their suspicions of fiction and utopian speculation and to emphasize the ways Bellamy's vision could reshape their lives and societies. Thus, one anonymous reviewer helped initiate a process that made Bellamy's one of the most powerful examples of book reviewer/reader power in the nineteenth century and in the history of utopian literature.

# Seven

# 733 Aliens Transforming Utopia
*Preliminaries*

Several years ago, I was standing on a corner in Hiroshima, telling a German biologist about nineteenth-century book-reviewing strategies and the wonders of competent, implied, and ideal readers, as well as the intricacies of interpretive communities. He listened patiently, then responded: "But what experiments have you done?" Descriptive analyses of reception history and textual and social constructions of readers were, for him, no substitute for "tests with live readers." He went on to remind me that I had "captive" and readily available "subjects" for such "experiments"—my students.

The biologist's question is certainly not a new one, nor has it been ignored by reader-response critics, despite the warning of W. K. Wimsatt: "The purely affective report is either too psychological or it is too vague" (qt. in Freund 4–5). One of the first twentieth-century critics to shun this warning was I. A. Richards. In England during the 1920s, he collected students' responses to poems and discussed many of their responses, along with his reactions, in part 2 of *Practical Criticism* (1929). In America during the 1930s, Louise M. Rosenblatt emphasized the importance of the "personality traits, memories of past events, present needs and preoccupations, a particular mood of the moment and a particular physical condition . . . and many other elements in a never-to-be duplicated combination" that actual readers bring to a reading experience (*Literature* 30). More recently,

Gerald Prince has stressed the complexity of that "bringing" ("Notes" 229), and Susan R. Suleiman has urged "that there must be room in audience-oriented criticism for descriptions of the reading process that go beyond the supposed experience of a generalized reader . . . that focus on the actual reading experiences and responses of specific individuals to specific works" (26–27).

And there has been some room made. In "Epistemological Assumptions in the Study of Response," David Bleich has offered a concise overview of several studies completed during the 1950s and 1960s, especially James R. Squire's and James R. Wilson's work with high school and college students (138–41). In *Subjective Criticism* (1978) Bleich himself analyzes student responses; and, of course, there are Norman N. Holland's intensive psychological study of five students (*5 Readers Reading,* 1975), Janice A. Radway's cultural and psychological study of a dedicated group of forty-two readers of contemporary romances (*Reading the Romance,* 1984, 1991), and Michael Steig's analyses of student papers in *Stories of Reading* (1989). If we add to these well-known titles the empirical studies listed in the bibliography of Elizabeth A. Flynn and Patrocinio P. Schweickart's *Gender and Reading* (1986, esp. 299–303) and cited in the footnotes of Ellen J. Esrock's *The Reader's Eye* (1994), the previously mentioned essay collections that examine the documented readings of historical readers, as well as the general reader surveys described by Helen Damon-Moore and Carl F. Kaestle in *Literacy in the United States* (180–203) and recent MLA convention sessions devoted to "real" historical and current readers and reception theory (for example, session 681, 1995; session 409, 1997; session 178, 1998; session 486, 1999)—then the room for studies of "actual reading experiences" seems rather expansive. Furthermore—and more directly related to this study—several of the contributors to the special "Science Fiction in Academe" issue of *Science-Fiction Studies* (23 [1996]) noted student responses to SF and utopian texts.

Nonetheless, in reader-response criticism in general and in the study of utopian literature in particular, the systematic study of actual readers has never achieved a privileged room. This utopian lacuna is strange, since the complex hybrid nature of utopian discourse and utopian literature's intricate combinations of de- and re-familiarization "challenge the reader and require her active participation and intervention" (Ruppert 13), making the study of actual utopian reading experiences seem particularly inviting.

In part, the relatively low profile of studies of actual readers of utopian literature can be attributed to the dominance of critical orientations that either deem irrelevant or look askance at empirical reader-response studies. A New Critical emphasis on the text in a vacuum certainly makes studies of readers irrelevant, as do, to some degree, interpretive strategies that focus on theoretical constructs of competent or ideal readers. From his critical viewpoint, I can understand, for example, why Jonathan Culler could believe that "as a reader oneself, one can perform all the experiments one needs" ("Prolegomena" 51) and that the "purely personal associations" used by readers are "irrelevant factors," since the "question is not what actual readers happen to do but what an ideal reader must know" ("Literary Competence" 111). The poststructuralists' valid skepticisms about the pretense of scientific objectivity also cast doubt on the necessity of empirical studies of readers. Just imagine how Stanley Fish would respond to Robert Escarpit's confident proclamation: "It is only through the study of objective data, systematically exploited without preconceived ideas, that we may approach the literary fact" (18).

New Critical and poststructuralist orientations were not the only serious obstacles to the type of study I envisioned, which required readers to read an almost forgotten book and to complete a biographical profile, a long questionnaire, and a reader-response analysis. If the only requirement had been the completion of a simple, multiple-choice questionnaire about a familiar text or issue, then I could have achieved a larger sample, especially if I had supplemented written responses with responses to an interactive website. I might have been able to generate a sample as large as or larger than the 1,217 readers discussed by Pierre Bourdieu (*Distinction* 512–18). Or if I had discovered a ready-made group of readers (like the Bellamy Clubs of the 1890s or Radway's modern romance readers) who were committed to reading *Looking Backward* "on their own," then I would not have had to create the artificial situation of assigning this reading-writing experiment to students, a local reading group, and a retirement community.

Because my study involved the complex procedures suggested above and described in some detail below, the primary candidates for the survey were those captive subjects used by Richards, Rosenblatt, Squire, Wilson, Bleich, Holland, Steig, Flynn, and others—students. The great majority (98.4%) of my sample were high school, undergraduate, and graduate students. (The rest of the sample consisted of two small but important groups:

a retirement community reading group in San Diego and a women's read-ing group in Arlington, Texas.) I certainly did not achieve a random or rep-resentative sample of contemporary readers. Because of the size of my sample and my lack of expertise in psychology, I also cannot offer the types of psychological analyses Holland presented as he defined reading and identity patterns for his five students.

Furthermore, the entire experiment is vulnerable to Jonathan Culler's cri-ticism of classroom response studies: "The form and content that emerge are controlled by the instructions . . . or the questions asked by the teacher, as well as the consciousness that one is engaged in the formal process of writing" (paraphrased in Steig 10). In my case the readers were required to read a particular text in a particular way in anticipation of completing the questionnaire and reader-response analysis, which placed further boun-daries on their responses by requiring them to limit their discussion of transformational associations (e.g., prior or immediate experiences, prior knowledge and readings, general attitudes and feelings) to the five that were most critical in shaping their responses. To borrow one of Gerald Prince's phrases, these readers were clearly reading "out of a sense of duty" rather than "fun" (229). And to use the type of language familiar to that German biologist in Hiroshima, this study is infinitely closer to the "ex-ploratory" than to the "conclusive" end of the investigatory spectrum.

## Portrait of an Audience

Despite the limits of my experiment, I was able—with the generous help of the Wesley Palms, California, retirement community; an Arlington, Texas, women's reading group; and students and teachers in seven states and four countries—to put together an interesting sample of readers who attempted to describe important aspects of their readings of *Looking Backward*. As I indicate below, I make no pretense of revealing their "ac-tual" reading processes. I agree with Stanley Fish: the reading "experience" is "immediately compromised the moment you say something about it" (qt. in Freund 94–95). This is a study of how readers perceived and articulated their encounters primarily with one utopian text within the contexts defined by the study. I say "primarily" because other utopian and nonu-topian texts were also used for comparative purposes.

The size of the combined sample (see appendix A) was large enough to accommodate, or at least tempt one toward, speculative generalizations:

733 readers and more than 3,100 specific transformative associations described in the reading analyses (see appendix B). The time span for the University of Texas at Arlington (UTA) portion of the sample was broad enough (1983–1996) to allow limited observations about the impact of changing historical conditions. There were also two small UTA "control" groups in 1999 and 2000, but they were not counted as part of the survey because they focused on utopias other than on *Looking Backward*. (See below.)

In a utopian world, all the readers would have completed all the aspects of the project. In this real world of busy and, often, working students, 668 provided biographical information (64 of the missing biographies were from UTA); 651 completed the reading analyses (most of the incompletes came from the 1989 University of Minnesota sample [33] and the 1996 UTA class [21]); and 541 completed the questionnaire. The questionnaire was not developed until the fall of 1987; the fall 1993 and spring 1996 UTA classes were not asked to compete questionnaires; and seven other UTA students failed to turn in questionnaires. Hence, most of the missing questionnaires can be accounted for by UTA students. Fortunately, I did collect a sizable sample from UTA (see appendix A.) I had direct knowledge of the follow-up discussions with my UTA and Japanese students; I had to depend upon secondhand reports from the professors at the other universities. Despite the flaws in administration and completion rates, there were enough readers who conscientiously completed all aspects of the experiment to allow qualified interpretations of the interrelationships among the biographical information provided, the reading analyses, the questionnaire responses, and (to a limited degree) the discussions.

Besides its size, another advantageous characteristic of the sample was its diversity, especially for a college student sample. Compared with the American adult population, the sample was young (average age: 23), single (80%), and underemployed (only 10% had full-time jobs). But the age range was impressive (16–89), and at least 42 of the UTA students were 30 or older. The age diversity facilitated comparisons between distinct groups of "younger" and "older" readers" (e.g., Arlington High School [average age: 16.5], International Christian University [average age: 22], a freshman class at UTA [S '88] and the Rensselaer Polytechnic Institute [RPI] class [both late teens and early twenties] vs. a spring 1989 night class at UTA with many students over 30 and the Wesley Palms retirement community [average age: 80]). Singles dominated the sample. Still, more than 100 who provided biographical information were either married (86), divorced (12), or widowed (4), and that count does not include the seven UTA classes (205 students) who were not asked to provide information on marital status. From 1979 to 1999 the marriage rate among UTA students was approximately 27% (Moorer). Hence, the actual number of married participants was probably closer to 150, if not higher. The underemployment figure noted above is also misleading. As several RPI engineering students responded, they were "*full-time* students" who "worked hard" at their "jobs." Furthermore, almost 60% of the sample worked part-time, and many of those jobs required twenty to thirty hours of work per week. The employment diversity within the sample allowed for comparison. Only 2 (10%) of the Japanese students had any sort of employment; at the other extreme, only 3 members (11.5%) of the UTA night class (S '89) did not work, and of those employed, 17 (65%) held full-time positions.

The gender balance was inclined, by a 58: 42 percent ratio, toward women, primarily because most of these captive subjects had enrolled in liberal arts courses, especially English, and at the institutions surveyed these courses typically attracted more women than men. Four of the groups were all-female: Hood College, Wesley Palms, the Arlington reading group, and Campion College at the University of Regina, Saskatchewan. (The Campion class was mixed, but only women completed the survey.) At RPI most of the students (75%) were male engineering and science majors. Excluding the Austrian professor (only one person, a woman, completed the experiment in his class), there were five male and six female professors (or, in the case of Wesley Palms, an activities director), who conducted the survey. At RPI, one course was taught by a man (F '89), the other by a woman (S '91). At UTA, I taught thirteen of the courses; a female historian taught one (S '91); and I administered the questionnaire to the Arlington women's reading group.

Most of the students (77%) identified themselves as Caucasian. In comparison with the general American population, Hispanics and African Americans were underrepresented (both 4%), and Native Americans were overrepresented (6%). (The remaining 9% of the "minority" students were primarily Asian American.) A "Minority Enrollment" article in the *Chronicle of Higher Education* (17 December 1999) suggests that the recent "minority" college population (26%) is approximately the same as the percentage in my sample (23%) (Carlson A53). My sample included several classes with high American minority percentages (e.g., UTA, F '89: 52% non-Caucasian) and one group, from Japan, that was 100% Asian. (By contrast, the small group from Campion was 100% Caucasian.)

More than 60% of the readers were raised in either Texas or the Midwest, reflecting the fact that a majority of the students attended two large state universities in Texas and Minnesota. Northwesterners and Far Westerners were scarce (2%). Considerable northeastern (Hood, RPI, Harvard) and southern (Louisville) representation did, nevertheless, provide provocative hints about regional-cultural influences, especially with regard to religious experiences and attitudes. As small as they were, the Japanese, Canadian, and Austrian samples also helped to define probable geographic and cultural forces that shaped reading responses.

The variety of institutions represented ensured some degree of socio-economic diversity. During the period surveyed at UTA (1983–1996), the students and their families were typically defined as "working" or "middle" class; many of the students are the first in their families to attend college. At the other extreme was International Christian University, a small, prestigious, and expensive Japanese liberal arts college. (Of course, Harvard is also prestigious and expensive, but the class surveyed was a summer class. Five of the twelve students were not Harvard students. Still, two of these came from MIT and Oberlin, schools that certainly fall into the "prestigious and expensive" category.) In between these extremes are the samples from two large and respected state universities (Minnesota and Louisville), the high school sample, three small and competitive science and engineering and liberal arts colleges (RPI, Hood, Campion), the Arlington reading group, and the Wesley Palms retirement community.

## The Advantages of Alien Readers

Now that I have outlined the basic characteristics of the sample, obvious questions remain: What can we expect to learn from such readers? In a reader-response study, what can we learn about reading a nineteenth-century utopia from late twentieth-century readers? By their own admission (see Q 3, appendix C), many of them are incompetent readers of utopia, unfamiliar with specific utopian texts and the genre's conventions that many nineteenth-century reviewers of *Looking Backward* deemed important. Half of them indicated that they had never read a book like

*Looking Backward*. The other half tended to identify a narrow range of twentieth-century works that represented dystopian (e.g., *Brave New World, Nineteen Eighty-four*) or, to a much lesser degree, Renaissance (e.g., *Utopia*) and feminist (e.g., *Herland, Woman on the Edge of Time*) texts quite different from Bellamy's. Furthermore, many of the historical and cultural situations discussed in chapter 3, many of the reading attitudes expressed by the reviewers examined in chapter 6, and many of the specific conventions of the nineteenth-century domestic novel analyzed in chapter 4 that enabled nineteenth-century American readers to "see" utopia would be foreign to these modern readers. Fredric Jameson's general comments about modern readers of nineteenth-century utopias seem to apply. He argues that for many contemporary readers, a traditional utopia is "desperately unreadable," its "content as irrelevant to consumer society as the draft constitutions and natural or contractual theories of the classics of political science. What had actually become obsolete, however, was a certain type of reader, whom we must imagine just as addicted to the bloodless forecasts of a Cabet or a Bellamy as we ourselves may be to Tolkien, *The Godfather, Ragtime,* or detective stories" ("Of Islands" 2).

We might even go beyond Jameson's proclamation of obsolescence, Culler's view of incompetence, and Peter Ruppert's depiction of modern readers as "strangers" to utopia or Henry Jenkins's "poachers" of mass media, to recall I. A. Richards's negative term "mnemonic irreverence," since more than occasionally modern readers' "preoccupations and past experiences" shape responses that are "unsupported by the text" (Rosenblatt, *Literature* 77). Or we could go one step further and invoke Robert Escarpit's notion of "alien" readers. His aliens are so far removed from the "community of assumptions" that linked the text to its initial audience that they cannot "penetrate" the text, cannot perceive its "reality." They can only produce "distorted" readings (78, 81).

The very alienness of these contemporary readers may prove an advantage. As Peter Rabinowitz argues convincingly in *Before Reading* (1987), "distorting presuppositions lie at the heart of the reading process" (26). Hence, studying these readers' descriptions of how and why they transformed *Looking Backward* should help us to understand important "forces in society" that shape presuppositions that affect reading processes (*Before Reading* 195).

If portraits of these alien readers (based on their questionnaire responses, reader-response analyses, and comments) are really so different from the constructs of the nineteenth-century readers presented in chapters 3 through 6, then we should also be able to make comparisons that say something about the evolution of utopian reading audiences since 1888. This approach seems more fruitful than a heavy emphasis on how modern readers "distort" *Looking Backward*—an approach that assumes that there is a fixed and correct meaning to the text and also obscures the fascinating ways both nineteenth- and twentieth-century readers have appropriated Bellamy's utopia for their own uses.

Another advantage of studying these alien readings is the potential for discovering how the modern appropriations of Bellamy's text are built from a complex network of negotiations (to again borrow Bleich's term) between personal and social constructions of reality as perceived "now" and "back then" and in the future. These acts of transforming utopia into a personal-ized and acculturated text can be very difficult to define when our only sources of evidence are the indirect leads offered by documented read-ings such as book reviews of *Looking Backward* or Bellamy's own changing responses, examined in chapter 5. The transformations and negotiations become more accessible when we can construct questionnaires, reader-response analysis exercises, and discussions designed specifically to ex-plore how readers use "private" feelings, thoughts, and experiences and more publicly shared attitudes to give meanings to the utopia Julian West discovers after his long sleep.

## Tools and Terminology

As suggested previously, I constructed several written tools designed to re-veal insights about how the readers in the sample transformed *Looking Backward*. The readers completed a brief biographical page: sex, age, place raised, ethnic background, marital and employment status, academic level and major, and reading, listening, and viewing habits in terms of time devoted to these activities. They read *Looking Backward*. I recommended that as they read, they identify sections of the text that evoked particularly strong positive or negative responses and jot down possible reasons for their responses. A third component was the questionnaire, composed of several different types of queries (see appendix C), some of which parallel the interests and concerns of the nineteenth-century reviewers. A few questions concentrated on the students' knowledge of basic reading-writing conventions and their ability to communicate information about a reading experience (e.g., Q 5: "How is this book 'told' [1st person, 3rd person . . . ]?" Q 1: "What is the book 'about'?") More questions focused on utopian reading-writing conventions (e.g., categorization [Q 2], associations with similar books [Q 3], the assumed audience and functions for these books [Qs 17–20], and the appeal or lack of appeal of the guide-visitor dialogues, the romance, the dream episode, and typical utopian character types [Qs 7–11]). These conventions and relevant episodes were often mentioned in the nineteenth-century reviews, and thus the students' responses set up possible historical comparisons. Other, more open-ended questions in which the readers were asked to identify episodes and ideas they especially liked or disliked could also be used for comparisons. Another type of question specifically requested information about how these readers used *Looking Backward* (e.g., questions that related Bellamy's viewpoints to their personal opinions [Qs 13–16] and that measured the "relevance" of the text [Q 17] and its ability to alter personal views of society and self [Q 20]). The section of the questionnaire on *Looking Backward* concluded with two open-ended questions that offered readers the opportunity to add anything they wanted to write about their general reading attitudes and their reading of *Looking Backward*. (The remainder of the questions concentrated on reading habits and biographical background. The former was not used in this study; the latter was presented above, is summarized in appendix A, and discussed where relevant in chapters 8 and 9.)

I designed the fourth written component to help the readers "to reflect self-critically" on how they transformed the text and vice versa (Rosenblatt, *Literature* 26). The reader-response analyses built upon the notes jotted down during the reading experience. The readers examined their notes, looking for patterns of interrelationships between parts of the text and their beliefs, their knowledge, their prior and immediate experiences and circumstances. They then selected the five most important attitudes/experiences suggested by the patterns. I knew that requiring five was outrageously arbitrary. But the requirement did encourage the readers to consider multiple associations and also facilitated comparisons among the written analyses. I emphasized that they were the experts on the combination of the five influences on their readings. There was no "correct" distribution of attitudes and experiences. I did require, however, that each of the five sections of their analyses include a description of the attitude/experience, identification of the part or parts of the text affected, and the nature of the response. I further asked that the most important of the five transformational associations be identified. (The UTA and Japanese students presented these reading analyses in the form of papers. The other readers wrote analyses on the backs of the questionnaire pages. These averaged one or two pages, though several residents of Wesley Palms sent me several single-spaced typed pages of analyses.) In all cases the questionnaire and reader-response analysis had to be completed *before* any class or reading group discussion. I hoped that this requirement would minimize the teachers', students', and reading groups' influence on each reader's reading-writing experience.

I had no idea what to expect, in 1983–84, when I first asked students to follow the processes of reading, note taking, and self-text analyses. I assumed that the hybrid nature of utopian discourse, with its combinations of many fictional and nonfictional forms of writing, would invite diversity in the types of associations readers perceived that they used to transform Bellamy's text into images and concepts meaningful within their personal and cultural contexts. I wasn't prepared, however, for the extent of the diversity (see appendix D). I realized that I needed a tentative system of categorization of the associations the readers defined if I were going to make comparisons among different groups of readers of *Looking Backward* or other texts. The reading analyses by the first 104 readers (all from UTA) provided me with categories which, though simple and reductive, have proved extremely useful in uncovering broad trends that characterized the 3,158 associations discussed by the 651 readers who wrote the analyses. (See "104 + 1 Readers.") Almost all of the associations fell into five categories: prior academic experiences (a reflection of the age and situation of the readers), immediate circumstances (physical, psychological, situational), reading and viewing experiences/tastes, prior specific nonacademic experiences (including events and contacts with particular individuals), and general attitudes and beliefs. (In appendix B and in some instances in this and the next two chapters, these five are abbreviated as AC, IC, RT, PE, and AB.)

The potential for overlap among these five categories is enormous. How long must "immediate" last before it becomes "prior"? Should associations with an assigned course text "go under" prior academic or reading taste/experience? Aren't all attitudes and beliefs reflections of complex networks of prior experiences? To answer these and many other similar questions, I had to let the readers' emphases be my guide. If a reader perceived a current mood or situation as having strong and consistent influence during the reading, I considered it an immediate circumstance even if that mood or situation was of long duration. If a student stressed the impact of a past class environment over specific texts, I defined the association as prior academic experience. If attitudes about women's roles were expressed in relation to a particular incident or person (e.g., a job as a waitress or memories of a mother's frustration), I classified the association as prior (nonacademic) experience. If, on the other hand, the student articulated a perception of women in abstract terms ("I believe that women and men should have equal career opportunities"), I listed this association as an attitude/belief.

So that the readers' analyses of *Looking Backward* would not exist in a vacuum, I set up a few modest "control" experiments. (The results were not, of course, included in the statistics related directly to *Looking Backward*.) In four UTA classes, I required students to write similar reading analyses of other utopian works: *Blithedale Romance* (34 honors freshmen, S '88); a selection of several utopias, including *Utopia, Walden Two,* and *Herland* (23 upper-level undergraduates, S '90); *Woman on the Edge of Time* and *Always Coming Home* (9 graduate students, F '90); and *Herland* (8 upper-level undergraduates, S '99). In seven other UTA classes, each student analyzed the impact of five associations on reading nonutopian texts that they selected. The texts were varied: late nineteenth- and twentieth-century American literature, mostly fiction (three sophomore surveys, 102 students, F '83, S '84), eighteenth- and nineteenth-century American literature (the honors freshmen), contemporary American Indian fiction (30 upper-level students, S '88; 12 upper-level students, S '00), and American oral and written literature before 1800 (8 graduate students, S '91).

Terminology posed a problem. I began by using the word *influences* to identify the five shaping forces described by each reader in the analyses of *Looking Backward* and the other texts. *Influence* is a broad term that captures a sense of the processes identified by the students, but it is also vague and suggests a simplistic, one-way cause-and-effect relationship. Concepts frequently used by reader-response critics—for instance, pre-understandings, prior experience, prior knowledge, intertextuality, symbolizing—are more precise and complex but do not cover the diversity of responses analyzed by the readers in my sample. *Interaction*—a term used by Susan Feagin (11)—and *transaction*—a term used by Rosenblatt, Holland, Steig, and others—come closer to describing the utopian reading process, since both emphasize "relationships between reciprocally conditioned elements," a "dynamic to-and-fro relationship" between text and reader (Rosenblatt, *Literature* 291, 292.) *Feedback*—a term used by Suvin and Moylan—captures the dynamic of an encounter with an alternative reality narrative that alters readers' perceptions of their own realities (Moylan, *Scraps* 8). I prefer *transformational associations,* a concept that suggests the complexity and reciprocity of the process, the diversity of the readers' perceptions of their reading experiences, and the transformational powers of utopian texts and readers implied in many of the nineteenth-century reviews and some of the twentieth-century scholarship. The concept emphasizes the active role of the readers (as does Holland's use of the term *transformational* [Freund 119]), without making readers the exclusive masters of the text. They couldn't transform without the potentially transformational invitations of the text. Readers also could not transform without a ready network of associations, and those associations are determined by personal, family, community, regional, and cultural conditions. Transformational associations are dynamic and recursive. What readers bring to a text affects how they respond to the text's invitations. But that transformation will also alter those readers' perceptions of the experiences and attitudes they used to activate/personalize the text. The next time they read that text, what they bring to it will thus be altered and will bring about altered textual transformations.

In chapter 8, I will use the readers' descriptions of their transformational associations, the questionnaire responses, the biographical information, and, where relevant, observations about the class discussions, to delineate general reading attitudes and processes. In chapter 9, I examine responses to significant issues that—according to the first reader, Edward Bellamy, the nineteenth-century reviewers, and my 733 readers—constitute key elements in Bellamy's vision of utopia. The German biologist would no doubt grumble about the limits of my sample and my nonscientific procedures. I hope, nonetheless, he would concede that I am beginning to make more room for studies of actual readers (though they be captive and alien) as they transform Bellamy's utopia.

# 733 Aliens Transforming Utopia
## Utopian Closings and Openings

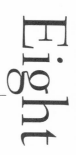

# Eight

What they saw when they read *Looking Backward* was certainly different for late nineteenth-century reviewers, late twentieth-century critics, and the 733 readers in my sample. In one significant way, however, their perceptions were similar. They were all interested in how a literary utopia could invite readers to see an imaginary world as a means of changing their perceptions or as a meaningful guide to reconstructing their worlds. How does reading a utopia "break . . . up" readers' "minds" and "open . . . space" for utopian syntheses, to once again borrow the words of the nineteenth-century reviewer and reformer Henry George and the twentieth-century critic Fredric Jameson? To be more specific, what are the characteristics of literary utopias that block or foster readers' entry into the imaginary worlds of the texts? What specifically do modern readers bring to Bellamy's text that enables them to accept, reject, or modify his criticisms of America and his hopes for a better America?

This chapter will attempt to answer some of these questions, first by highlighting the types of discourses and conventions "in" *Looking Backward* that were inaccessible and accessible to my 733 readers and then by delineating the diversity of transformational associations they used to construct their responses to Bellamy's utopia. I will place emphasis on associations that facilitated the "opening up" process and on the hierarchies of associations that helped to shape the strongest responses to *Looking*

*Backward.* My concentrations on the discourses/conventions and on the transformational associations suggest the complexities of utopian reading processes that can engage readers as different as Henry George, Fredric Jameson, and a sophomore making a forced read of utopia.

## Categorization and Discourse Accessibility

Many of the reviewers discussed in chapter 6, as well as modern critics such as Gary Saul Morson and Janice Radway, have proposed that a crucial aspect in gaining the confidence to accept invitations to co-create a text is the ability to identify—or rather to articulate an understandable identity for—what one is reading. Morson even makes the ability to perceive connections between a particular text and "the traditions of previous utopian literature" the first element of his definition of a literary utopia (74). Radway advances a similar position for a different genre, the popular romance novel. As she argues convincingly in *Reading the Romance,* "Dot's" faithful group of romance readers had the confidence to judge and then to use romances to create hopeful meanings in part because they had become so adept at decoding and categorizing various types of romances. My 733 readers were not as competent at utopian categorizing as Radway's readers were at romantic categorizing. Still, without explicit guidance in class discussions or from the questionnaire (Q 1 was stated in vague terms—"What is *Looking Backward* 'about'?"—and the questionnaire and reading analyses were to be completed *before* class discussions), they knew that two acceptable ways to understand and to communicate what a utopian text is "about" were to formulate a concise summary of the narrative sequence and to construct a brief statement of an ideological concept they perceive "in" the text. The former response typically began with "A man falls asleep for 113 years . . ."; the latter took the form of a succinct statement, for instance, "an ideal socialist society." The responses to question 1 (see appendix C) suggested either one or the other approach (there was little overlapping) in almost equal proportions for the combined sample: 46% narrative sequence; 54% concept. In part this split reflects the hybrid nature of *Looking Backward* and utopian literature in general that reviewers had emphasized a century earlier. Readers inclined toward seeing texts in terms of narrative sequence could find ample evidence in West's sleep voyage and awakening, in the Edith Leete–West relationship, and in the nightmare return to 1887. Readers inclined toward extracting concepts could look to the Dr. Leete–West dialogues.

The most striking exception to the balanced splits in the individual samples reveals the strong impact of the immediate interpretive community of readers. In the University of Louisville political science course ("Modern Political Thought") 96% of the students described what *Looking Backward* was "about" in terms of broad sociopolitical concepts. The stated goal of the course was to introduce "main currents in postmedieval political theory." Just before reading *Looking Backward,* the students studied "dominant themes" in socialist thought. Obviously this context encouraged them to perceive Bellamy's narrative as an example of a political theory. The fact that more than half of the students were political science majors (the closest to an English major was a political science/English major) further inclined these readers toward conceptual readings. In other political science classes they had presumably been trained to extract concepts rather than examine narrative structure, though in an English class, with its different expectations and reading conventions, these same students might have read differently (as did the political science majors in some of the UTA English classes).

The influence of immediate interpretive communities was also evident in the responses to categorizing *Looking Backward* (Q 2). As was the case with many of the nineteenth-century reviewers, most of the modern readers in my sample (74%) used terms such as "utopian fiction," "utopian literature," or "utopia" to define the text. Many of the other terms used, for example, "science fiction," were closely associated with utopian literature. This consensus demonstrates the appeal of one of Rabinowitz's "rules of coherence," naming: to make literature "manageable by putting it in a category" (*Before Reading* 158). The strong consensus also typically reflected immediate contexts and expectations rather than expertise in utopian literature. Most of the courses were literature courses; 13 (14 counting the Austrian tutorial) used some form of the word *utopia* in the class title. In many of the other courses, *utopia* was mentioned in the syllabus. In other words, these readers had a ready-made, authority-blessed category to use. Even if they didn't understand exactly what *utopia* meant, they at least had the power to name the text, and that act of naming gave them confidence to talk about and use the text.

So did prior reading experiences. The importance of both interpretive community and intertextuality was emphasized in the responses of one UTA class that was not a literature class, did not use the term *utopia* in the title or syllabus, and was not taught by me. Only 38% (the lowest in any sample) in this late nineteenth-century American history class (S '91) used some form of the word *utopia* to categorize Bellamy's text. Only 13% (again the lowest) indicated that they had ever read a book like *Looking Backward* before (the combined sample response was 48%). Conversely, the sample with the highest percentages indicating prior reading of utopian literature (Hood, 89%), also had a high usage of the word *utopia* as a means of categorization (83%). Many of the intertextual associations examined in the reading analyses inclined readers toward negative responses. This was especially the case with those who had read contemporary feminist utopias and Orwell and Huxley. The prior readings sensitized them to perceiving sexism and authoritarianism in Dr. Leete's world. But in general, the previous readings of utopian or dystopian texts were associated with positive responses even if those texts were perceived as being ideologically or stylistically antithetical to *Looking Backward*. The attitude, often expressed in the class discussions following the completion of the questionnaires and reading analyses, was that the previous readings made *Looking Backward* more accessible, more usable. Most of these modern readers were using an interpretive technique similar to the nineteenth-century reviewers' attempts to make comparison between *Looking Backward* and other utopian or reform literature such as *Uncle Tom's Cabin*.

The UTA history students found different means and uses. They used their prior historical readings, and, not surprisingly, their interpretive community inclined them to label *Looking Backward* as "historical fiction." When asked if they would recommend *Looking Backward* to someone else (Q 21), they, like the readers in the other samples, said yes, overwhelmingly. But to justify that response, they tended to emphasize insights gained about late nineteenth-century American social and economic conditions, rather than the way *Looking Backward* provoked thought about alternative societies and about flaws in the present society—the two functions of Bellamy's utopia most frequently emphasized in the other samples.

The expectations raised and reading conventions established by clearly defined interpretive communities (particularly classroom communities) can help readers to gain access to many but not necessarily all parts of a utopian text. The fable-manifesto hybrid of *Looking Backward*'s discourse is a conglomerate of many discourses. In chapter 4, I examined one, the love-story narrative of the domestic novel. As I suggested in chapters 1 through 3, other types of discourse in *Looking Backward* and other late nineteenth-century American utopias include travel, exploration, and settlement accounts, as well as adventure tales, captivity and conversion narratives, the realistic novel, muckraking exposés, science fictions, economic and social treatises and manifestos, philosophical dialogues, prophecies, parables, sermons, lectures, election speeches, how-to manuals, and blueprints (verbal and visual). These texts are virtual encyclopedias of late nineteenth-century Anglo-American discourse types. The tremendous popularity of *Looking Backward* suggests that this polyvocality spoke well to Bellamy's initial readers; even if they disagreed with Bellamy, as reviewers often did, they respected the book's potential to profoundly influence many people. But, as Jameson has suggested, to a late twentieth-century reader, a traditional utopia might be "desperately unreadable"—a boring babble of different voices ("Of Islands" 2).

The reading analyses and the responses to question 6b ("Are there any particular episodes that you especially disliked?") suggest which forms of discourse were inaccessible to these modern readers and why. A strong consensus—that cut across gender, age, geographical, ethnic, and interest boundaries—criticized Rev. Barton's sermon (274–85), and, to a lesser degree, the long guide–visitor talks. (The only clear exceptions to the sermon critiques were two women from Campion College who praised Barton's attacks on "false Christianity.") Readers found fault with the sermon in terms of reading conventions and religious attitudes. Readers who wanted *Looking Backward* to be a novel perceived the sermon (and sometimes the Leete-West talks) as preachy "interruptions," "deviations," or bothersome "switches." As one UTA undergraduate put it, the "action" and "almost all the dialogue [were] stifled while Bellamy, through his characters, stood up on a literary soapbox" and delivered "a sermon or stern lecture."

These modern readers used a broad spectrum of religious associations to criticize the sermon. (I did not ask them to identify their religious preference, but almost all who discussed the sermon did.) Because it was broadcast into homes, the sermon reminded readers from all the geographical areas of TV-evangelist scandals. Several northeastern engineers at RPI, who identified themselves as atheists, thought that the inclusion of "religious" discourse was totally out of place in a book set in the future. In terms surprisingly similar to the critiques used by nineteenth-century reviewers who disliked the sermon, fundamentalists from Texas, the Midwest, and the South protested the lack of "religion" in the sermon. They claimed that there was no mention of Jesus or the Bible. Instead there was a suspect emphasis on human progress that smacked of secular humanism. Actually, there was mention of Jesus (279), and biblical styles (the rosebush parable, for example) and references (the ten commandments) do appear. But Rev. Barton's sermon was not identifiable with their concept of a sermon, so they distanced themselves from his text, and this distancing obscured or even rendered invisible familiar "religious" characteristics of Rev. Barton's words. (In discussions after the completion of the questionnaires, the fundamentalists were shocked to discover that Bellamy was the son of a Baptist minister.) Some of the most interesting negative responses to the sermon came from readers—Protestant, Catholic, and Jewish—who associated religion with communal experiences. Like Michael Maher, the previously quoted reviewer for the Catholic magazine *Month,* these readers believed that to be a real sermon, the speaker's words had to be shared with other people in the same room. As one Filipino Catholic living in Texas proclaimed, people should not turn God "on and off like a switch button" in their homes. This group of readers did not want a couch-potato worship service.

No doubt Escarpit would label these criticisms as unfair distortions. Many of the readers were certainly incompetent in the sense that they did not know the contexts that rendered Barton's sermon meaningful to many of Bellamy's first readers and to twentieth-century American studies scholars. They were unaware of authorial contexts (Bellamy's family background and his essay "The Religion of Solidarity," for instance), historical contexts (the Social Gospel and Reform Darwinist movements), and genre contexts (portions of nineteenth-century literary utopias were expected to be preached). Their strong negative associations also blocked the perception of textual contexts. For example, within the framework of Dr. Leete's world, having the very best religious leaders available to every home represented a great egalitarian advance over the limited access to prestigious preachers during the nineteenth century. (After acquaintance with these contexts, my students still didn't "like" the sermon. But our discussions did at least transform the sermon from being an incomprehensible intrusion to a conceivable inclusion.)

With the significant exceptions of important French and British reviewers, many of the nineteenth-century reviewers had greater tolerance for the long Leete-West dialogues than they had for the sermon. The modern readers, who were less accustomed to socioeconomic dialogues interrupting their "novels," were less tolerant. Part of the problem was that West was often a "dry and inadequate foil" (Pfaelzer, "Immanence" 59); hence, monologues often masqueraded as debates. The readers in my sample didn't have to be disciples of Mikhail Bakhtin to perceive the monologic nature of these supposed dialogues. One UTA night student characterized Dr. Leete as an "obnoxious know-it-all" who was forever "rubbing his nose in the follies of the nineteenth century while feigning objectivity and sympathy" for West's contemporaries. Responses to question 11 supported the criticisms in the reading analyses; Dr. Leete was the least liked of the dominant characters (West, Edith Leete, and Dr. Leete).

Nevertheless, there were a substantial number of readers who had positive responses to the West-Leete conversations (43%), and a clear majority did like Leete (74%). These cases demonstrate the power of assumptions about the functions of reading and of associations with intense personal experiences. Many of the male RPI engineers indicated that for them books were "sources of information." Leete's descriptions of the old and new world came closer than any other parts of the text to fulfilling their expectations. Since the RPI sample had the highest percentage of males (75%), the engineers' emphasis on information gathering may lend support to the model of male readers as cognitive, efferent readers (Flynn x, 234–66, 267–88), though interpretive strategies used in specific classroom situations, as well as strong personal associations, also influenced positive responses to the dialogues. The UTA history class's positive response to the historical value of the dialogues and that of one female African American student make this clear. In the history class the book was presented and perceived as a source of information, and the African American student transformed the dialogues by associating them with her grandmother. She had great difficulty relating to her grandmother, a woman who raised sixteen children, was a "cleaning woman," and suffered discrimination. As the student put it, "cleaning was her life and 'colored' was her first name." She believed that she had earned the privilege of knowing right from wrong, and she often lost her patience when her granddaughter didn't fully respect that privilege. In Dr. Leete, this student perceived a model of a patient and understanding grandparent. She saw in Leete what she wanted in her grandmother. Certainly this is a highly personalized reading. But besides providing a comforting image of a grandparent, it also gave her insights into the ways Leete might have nurtured troubled nineteenth-century readers into finding hope in his world.

In chapter 4, I emphasized the importance of nurturing intermediaries. Directly or indirectly the need for identifiable intermediaries is indicated in the numerous comments about the "love story" in the nineteenth-century reviews and in comments by modern critics, for instance, Peter Ruppert's view of readers of utopias as "strangers" in a "strange" land, in Darko Suvin's emphasis on "cognitive estrangement," and in other scholars' interpretations of how the jarring "other" and reassuring "familiar" vie in utopian texts. Nowhere in the responses of the 733 readers was the importance of nurturing intermediaries reflected so clearly as in their comments about the types of discourse they found most accessible in *Looking Backward*. Ninety-one percent of the combined sample indicated that they liked Julian West. The most frequently mentioned episodes designated as best-liked were those involving West's encounters with Edith Leete, and only 14% of the combined sample indicated that they disliked the "love story." (For an examination of this minority opinion, see the discussion of women's roles in chapter 9.)

There were dissenters who focused on West's "snobbery" before his sleep and his "spineless" resistance to Leete's views. All but one of the all-female samples (Campion) had reservations about Edith Leete, and a few students in each sample, and most of the readers in the Wesley Palms retirement community, picked the Edith Leete–West scenes as the most disliked episodes (they were annoying "interruptions" for those who wanted "information") and labeled Edith Leete as an "air head," a "silly Victorian," or "sentimental whiner." Their terms of derision were not unlike the labels voiced by the few Edith Leete detractors among the reviewers, for instance, Geraldine Meyrick, who called the love interest "sickly sentiment" (567). Still, for the clear majority of the modern readers, West's personal conversion narrative and, to a lesser degree, the romance narrative were the easiest access routes to Bellamy's utopia. They represented the most familiar forms of discourse in an imaginary world that, if anything, was less familiar, more estranged, than it was to nineteenth-century readers. True, some of the technological devices were more familiar to them. But even these were unfamiliar, since we have already "surpassed" so many of the inventions depicted. Hence, they were antiquated and curious rather than familiar.

As suggested above, the mixtures of nonfictional and fictional discourses were less familiar to these readers. Most important, we seem just as far from an era of universal brotherhood/sisterhood as were Bellamy's first readers, and the modern readers' close proximity to the fictional time setting of A.D. 2000 made Bellamy's timetable seem more unbelievable today than in 1888. This seemed especially so for readers who participated in the experiment during the late 1980s and 1990s. During the early 1980s, most of the objections raised against a centralized economy and socialism were based on ethical or theoretical associations. Beginning in the late 1980s, the transformational associations relating to Leete's celebrations of the industrial army took on much more of an inductive air, with students pointing to the breakup of the Soviet Union and the decline of communism in Eastern Europe as "proof" of the impossibility of Bellamy's utopia. If the readers from the early 1980s rewrote their analyses today, I'm certain they would find much use for the example of the collapse of Soviet communism and the dire state of the Russian economy at the dawn of the new millennium. The change in the nature of transformational associations used to critique centralization and socialism was the most striking evidence of the impact of changing historical conditions on the way the readers in the combined sample perceived *Looking Backward*.

In the midst of all the unfamiliarities and unbelievabilities of Bellamy's utopia, West's personal addresses and questions, his emotional outbursts, and his romance with Edith seemed reassuringly familiar, or at least they were reprieves from the other forms of discourse and the increasingly distant possibility of a grand and rigidly centralized route to universal harmony. With great consistency, these readers linked their perceptions of West alone and Edith and West together to specific, personal, and familiar experiences: having insomnia, waking up disoriented in a new locale, memories of relationships with family members and recollection of the highs and lows of romances.

The Japanese sample offered a striking example of this process of personalizing utopia—in this case a process of personalized acculturation.

Bellamy's American vision (which these students read in English) was literally and figuratively foreign to these readers. They had strong needs for intermediaries and translators. It is not surprising that they were attracted to the openly confused voice of West and the nurturing sentiments of Edith Leete. (They expressed the highest approval rating for Edith [94%].) These sixteen young women and four young men perceived the West–Edith Leete relationship in terms of an idealized but modern Japanese relationship in which a troubled man is nurtured by a sympathetic, kind, and extremely patient woman. There were particular elements of the West–Edith Leete relationship that were imminently translatable into a Japanese worldview. These include Edith Leete's great dismay over (and even a hint of lack of tolerance for) West's public outburst of emotion in the streets of Boston and her great sympathy for West during the other outbursts, which, as indicated in chapter 4, all occur in the privacy of the domestic sphere. The sermon, Dr. Leete's long talks, and many other parts of the text were almost as untranslatable for these readers as they would have been for the dinner guests at the Bartletts' luxurious home in 1887. But the Japanese readers could use their belief in the beauty and power of female compassion for a troubled man to transform the West–Edith Leete romance into an accessible and moving reenactment of an idealized Japanese vision.

## The Diversities of Transformational Associations

The questionnaires provided the most information about the ways the readers categorized Bellamy's text and the specific types of discourses that were least and most accessible to them. The reading analyses were my primary means of investigating the following general questions about perceptions of reading processes: What types of experience, knowledge, and attitudes did the readers use to transform the text's invitations into personalized meanings? Do the natures of the transformational associations described differ when some of these readers turn to other utopias or to nonutopian works of fiction and nonfiction? Are certain types of associations related to positive or negative responses, to "quick entry" into the text or to the processes of "opening up" to an awareness of "different" realities and possibilities? Are any types of associations used more frequently than others? If there are, then are there any correlations between gender, age, ethnic background, or other biographical characteristics and these frequency patterns?

As noted in chapter 7, as early as 1983, I was already impressed with the diversity of transformational associations discussed by the readers and had identified five broad categories to define this diversity: past academic courses (AC), immediate circumstances (IC), reading-viewing tastes (RT), prior nonacademic, nonreading experiences, including memories of events and relationships with people (PE), and general attitudes and beliefs (AB). (See appendixes B and D.) I was tempted, even when I received the first reading analyses of *Looking Backward,* to assume that those analyses demonstrated that the conglomerate nature of utopian texts invited, and indeed activated, a diversity of associations more pronounced than would be found if the readers were encountering nonutopian texts.

During 1983 and 1984, as a modest test of my tempting assumption, I asked 104 students in three American literature surveys (1860–present) who had done reading analyses of *Looking Backward* to select another text for a similar analysis. (Allowing them a choice almost ensured that the responses would be more positive than they were for the Bellamy reading.) Most of the students selected works of fiction by established authors, for example, Crane, Dreiser, Jewett, Hemingway, Fitzgerald, and Faulkner (see Roemer, "104 + 1 Readers Reading"). The results reinforced my assumption. In both the tabulations of the overall (i.e., all five associations identified by each reader) and most important associations identified by each reader, the perceptions of the readings of the nonutopian fictions were dominated by memories of prior nonacademic, nonreading experiences (overall: 52% of the associations described; most important: 59%), whereas the distribution was more diversified for the *Looking Backward* readings (overall: 5% AC, 14% RT, 16% IC, 30% PC, 35% AB; most important: 4% AC, 10% RT, 11% IC, 30% PE, 45% AB). Very brief descriptions of transformational associations collected on simple forms for many texts in an American literature survey (S '84) and in the freshman honors course (S '88), as well as reading analyses of texts in contemporary Native American fiction courses (S '88, S '00) and a graduate early American literature course (S '91), tended to support my early "findings." For example, in the Indian fiction classes, the statistics were S '88—overall: 57% PE, most important: 81% PE; S '00—overall: 67% PE, most important: 73% PE; in the early American class—overall: 46% PE, most important: 50% PE.

Before I turn my tempting assumption into a convincing hypothesis, I must allow for two significant qualifications. In general, when the students made their own choice of text, the percentage of prior nonacademic, non-reading associations increased, which seems natural. They picked works they could "relate to," and this relating frequently took the form of associating parts of the texts with memories of personal events and relationships. Moreover, other experiments with different utopias and with provocative nonfictional texts demonstrated that the nature of transformational associations described can vary substantially from utopia to utopia and that provocative nonfictional texts can certainly activate diversified mixtures of associations. For example, the freshman honors students did reading analyses of *Looking Backward* and Hawthorne's *Blithedale Romance.* For *Blithedale* they used many more personal memories about people and personal relationships (e.g., most important: *Blithedale,* 36% PE; *Looking Backward,* 9% PE), reflecting Hawthorne's much stronger emphasis on character development and interrelationships. I discovered similar responses in a small sample (S '99, eight upper-level students) who voluntarily selected Gilman's *Herland.* The higher percentage of personal experience associations (overall: 40%, most important: 62%) may well have reflected Gilman's emphasis on interpersonal relations, especially the bonds between mother and child. The emphasis on personal experience also suggested the obvious fact that they selected *Herland* because they could personalize the text, though the processes of personalization were as different as one male student's memories of warm, ironed shirts wrapped around him by his mother on cold days and an exotic dancer's annoyance at people who seemed incapable of recognizing intelligence in someone who takes off her clothing.

When graduate students at UTA compared their reading analyses of *Looking Backward* and Ursula K. Le Guin's *Always Coming Home,* they discovered a significant difference between the low rate of reading taste associations with Bellamy's text (overall: 10%; most important: 0%) and a much higher rate for Le Guin's (overall: 37%; most important: 33%). Again this was predictable. Le Guin's experimental, discontinuous form invited numerous comparisons with oral literatures, as well as modernist and post-modernist written texts. In the reading analyses by the honors freshmen of provocative, multigenre autobiographical texts, such as Franklin's *Autobiography,* the mix of associations (e.g., most important: 31% RT, 34% PE,

34% AB) approached or even surpassed the diversity of the association mix found in some of the other samples focusing on *Looking Backward.*

The temptation of my initial assumption has been tempered by the subsequent reader analyses of nonutopian and other utopian texts. But the limited comparative studies I have made still suggest that readers will draw upon a greater variety of associations when reading a traditional utopia such as Bellamy's than when reading other types of texts, especially "realistic" fictions. This may help to explain why, over the centuries, readers have disagreed so violently about the meanings and values of specific utopias and why so many different nineteenth-century readers saw many different "things" in *Looking Backward.* Bellamy's text expresses so many different types of invitations that can activate so many different types of associations that in turn can transform the text in so many ways that we should not be surprised that the initial reviewers violently disagreed about the meanings and potential effects of *Looking Backward* and that there were retired generals, Christian Socialists, Theosophists, Populists, women's rights advocates, educational reformers, and many other types of reformers rubbing shoulders in the Bellamy and Nationalist Clubs of the late 1880s and early 1890s.

## Associations That Open Utopian Spaces

Besides the diversity of associations, two other significant trends revealed in the reading analyses of *Looking Backward* were the consistent relationship between associations with past personal experiences and positive responses (see appendix B) and the tendency of certain types of associations to facilitate entry into the text and invite new ways of perceiving the present and future.

The relationship between the positive responses and the personal memories reflects the desire to, indeed the necessity of, personalizing utopian texts. Although this process characterizes to some degree all reading experiences, it is especially important to readers of utopias. The imaginary worlds described can seem so far removed from the readers that they need personal linkages to tie the utopias to their notions of reality. Thus, I was not surprised that when readers could associate a character with a friend, or an episode with a past experience, they tended to describe their responses to the reading experience in positive terms. In the large UTA sample, for instance, in the personal experience category of associations, the students described 449 of the associations in positive terms, 199 in negative. In the four other categories, the ratio between positive and negative responses was much more balanced (AC: 67/61; IC: 98/68; RT: 162/137; AB: 383/503).

I was not surprised by this trend, since I assumed that associations that helped to personalize utopia would be seen in a positive light. I was also not surprised to discover that certain specific types of associations with prior experiences almost ensured a strong engagement with either part or all of *Looking Backward,* though they did not guarantee a positive response. Some of these associations mentioned most frequently include memories of insomnia or waking up disoriented (related to West's experiences), romances (related to the Edith Leete–West romance), friendships with handicapped people (related to the "invalid corps" in the industrial army), involvement with science and engineering projects (related to the technological wonders), direct knowledge of the legal system and criminal behavior (related to Leete's explanations of the disappearance of crime), and experiences with poverty.

The latter association was especially important. Only five students in the combined samples described their substantial wealth as a significant association. (Four felt guilt; one, the youngest, feared the changes to his lifestyle that Bellamy's equality would require.) On the other hand, more than a hundred readers, mostly from the UTA and Minnesota samples, identified experiencing poverty as an important association inclining them toward approval of Bellamy's reforms. (Most of these associations included personal suffering, though several involved the witnessing of poverty by economically secure students; for instance, one student discovered a homeless man in a dumpster on a Christmas morning.) Some of the periods of poverty were short; an RPI student reported living in a tent for three months because his family could not afford a house. Others seemed endless. One UTA mother recalled her childhood growing up with fourteen brothers and sisters. She wore flour-sack dresses through her teens, and had powerful recollections of her first visit to a rural grocery store at twelve: "There were things there that I didn't know existed." Her former poverty made her very sympathetic to Bellamy's sense of equality. But the recalled excitement of that first store visit was still with her and made shopping an "exciting sport." Edith Leete's efficient warehouses didn't appeal to her. But whether her responses were positive or negative, it was clear that her past experiences with poverty transformed Dr. Leete's treatises on nineteenth-century inequality from dry abstractions into lived experiences.

Whereas the previously mentioned types of associations opened up particular parts of *Looking Backward,* one type of recalled experience—a sudden and profound change of environment—almost always facilitated entry into the entire world of Boston A.D. 2000. The memory of the change helped the reader to "identify" with West. It also provided a personalized paradigm of a comparative mode of perception so essential to the utopian reading experience. These readers were saying, in effect, we can read utopias because we've already thought that way before.

In several instances the change in environment was transitory and did not involve a significant geographical move—an Austrian student's stay in a psychiatric ward, a return to a nearby but radically altered hometown in Texas, for instance. More frequently the alteration involved a change in environment lasting from a few weeks to years. Several students at UTA, Hood, and Minnesota, for example, had lived in countries governed by various forms of socialism or strong centralized governments: West Germany, Finland, Honduras. The former two associations created powerful positive biases toward Bellamy's utopia; the latter, a negative response. Visiting a cousin in an Israeli prison strongly inclined a UTA student to support Bellamy's judicial system. Living in Taiwan during the Tiananmen Square massacre and reading *Looking Backward* within view of the extremes of wealth and poverty in Cancun set up criticisms of Bellamy's authoritarianism and enthusiastic support for Bellamy's egalitarianism for two other UTA students.

As to be expected, readers raised in another country were the most adept at seeing comparatively. The associative transformations they performed were often surprising to the students raised in America. For example, one UTA student read *Looking Backward* through multilayered comparisons to Filipino, Chinese, and metropolitan Texan cultures. Her response to Mr. Bartlett's railing against workers early in the second chapter (104) was particularly interesting. Whereas in discussions most of the students found his views deplorable, she had a strong positive response, primarily because he praised the stability of China. In the other works we had read, the Chinese were either invisible or depicted unfavorably. She relished Bartlett's brief comment as a sign of recognition of her background, and that small act of recognition made her pay more attention to Bellamy's book than to the previous readings.

One other international association deserves special note. Reading tastes often affected responses to an episode frequently discussed in the nineteenth-century reviews—the well-known coach analogy (96–98). One reader associated the coach with analogy writing and the "clever and entertaining people" who thought up analogies. A more common response was the act of transforming West's "prodigious coach" into a stagecoach associated with Westerns. This tended to make West's analogy seem not only figurative but also romantic and removed from the present. One of the UTA night students went even further with this distancing process. He disliked Westerns, analogies, and most "figurative language." The coach analogy "left me flat. I wanted something more realistic, less metaphorical, more detailed." In stark contrast to this and the other distancing associations described by readers raised in the United States was the response of a Pakistani student living in Texas. For him West's coach was "a fact of life." He had been raised in an area characterized by extremes of wealth and poverty; his family was extremely wealthy and had been for several generations. He was used to great luxury as a child. A sudden and disastrous business turn depleted the family's money and forced them to leave Pakistan. For him the coach was factual, not figurative, proof that "accumulated wealth can never stay forever."

Of course, that lesson is taught in America too. One native Texan reader began *Looking Backward* on the day his home loan was turned down and a big business deal collapsed. But the Pakistani's transformation of analogy into fact goes beyond a process of forming socioeconomic associations. His luxurious childhood in a "distant land" had, in effect, become a utopian text for him—a radically better alternative far removed from his present situation. His present experience, his memories of past good and (suddenly) terrible experiences in Pakistan, and the way he used the present and past to transform West's coach, bespoke a reader who believed he could respond to the text on bases of "fact" and by using cross-cultural perceptual skills developed during the years of luxury, misfortune, and gradual rebuilding. His degree of confidence was pronounced, but not untypical of the readings offered by international students who appealed to the "facts" of their cross-cultural experiences.

## Hierarchies of Transformational Associations

Despite the tremendous diversity of transformational associations described in the reading analyses, a pattern emerged that reflected preferences for using certain types of associations more than others. The pattern defined a hierarchy of increasing use in the following order: past academic experiences, immediate circumstances, reading-viewing tastes, prior (nonacademic, nonreading) experiences, and general attitudes and beliefs. (See appendix B.)

Transformational associations described in terms of general ideas, attitudes, and values repeatedly, though not in every case, topped the hierarchy, accounting typically for 30 percent to more than 50 percent of the associations described. (For the most important associations, the percentages were slightly higher than for the overall count of associations.) This emphasis establishes a strong link between these modern readers and Bellamy's initial readers, the models of discoverer-exposé readers discussed in chapter 5, and many of the nineteenth-century reviewers who, like William Morris, believed that the task of the reader of utopias was to get beyond the narrative surface to reveal the underlying "serious essay" ("Looking Backward" 287). For past and present readers, *Looking Backward* was most significantly an expression of ideas and beliefs designed to provoke thought about past, present, and future realities and possibilities. Significantly but not exclusively: comparisons with responses to texts such as *Walden,* which were almost entirely dominated by attitude-belief associations, remind us of the diversity of associations used by the modern Bellamy readers. Nonetheless, the reading analyses suggested that, like readers more than a hundred years ago, these readers believed that perceiving *Looking Backward* most frequently through a network of general values and beliefs and as a close relative of the "novel of ideas" was much more appropriate than readings dominated by associations with memories of other texts or immediate and past academic and nonacademic experiences.

The exceptions to the typical hierarchy reflect the importance of reading environments created by local interpretive communities and the significance of the ages of the readers. The honors freshman American studies class at UTA and the "American Novel" class at Hood demonstrate the former influence. Compared to the other students at UTA, the honors students used intertextual associations much more frequently and personal experiences less frequently: overall associations, honors: 3.3% AC, 8% IC, 17% PE, 28.3% RT, 43.3% AB; combined UTA sample, overall: 6% AC, 8% IC, 14.3% RT, 29.3% PE, 42.3% AB. In their past academic environments, the honors students had been rewarded for reading more books than their classmates. Indeed their elevated academic identity was firmly grounded in their belief that they were reading more than their colleagues. It is not surprising, therefore, that they tended to read *Looking Backward* through other books more frequently than other UTA students. Ellen J. Esrock might relate the lower frequency of personal experience associations to the denigration of personalized imaging in academic settings (180–81). Teachers often criticize such visualizations as inappropriate or even childish responses to reading. Many honors students would have been conditioned to avoid such "immature" behavior.

The Hood College reading analyses represented an even more striking departure from the typical hierarchy. In both the overall and most important tabulations, associations with past academic class work (which was usually the lowest or second-to-lowest in the hierarchies of the other samples) ranked near or at the top: overall: 6% IC, 20% RT, 23% PE, 25% AC, 26% AB; most important: 6% RT, 18% IC, 18% PE, 23% AB, 35% AC. Hood has a long tradition as a women's college and strong offerings in women's studies. Although the class surveyed was not one of these offerings, the professor was a recognized feminist scholar, and most of the students were juniors and seniors who had taken women's studies courses. Both college and classroom environments at Hood provided these students with expectations and interpretive skills that encouraged them to see *Looking Backward* (especially the descriptions of Edith and chapter 25 on women) through their college tradition and academic awareness of women's issues.

I had not particularly noticed the other significant variable—age—until I reexamined the reading analysis of my oldest UTA student. (He was 74 when he read *Looking Backward*.) He responded to my request for descriptions of five transformational associations by examining twenty personal memories, including his merchant marine and navy careers, his witnessing of the Marines' refusal to break up a hunger strike in 1932, his contacts with famous people such as the Socialist presidential candidate Norman Thomas, and his struggles to desegregate hospitals and nursing homes in the South. His life was exceptionally rich; but his analysis made me reexamine other more typical older readers to see if, like he, they also emphasized nonacademic personal experiences more than the younger readers did. By coincidence his class (S '90) was above the average age of my combined UTA sample (average: 23.4; S '90: 26.5). Almost half (44%) of the students were 24 or older. So I began by examining the figures for his class. Memories of specific past experiences and personal relationships were mentioned more frequently than general attitudes and beliefs in both the overall and most important tabulations: 36% AB, 38% PE; 38% AB, 43% PE, respectively.

The relationship between higher age and increased use of associations with specific past experiences did not always appear. The relatively young (average age: 22) 1983 UTA sophomore class used personal experience more frequently than did many older UTA classes; and in the spring 1989 night course (average age: 29) and the spring 1991 history course (average age: 30) general attitudes and beliefs topped the hierarchy. Nevertheless, the pattern was evident in most of the samples. Compared to the combined UTA sample (overall: 30% PE; most important: 29% PE), the younger samples reflected less emphasis on associations with specific personal experiences: high school (average age: 16.5): overall: 15%, most important: 16%; University of Minnesota (average age: 20): overall: 16%, most important: 6%; RPI (average age: 20): overall: 11.5%, most important: 5%. Conversely, most of the older samples placed more emphasis on associations with personal experiences: for example, the fall 1990 UTA graduate course (average age: 31): overall: 34%, most important: 63%; Harvard (average age: 25): overall and most important: 34%. The oldest sample, the group from Wesley Palms retirement community (average age: 80) reflected the strongest emphasis on reading Bellamy through past personal experiences: overall: 58%, most important: 60%. A particularly interesting contrast appeared in the Japanese sample composed of 15 young undergraduates (average age: 20) and 5 graduate students (average age: 27). The younger readers placed little emphasis on personal experience associations (overall: 12%, most important: 18%). The older group equaled the combined UTA emphasis on personal experience for overall count of associations (29% PE) and more than tripled that emphasis when they discussed the most important associations (100% PE).

To explain why he did not mention any personal experiences, one young RPI student wrote, "personal experience—not applicable." To explain why he dwelled upon personal experiences, one older UTA student admitted that "my age tempts me to use life as the basis for all my influences." It should come as no surprise that the older the reader, the denser and richer the networks of memories of specific experiences, and hence, the increased likelihood of reading *Looking Backward,* or any text, through specific experiential associations. But the contrast between the reading analyses by younger and older readers was not simply a matter of smaller versus larger storehouses of recalled experiences. Many of the older readers used a different way of perceiving past experiences that gave these experiences special meanings beyond the mere remembrance of specific events and people. The younger readers tended to perceive prior experiences as individual events that could facilitate transformations of specific portions of the text. The older readers tended to place memories of specific past experiences within the contexts of life patterns that could open up general issues that dominated the text.

Two statements—one by a thirty-plus UTA student, the other by one of the residents of Wesley Palms—indicate important characteristics of this attitude: "Life seems to become more and more a composition of past experiences brought together to deal with a current situation"; "There seems to be a common thread in all that has influenced my life." In several cases the elevation of a particular event to paradigmatic or even archetypal stature gave readers this kind of grand overview perspective on past experience. These paradigm experiences were often described in imagistic language that tends to confirm Esrock's contention that visualization intensifies the reading experience (vii). For example, one upstate New Yorker transplanted to Texas responded to the regimentation of Bellamy's industrial army by evoking the memory of a contrasting paradigmatic experience articulated with strong sensory imagery:

> [I] *rode horses throughout gorgeous countryside wedged between picturesque lakes. . . . I still smell the lush vegetation, still see the vividness of the colors, still feel the freshness of the air, and still hear the hypnotic sounds. I also remember that feeling of complete freedom from rules and expectations. . . . And now, . . . every feeling that I experience . . . will in some way ultimately be compared with the intense feelings I have for natural beauty and freedom. . . . [Bellamy's] efficient social organiza-*

*tions, machines, factories, stores, and bureaucracies all make me feel as if my body is swaddled in heavy chains.*

The older readers' emphasis on associations with paradigmatic experiences cuts across boundaries of gender, race, class, and geography. They remind us that attempts to determine how readers locate utopia must go beyond discoveries of which forms of discourse invite and repel readers, which experiences—notably poverty and living in another country—facilitate entry into utopia, and which types of transformational associations readers use most frequently. They must also include an appreciation of how age relates to the ways readers give meanings to the events and people in their lives and an awareness of how readers use these meanings to include or exclude utopia from their personal domains of memory.

# Nine

# 733 Aliens Transforming Religion, Women, Equality, and Utopia

The 733 readers were postmodern and old-fashioned. Like Fredric Jameson and Louis Marin, they perceived utopia as a perception-altering agent. But unlike Jameson and Marin, who emphasized the "opening up" processes and the shapes of utopia (Marin even proclaimed that "the way to tell the story constitutes the story" [115]), these modern readers were as interested in the "filling in" as in the "opening up." Like William Morris, most of the nineteenth-century reviewers, and critics excavating for a utopian core, they wanted to evaluate the "serious essay" beneath the shapes ("Looking Backward" 287); they wanted answers—representations of better worlds to fill the gaps left by the invitations to "break up" their familiar notions of their world.

Also like most of the reviewers, the modern readers concluded that equality was the cornerstone of Bellamy's representation of utopia, though both reviewers and the 733 aliens disagreed among themselves about the desirability of absolute economic equality and the institutionalized bureaucracy and socialistic ideology that sustained equality in Dr. Leete's world. The reviewers and the modern readers would agree with Bellamy that religion was a key element in his and their concepts of utopia, but the 733, like some of the reviewers, often had difficulty appreciating the spiritual center of Bellamy's utopia.

The role of women in society and the function of utopian literature—

these were the great divides separating the nineteenth- and twentieth-century readers. The striking differences in composition between the practically all-male group of reviewers and the more-than-half female sample of modern readers help to explain why "woman" was noticeable by her absence in the reviews and prominent in the modern responses. The contrast between the ways the reviewers celebrated/feared the mass impact of *Looking Backward* and the modern readers' doubts about the impact of reading a literary utopia on self and society suggests the declines of the Victorian "moral community of discourse" and belief in book power. Still, the 733 readers' concern about Bellamy's views of religion, women, equality, and the utopian destiny of America demonstrate the continuing appeal of Bellamy's invitations to conceive of America as utopia. And their ability to use transformational associations to personalize Bellamy's utopia demonstrates the power of modern readers to recreate Bellamy's millennial vision in their own images of the year 2000.

## Too Much, No, the Wrong, and the Right Religion

In an intellectual and historical sense, the 733 readers were not competent judges of the religion of Dr. Leete's world. As indicated in the previous chapter, they found Rev. Barton's sermon inaccessible. They were also unfamiliar with Bellamy's "Religion of Solidarity" essay; unfamiliar with Bellamy's religious family background; unfamiliar with the Social Gospel movement; and in some cases even unfamiliar with the Bible. Nonetheless, these incompetencies did not stop them from consistently responding in personal and inventive ways to the text's invitations to associate religious attitudes and experiences with utopia.

This was not a consensus consistency, however. How readers used religious associations typically depended upon how they defined their religious identities. (The biographical questions did not request information on religious preference. But, as noted in chapter 8, those who discussed religious associations almost always mentioned their religious background.) Students—especially, though not exclusively, those from Texas and the South—who defined themselves as Southern Baptists, "born-again" Christians, "fundamentalists," or "strong" believers (including Protestants and Catholics and a few Jews and Moslems) tended toward negative responses to the religion preached by Barton and described or implied by Dr. Leete, West, and Edith. To many of these readers, religion was very hard to see in

Bellamy's utopia. One UTA student flatly proclaimed that there was "no religion" there; a United Church of Canada member at Campion College asked rhetorically, "Where's God?" Like many of the first Spanish explorers of Central and South America, these readers couldn't see the religion of the natives because they were looking for familiar names, customs, and situations that seemed absent in Bellamy's A.D. 2000. Specifically, they searched for an explicit emphasis on Christ as the sole means of reforming depraved humans, and for specific mention of the Bible as the ultimate guide to change, communal worship, and institutionalized religion. (Most of these critical readers were Protestant and Catholic, but one Harvard student, who by birth was "half Jewish" and by choice a "strong" Jewish believer, advocated belief in human depravity as a necessary means of understanding historical realities such as the Holocaust.) Instead of seeing these essential elements of religion in Dr. Leete's utopia, they saw an emphasis on the innate goodness of humans, reason, human agents, "couch potato" worship, and even blasphemy. One Texas student was "outraged" by West's proclamation, during his nightmare return, that "I have been in Golgotha. . . . I have seen Humanity hanging on a cross!" (307). To her this was a "blasphemous" comparison between West and Christ.

The few readers who identified themselves as atheists or agnostics (primarily from the Northeast and at RPI) viewed the religious passages in the text either as clever descriptions of a convenient "dial-a-church" religion, as annoying intrusions, or as misplaced anachronisms. The latter view was expressed by a Canadian who had left Christianity for belief in a "Life Force." For her, the Leetes' religion was "obsolete"; there was simply "too much God in the text."

Bellamy's original supporters might have had difficulty understanding the responses of the fundamentalists, atheists, and the believer in the Life Force. Many of the sympathetic reviewers examined in chapter 6 and the members of Bellamy Clubs—who often came from strong Protestant backgrounds (Howe 425–29), especially those who defined themselves as Christian Socialists, Social Gospelers, and religious activists (W. D. Howells and the Rabbi Solomon Schindler, for example)—would probably have felt much closer to another group that was smaller than the fundamentalists but larger than the atheists. Primarily international students or from the Northeast and Midwest, these readers placed emphasis on Christian or (in the case of the Japanese) non-Christian "brotherhood" and "unselfishness." Even though most of these readers did not enjoy Rev. Barton's sermon, their concept of religion sensitized them to Bellamy's belief in the dignity of human life and the necessities of social action and cooperation. One Harvard student, raised in Africa and France, articulated this view by equating her "basic" notion of "politics and Christianity" with "humanity and equality." She would have been a sympathetic reader for Bellamy's "Religion of Solidarity."

## Women and the Interpretive Communities of Classrooms and Cultures

The modern readers' responses to Bellamy's utopian religion offer insights into the ways strongly felt beliefs can illuminate and obscure parts of a utopian text. If we limited our view to the Hood and RPI responses to Bellamy's women, we would most likely conclude that the gender of the reader is an equally strong shaper of perceptions. Both these groups were composed of young (Hood's average age: 21 [plus two in their fifties]; RPI: 20) Northeasterners attending small, competitive colleges. The Hood sample was all female. In their reading analyses and especially in their questionnaire responses, there were many comments about Edith and chapter 25, in which Dr. Leete describes the women of utopia. Most of the comments were negative. The responses to the separateness of the women's industrial army and the limits placed on women's career opportunities were particularly harsh. The fact that Edith Leete didn't seem to have a job didn't help matters. The RPI sample had the highest percentage of males (75%). As was the case with the (almost) all-male sample of nineteenth-century reviewers, these readers paid very little attention to the role of women. In the RPI reading analyses, only one of the 38 males included a discussion of women's roles. On the other hand, all but two of the RPI women who wrote analyses mentioned the issue. Further support for the influence of gender can be found in the strong negative responses to the love-story narrative and to Edith in the all-female Wesley Palms sample. They expressed the highest "dislike" percentages for both: 67% and 60%.

When we expand the number of samples to include the all-female Arlington reading group, the all-female Campion class, and the other mixed groups, we see the truth of Elizabeth Flynn and Patrocinio Schweickart's warning in their introduction to *Gender and Reading* (1986): rigid gender "categories obscure considerable individual variation" (xxix). The Arlington women's group's response to Edith Leete was one of the most positive (83% liked her), and this was the only sample that did not register one "dislike" vote for the love story. At Campion, only one student disliked the love story; only one disliked Edith Leete. More important, in the reading analyses there was almost no mention of issues relating to women. Instead, they placed much emphasis on religious questions. Similarly in the Minnesota sample, which had a relatively high female percentage (71%), there was strong approval of Edith (89%) and not much mention of women's issues in the reading analyses. The differences between the Hood College readers and the other groups demonstrate what Elizabeth Long and other feminist critics have stressed: the importance of the classroom environment (191). At Hood, the traditions of a women's college, the strong women's studies courses, and the presence of a respected feminist professor set up types of expectations and sensitivities very different from those found in mixed classes taught by male professors at universities with a less pronounced emphasis on women's studies. (As noted earlier, the Campion class was mixed, but only women participated in the survey.)

Surveying all the responses also reveals the impact of cultures, work experiences, and ethnic backgrounds on women responding to Bellamy's women. A typical response (expressed in terms of associations with general concepts of womanhood and specific prior experiences) was sympathetic criticism. For example, one of the freshman honor students in Texas concluded that for "the 19th century, the separate woman's work force must have been radical indeed, but in the 1980s, prejudice such as this is disappointing." A more biting version of this response came from a Texas woman in her thirties:

> *I tried to remind myself that Edward Bellamy wrote this book in 1888 and that the equality he gives women must be considered remarkable. . . . [Nonetheless,] I do not accept the theory that there is any work that a woman should not be allowed to do based on her "delicate" strength. . . . [This limited view of women] crawled under my skin and ran up and down my spine in the most irritating fashion.*

These two women readers give a good sense of the typical responses from white, middle-class, female readers raised in America in my combined sample, though they omit the mention of less housework and equal educational opportunities that pleased many of the women readers.

Some of the female international readers expressed attitudes that shared the tone of sympathetic criticism revealed in the comments of the two women from Texas. But the types of transformational associations they used were quite different. Edith's character (as noted in chapter 8), women's economic equality, and the structure of the industrial army all struck positive chords with the young, female Japanese readers. The combination seemed to be a commendable mix of traditional emphases on separate spheres, the importance of nurturing woman, and the new desires among Japanese college women for independence and career opportunities. One Palestinian student living in Texas also associated Bellamy's women with a transformed version of traditional roles. She came from a small town where woman's work was "housework." She not only was delighted that there was less housework in A.D. 2000 but was also pleased that the housework of cooking and cleaning was "no longer considered women's work, but . . . real work done by men and women" in public facilities.

Perhaps the most complex international response to Bellamy's women came from a woman with one of the most complex cultural backgrounds in the combined samples. She came from a Chinese/Filipino background; she had lived in Texas for several years and was supposed to wed a Sri Lankan and eventually move to Sri Lanka. (I've mentioned her previously in the discussions of responses to Rev. Barton's sermon and to Mr. Bartlett's comments about China in chapter 8.) The "Americanized side" of her appreciated the emphasis on "material opportunity" and "maternal leave" for women and made her critical of the separateness of the women's industrial army. Her critique of separateness also had an Asian and a family side. Two of her female cousins had medical degrees. One worked very limited hours. The other was "a simple housewife." The medical degrees were perceived primarily as symbols of accomplishment and distinction. Her cousins and she perceived being "a housewife [as] an act of service and love to your family." To her, this type of service was much more intimate and meaningful than impersonal service to an industrial army: she would rather "serve [her] husband" than "a country."

The responses to Bellamy's women indicated the tremendous impact of work experience associations and socioeconomic and ethnic backgrounds. The responses of three very different women were especially revealing. One was a young, single, white farm girl from Minnesota. The other two were African Americans: one a native of a poor rural Texas community (she was one of fifteen children), who was married with children and in her late twenties; the other was raised in Cleveland, divorced, and in her late thirties. One characteristic they shared was that they were all physically very strong. Basing my prediction on the responses of female athletes to *Looking Backward* at UTA, I assumed that physically strong women would be "resisting" readers, to borrow Judith Fetterley's term. I expected them to articulate forceful negative responses to Dr. Leete's comment about the "inferior" strength of women that "disqualified" them from certain types of work (263). I was wrong. Associations with past experiences inclined these three readers to downplay or completely ignore Dr. Leete's comments about women's physical limitations and instead to focus on the changes in women's duties and opportunities.

The Minnesota woman had powerful memories of her childhood frustrations. She was as strong or stronger than her brothers. But because she was a "girl," she was barred from most heavy labor. This discrimination would probably continue in Bellamy's utopia. (Even in *Equality,* where Edith actually is a farmhand, she does little muscle work. Everything is done by machines [43].) Nonetheless, the combination of her childhood frustrations and the comments about women's economic, educational, and career equalities that preceded chapter 25 had created such strong positive associations about Bellamy's women that she didn't even bother to note the existence of Dr. Leete's comments about female weakness in her reading analyses.

The African American mother concentrated on the domestic side of Bellamy's utopia, and like Bellamy, she perceived little joy in housework (Levitas, "Who Holds" 66, 70). She was married and pregnant at nineteen. "I went from making doll clothing to changing baby clothing. The transition was very hard for me, and it still gets sort of tiresome after nine years." She continued: "All my life I have worked my fingers to the bones trying to keep a clean house that never stays clean and trying to cook a delicious meal that is never good. Therefore, any relief from my painful and menial tasks, whether in fantasy or reality, is a welcome experience." She longed for the "same joys that Mrs. Leete and Edith have."

The Cleveland woman transformed *Looking Backward* with memories of urban occupational prejudices. Her comments deserve to be quoted at length:

*Some years ago, I worked as a laborer for a construction company, al-*
*though the executives in the company didn't know it at the time. This*
*company did not hire any females for that type of work. However, my*
*Dad was a brick mason for the firm and hired me to work under his*
*supervision. He had the authority to hire anyone he thought capable*
*of getting the job done with or without the knowledge of his bosses. He*
*was also ahead of his time in how he saw sex roles in industry because*
*with him, there were no differences, just abilities. Well, I used wheel-*
*barrows, broke up existing cement sidewalks with a sledge hammer,*
*laid new foundations, did everything required of me. This was such a*
*novelty back then that the curiosities of people caused a tremendous*
*amount of work delay. Sometimes crowds would gather and block the*
*sites under construction. I was concerned for my father that the com-*
*motion might get back to his bosses at the firm because someone had*
*called a reporter from the* Plain Dealer *to do a story. Therefore, without*
*my Dad's approval, I resigned.*

She acknowledged that there was "some separation" between male and f-
male workers in Bellamy's utopia. Still, the "relatively equal" job status of
men and women was so attractive to her that it outweighed the separation
(and blotted out Dr. Leete's comments about women's "inferior" strength).
Like the Russian workers from Petrograd who, in 1905, overlooked Leete's
negative comments about labor organizations and embraced *Looking
Backward* (Rosemont 158), this late twentieth-century reader downplayed
Leete's patriarchal views and emphasized her perceptions of equality in
Bellamy's utopia, so that she could imagine a world where her father could
hire her without qualms, and she could work without gawking crowds.

   If I were asked to predict what would happen when copies of *Looking
Backward* were placed in the hands of a male and a female reader today,
I would probably be foolish enough to predict that the woman would
pay more attention than the man to the descriptions of Edith and to the
descriptions of women in chapter 25. Beyond that, I'd have to dress more
specific predictions in numerous qualifications. I'd venture particulars
about the female reader only if I knew the nature of her immediate interpretive community; her cultural, socioeconomic, and ethnic backgrounds; her literary tastes; and her psychological profile. I'm sure she'd
still surprise me.

## Equalities

I might have more luck predicting how women and men today would respond to Dr. Leete's notions of equality. Like the nineteenth-century reviewers and most twentieth-century critics, these readers would notice the centrality of equality to Leete's concept of utopia. I would also predict that the American readers would have reservations about a system of absolute salary equality supported by a socialistic bureaucracy. Finally, I would predict that they would read the equality of Bellamy's utopia through associations with general attitudes and beliefs (particularly about motivation, selfishness, poverty, and injustice) and through specific memories about work experiences and close friends and family members. My bases for these speculations would be the reading analyses and the responses to questions 12 through 16 and 20a on the questionnaire (see appendix C).

In both the analyses and the questionnaire there was an emphasis on equality that cut across boundaries of gender, age, ethnic background, and socioeconomic situation. The responses to question 16 ("What, *in your opinion,* is the most significant improvement you'd like to see in the 21st century?") and 20a ("Did reading *Looking Backward* change your views about society?") and the class discussions also convinced me that the ways these readers transformed the text in turn encouraged transformations of how they perceived their societies. There was a marked increase in awareness of inequality.

Beyond these general predictions, I would have to be careful, since it was clear that different groups brought different concepts of equality to the text, and those differences affected the nature of the textual transformations. For example, the fall 1989 UTA sophomore class placed strong emphasis on racial equality. Fifty-four percent (the highest of any sample) of this group were American minorities (Hispanic, African American, Asian American, Native American). Since there was not explicit mention of racial segregation or discrimination in *Looking Backward,* these readers assumed that all races experienced social and economic equality. This assumption was reflected in the relatively high positive responses to *Looking Backward:* most important transformational associations for fall 1989—57%+, 41%–, 2%+/–; UTA combined sample—47%+, 49%–, 4%+/–. This trend toward positive responses was reflected in the reading analyses of minority students in other classes. For instance, an African American woman in the night course read Leete's advocacy of equality through memories of family stories about her grandfather's floggings and her father's anger whenever he was called "boy."

In class discussions, when students raise the issue of racial equality, I mention that in October 1891 in response to a letter to the editor in the *New Nation*, Bellamy admitted that African Americans were not mentioned in *Looking Backward*. He added that as far as he was concerned, the people in his vision of A.D. 2000 "might have been black, brown or yellow as well as white. . . . All men are brothers" (qt. in Rosemont 173). But I also explain that by 1898 he had apparently changed his mind. In *Equality*, Bellamy clarified his position by advocating economic equality for all races and by stressing that different races would be kept separate (in the industrial army and in residential areas) to a degree that would satisfy "the most bigoted local prejudice" (179). Both minority and white students were angered by this revelation. It was as if Bellamy had invited them to fill in the silences of *Looking Backward* with their views of racial equality, and then he withdrew the invitation and even abused their use of it. I'm certain that if I had asked for another reading analysis of *Looking Backward* in the fall 1989 class, the negative reactions would have risen sharply.

In another very different Texas sample—the two classes of predominantly white honors high school students—I discovered a tempting hint suggesting a strong link between gender and concepts of equality. In these reading analyses, there were more associations described involving equality in general and about sexual equality in particular than any other types of transformational associations in the attitudes and beliefs category. And *all* these descriptions were written by women. Such a striking trend seems to confirm theories articulated by Nancy Chodorow, Carol Gilligan, and other feminist scholars who posit different gender- (and cultural-) based perceptual styles, with women tending toward the interpersonal and cooperative and men toward the independent and competitive. (Indeed, many more men than women in this sample advocated independence and criticized socialistic cooperation.)

The connections between feminist theory and the high school responses are provocative. But they need some qualification. In the other samples, women often did comment on equality, especially sexual equality, more than men. There were, nevertheless, no other samples in which the split between male and female responses was as striking as in the two high school classes. To some degree—a large degree, I suspect—that split can be attributed to the local environment. In their analyses, several of the women expressed anger about how teenage boys perceived teenage girls. A typical observation came from one of them who was sick of hearing "teenage boys' jokes about what women are for." These were some of the brightest students in the school, taught by one of the best teachers (who was female). Sexist stereotypes rankled them and inclined them either toward appreciating Dr. Leete's descriptions of the "new" equalities for men and women or toward recommending that Bellamy should have gone even further in making men and women socially and occupationally equal.

Appreciation of the equalities of Bellamy's A.D. 2000 was clearly affected by socioeconomic backgrounds. For the UTA students in general, but particularly for the night students, equality often meant equal access to higher education and job advancement. (Sixty-three percent of the most important transformational associations described by the night students related to equality.) I quote two representative statements about educational equality: "Having each person educated is the first step in equalizing society." "Even the unborn child has the right to educated parents." For the UTA students who, in their analyses, identified themselves as "lower" or "working" class, educational equality was a key issue when they mentioned their children or the children they hoped to have. One older student observed that despite his anticipated college degree and his white-collar job, he would probably never shake his "truck mechanic self-image" that was reinforced by his family history. Only one person on either side of his family had even attended college. But he believed that getting a college diploma and a good job would enable his children to "escape" his mentality. He longed for a world like Bellamy's utopia, where equal educational and job opportunities and a classless society would free his parents, him, and his children from limited self images.

In the other samples, the readers typically defined equality in much broader social and economic terms. The most pronounced example of this trend appeared in the responses by the readers at International Christian University, which attracted upper-middle- and upper-class Japanese students supported by their parents. (*None* of the undergraduates in the Japanese sample had part-time or full-time employment.) These young students conceived of equality in terms of equally shared values and responsibilities. "We Japanese need a sense of public duty," wrote one, and a sense of international "cooperation." In the contexts of these assumptions, they lauded what they perceived to be Bellamy's commitment to "universal brotherhood." The contrasts between the UTA and ICU concepts of equality suggest that the younger and the further removed readers are from work experiences, and the higher the socioeconomic background, the greater the tendency to conceive of equality in terms of laudable abstractions instead of the nitty-gritty realities of who can afford to go to college and who gets promoted. (One important qualifying note: typically, Japanese universities are less expensive than American colleges, especially private colleges. Hence, the cost of a college education is less of an economic barrier in Japan than in America.)

More than any other specific invitation in *Looking Backward,* the invitation to consider the importance of equality displayed readers' abilities to project into Dr. Leete's world their perceptions of what they and people like them most needed. Reading *Looking Backward* thus became a means of reinforcing beliefs in racial and gender equality, open access to educational and job opportunities, and international cooperation. Considering Bellamy's advocacy of segregation, his hesitancy to condone physical work for women, and his limited concept of internationalism, he might have been surprised by the specifics of some of these transformational associations. (As Susan Matarese argues consistently in *American Foreign Policy and the Utopian Imagination* [2001], Bellamy's concept of internationalism was limited by an assumption that all nations would follow a reformed America.) Nonetheless, he would have been gratified to learn that more than a hundred years after its publication, *Looking Backward* still provoked anger about inequality and longings for equality.

## The Distances between Here and Utopia

One other issue that surfaced repeatedly in the reading analyses and questionnaires was the value of utopian literature. Responses to the questionnaire seemed to indicate a surprisingly strong confirmation of the relevance of utopias. In response to questions 4 ("Would you like to read a book like this again? If so, why? If not, why not?") and 21 ("Would you recommend this book to someone else. If so, why? If not, why not?"), 75% and 77% of the combined samples responded positively. The typical explanations in these responses were similar to Jameson's emphasis on invitations to open up thought processes. They believed that *Looking Backward* provoked thought about alternative possibilities, the flaws in our society, and comparisons between past and present visions of better worlds. An even higher percentage (81%) answered yes to question 17 ("Do you think *Looking Backward* is still relevant?"). "Relevant" did not translate into "a realistic and practical social criticism and a model for actual reform" (one of the descriptive options offered in question 18, which only 9% of the combined sample selected). Still, 63% of the combined sample agreed that *Looking Backward* was "a speculative work with some possible applications" (option b). The responses to question 19 ("Do you think Bellamy primarily wanted to: a. change social systems?; b. change individuals' feelings and thoughts?; c. both of the above equally?; d. neither of the above?") indicated that the readers believed that from Bellamy's viewpoint, two of his "intents" were to "change individuals' feelings and thoughts" (34%) and to "change both individuals' feelings and thoughts" and "social systems" (55%). The overlap between these two responses reveals that almost 90% of the readers thought that Bellamy wanted to change individuals' viewpoints. The responses to questions 4, 17, 18, and 21 suggest a strong consensus view, affirming the continuing power of Bellamy's utopia.

And yet, when these same readers were asked, "Did reading *Looking Backward* change your views about: a. society? (If so, how?); b. yourself (If so, how?)" (question 20), the consensus seemed to collapse, even to reverse. Sixty percent of the combined sample indicated that their view of society had not changed, even though, as I previously noted, their awareness of inequality had apparently increased. (The youngest sample, the high school classes, was the only one with more than 50% indicating an altered view of society. The oldest sample, Wesley Palms, had the lowest positive response rate: 17%.) Almost 75% of the combined sample perceived *no* change in self-image. (Again, Wesley Palms had the lowest reflection of change: 0%.) By far the strongest indication of a perception of personal change resulting from reading came from the Arlington women's group—the only sample composed of people who voluntarily and regularly came together because they loved to read. But even in this group of dedicated readers, only half indicated that their self-images had been changed by this reading experience.

The overall impression left by the contrasts between the positive responses to questions 4, 17, 18, and 21 and the negative responses to question 20, is strikingly different from the impression of book power voiced by the nineteenth-century reviewers. *Looking Backward* inspired both friendly and hostile reviewers to celebrate or warn readers about how reading Bellamy's book could transform their views of self and society and motivate reform activities that could change the world. To once again cite Jameson, these readers could perceive utopian blueprints as forceful agents of societal and personal transformation ("Of Islands" 2). The readers surveyed at the close of the twentieth century seemed to believe instead that the primary power of the *Looking Backward* reading experience was to provoke thought about "things out there" distanced either by time (comparative views of society) or impersonality (abstract social questions rather than personal reevaluations of interpersonal relations or self). Nineteenth-century readers might have taken *Looking Backward* to heart, but these readers held it at arms length.

This distancing may help us to understand why contemporary authors, notably Ursula K. Le Guin, Marge Piercy, Joanna Russ, Doris Lessing, and other feminist utopists, place emphasis on intimate interpersonal relationships in their visions of utopia. It also reveals an apparent contradiction. How can readers allow themselves to be provoked without changing some of their views—even if that change only takes the form of a new type of reaffirmation of beliefs held prior to the reading? The reading analyses often revealed ongoing processes of textual transformations that went beyond the reading experience to transform the readers' reality. The boundaries of an upstate New Yorker's freedom (horseback) rides are now more clearly (re)defined in contrast to the restrictions of Bellamy's industrial army system. As an African American mother continues to "work her fingers to the bones," she can ease her pain a little by escaping into her remembered images of Edith Leete's easy domesticity. A Texas high school student now has new ways to criticize socialism; he can use his criticisms of Bellamy's equal pay society. A native of Pennsylvania who read *Looking Backward* in his late seventies has a new perspective on memories of his meetings with Norman Thomas, now that he knows some of the American origins of Thomas's thought.

In other words, each one of the 3,158 transformative associations described reflect some form of altered view of self and society. Although these readers were willing, even quite pleased, to assume the role of utopian text transformers, only a minority of them were willing to concede that transforming the text meant transforming the reader. This attitude stands in marked contrast to the attitudes of thousands of nineteenth-century readers of *Looking Backward* who willingly transformed the text and willingly admitted to a degree of self-transformation sufficient to cause them to join a Bellamy or Nationalist Club, support Nationalist Party activities, engage in municipal reform movements, start a Nationalist communal experiment, or at least subscribe to one of the many magazines inspired by *Looking Backward*.

Some of the plausible explanations for the different attitudes are obvious. With the exceptions of the members of the Wesley Palms community and the Arlington reading group, these readers encountered *Looking Backward* as a school reading and writing assignment. That certainly set up a network of reading expectations (and frustrations) that block invitations to perceive reading as a means of self-transformation. (Along these lines, it is relevant to note that the biographical information revealed that at this point in their lives more than 75% of the combined sample associated reading primarily with school assignments.) There are broader cultural and historical explanations that are just as obvious and significant as the specific contrasting reading situations and obvious explanations relating to the modern readers' unfamiliarity with Barton's sermon discourse and the monologic guide-visitor dialogues. For example, many of the contexts discussed in chapter 3 that encouraged nineteenth-century readers to "see" utopia as a meaningful guide to their personal and public lives had changed radically by the end of the twentieth century. Especially evident is the waning of Victorian reading attitudes that defined serious books as powerful moral agents and social forces. The responses to the questionnaire and the reading analyses rarely if ever suggested that *Looking Backward* or any other book (with the exception of the Bible) should be read this way. This change in attitude reflected in my sample does lend credence to Jameson's claim that it is the obsolescence of "a certain type of reader" that makes traditional utopias seem so distant today ("Of Islands" 2).

Ironically, another explanation (offered by the students themselves) for the distance links them to their obsolete nineteenth-century predecessors. As discussed in chapter 6, even sympathetic reviewers sometimes perceived Bellamy's visions as all fine and good but unattainable by real human beings. In the Texas samples, from a fifth to a third of the transformational associations described implied limits on human nature that would cripple Bellamy's utopia. Sometimes they stated this view indirectly, noting, for instance, that humans simply weren't cooperative enough to build successful socialistic societies. More frequently the criticisms were expressed in modifiers that would be quite familiar to nineteenth-century reviewers who criticized Bellamy: "human nature" was "imperfect," "selfish," "greedy," "corrupt," "depraved." These claims were routinely associated with specific job experiences (the waitresses and IRS employees were confirmed believers in human corruption) and general attitudes, particularly religious beliefs. Because of the strong presence of fundamentalist religions in Texas and the South, the emphasis on human limitations was more pronounced in the UTA and Louisville samples. But the trend was evident in all the American samples, even in the reading analyses of the engineers from RPI.

Three of the Japanese readers briefly raised the issue of the limits of human nature. One in particular referred to her father's combination of "ego and avarice" that drove him and so many Japanese businessmen to work "day and night." But in their written and oral attempts to explain why *Looking Backward* seemed distant to them, most of the Japanese readers did not refer to human nature or to the obvious fact that they were reading a book in another language about another time and culture. Instead, they repeatedly noted the lack of a Japanese tradition of utopianism, specifically one that linked nationalism and utopianism. A mode of thought taken for granted by many of Bellamy's readers, and still assumed by many Americans today, was alien to these Japanese readers. As a result, the words they used to describe *Looking Backward* were often the same words some Americans still use to describe "alien" Asian cultures: "strange," "obscure," "mysterious." One student tried to perceive Bellamy's American utopianism through associations with the Chinese concept of *ki* forces. Most of the others expressed themselves in terms of suspicion and bewilderment: "I don't even think about Utopia and never think Utopia exists." "I didn't know much about the 'promised millennium.'" A student who had visited America wrote, "I was often surprised by the Americans' strong belief that the U.S. was the best country in the world." Another was suspicious of the way Bellamy combined passions for loyalty to the industrial army and desires for glory and honor with utopianism. This reminded her of what she had heard about the "dangerous" World War II enthusiasm of Japanese soldiers. Two other comments by other students are especially revealing:

*I, myself, have barely thought about utopia. This is partly because of the culture in which I have grown up. I guess we Japanese are not so strongly future-oriented or reform-oriented as Americans are.*

*I can understand the feeling which inspired a desire for a better society, but the concept of Utopia is too unnatural to understand for me.*

A comment by a Texas student with an Amish background would probably seem as unbelievable to the Japanese students as West's words were to the Bartletts' dinner guests during his nightmare reunion with his contemporaries: "I believe utopia is attainable and that God wants it for us [Americans]."

## Utopian Readers' Profile

The fundamental differences between the transformational associations used by the Texan and Japanese readers are reminders of the limits of my sample. With the additions of other American and certainly other international samples, my portrait of modern readers of utopia would surely change. Eugenia Kaledin has reported, for example, that her Chinese students concentrated on a part of the text that my readers virtually ignored: Bellamy's government by alumni/ae. Her students associated this with the oppressive rule of old Chinese bureaucrats. On the other hand, her female students envied Bellamy's women, who were free to choose their husbands. The Chinese readers did not emphasize human depravity, and links between nationalism and utopianism were not totally unnatural to them. It was the incomprehensibility of a peaceful evolution (rather than a bloody revolution) that distanced Dr. Leete's world and turned Bellamy's utopia into a "fantasy" ("Teaching Bellamy in China").

As the above-quoted comments extracted from Japanese reading analyses suggest, my portrait is, furthermore, a surface profile that lacks the psychological depth of Holland's and Radway's studies of much smaller groups of readers. And that surface outline was often created by downplaying numerous variables influencing specific responses and significant differences between the samples, for instance, the differences between the Texan and Japanese paper-length reading analyses and the other much briefer analyses from other parts of America and from Canada.

The portrait that emerged can be, nonetheless, a useful model for making comparisons between nineteenth- and twentieth-century readers of utopia and in making predictions about how certain types of readers will respond to traditional utopias like *Looking Backward.* This portrait suggests that the expectations readers have about a utopia, how they categorize it, and what they "see in" it depend heavily upon their immediate interpretive community. In my combined sample this community was most often defined by classroom traditions and expectations, possibly the most striking examples coming from Hood College, with its strong traditions of a women's college and women's studies courses, and the UTA history class, with its clear intent to extract historical information from utopia. Though sometimes less visible, the interpretive communities established by reader and editorial expectations exerted strong influences on what the nineteenth-century reviewers saw in *Looking Backward,* as I discussed in chapter 6. This was particularly obvious in the reform and religious journals.

The hybrid discourses of *Looking Backward* almost ensured that the generations of readers following the initial readers would find certain parts of the text "desperately unreadable," to borrow Jameson's words. For many in my sample, Rev. Barton's humanistic sermon and, to a lesser degree, the long guide-visitor (monologic) dialogues were alien discourses. I would predict, however, that the questioning and confused androgynous voice of Julian West will continue to appeal to modern readers. Bellamy's utopian world will most likely become stranger and stranger to future generations of readers. The need for an identifiable intermediary will, therefore, increase. Whether or not Edith Leete can also serve as a welcome intermediary will depend mostly upon each reader's assumptions about the role of women in society. I would predict, however, that female Japanese readers will find comfort in her well into the twenty-first century.

The hybrid nature of the utopian text will also continue to invite a diversity of transformational associations that makes my profile of a modern utopian reader different from my profile of a modern reader of more realistic forms of fiction. The reading analyses by readers in the sample indicated, however, that some associations are more transformative than others. Specific memories closely related to episodes in *Looking Backward* (for instance, insomnia) can open up particular passages or entire chapters. Prolonged travel in another country or being raised in another culture can set up a comparative mode of perception that carries the reader through the entire text. This compatibility between a mode of perception and a fundamental convention of utopian literature does not ensure that readers with a "comparative background" will like the utopia they are reading. But they will be more inclined to play the utopian game of comparisons. They've already lived this game, so they have the confidence to continue the play.

Another, even broader category of privileged transformational association is the association between textual invitation and a strongly felt belief or value. In almost all the samples, associations with beliefs stated in general terms were used more frequently than other types of associations, though the varied invitations of the text ensured that belief associations shared importance with the several other significant types of associations examined in chapter 8. These readers assumed that one of Bellamy's significant intents was to provoke thought about values and beliefs, so they, like many of the nineteenth-century reviewers, responded by articulating their beliefs alongside his. Since such joint journeys create situations in which Bellamy will inevitably tread on some readers' sensitive spots, it was not surprising that in my sample there were more negative responses resulting from associations with general beliefs than there were with specific, personal experience associations. The latter were typically used to familiarize the utopian text, to reassure readers that their notions of reality could be verified in a text and vice versa. The former, on the other hand, often allowed readers to distance themselves from some of the most troubling and unfamiliar aspects of Dr. Leete's world.

Although my general outline of a modern reader of *Looking Backward* would include a hierarchy of transformational associations topped by associations with general beliefs and attitudes, I certainly wouldn't expect that model to be an accurate predictor for all contemporary American readers or even all college students. The reading analyses of the UTA honors freshmen demonstrate how readers who have been rewarded for seeing books through other books will probably continue to do so as long as that reward system (or a positive memory of it) still functions for them. The Hood students' tendency to emphasize memories of past academic experiences in women's studies courses also demonstrates how "local" expectations and traditions can rearrange the hierarchy of associations. So can the readers' ages and their inclinations to perceive past experiences either as isolated events or as parts of a significant pattern. At one extreme, a young reader believes that memories of personal experiences are "not applicable" to the utopian reading experience; at the other, a request for five "influ-ences" generates associations with twenty intense memories spanning sixty years in a pattern of public service and commitment that creates a mutual validation of text and life.

From the appearance of the initial reviews through the responses of the readers I collected at the close of the twentieth century, there has been in-terest in the concepts of religion, equality, and utopia that readers discov-ered as they read *Looking Backward*. The scarcity of nineteenth-century woman reviewers of *Looking Backward* impeded sustained discussion of the "woman issue" in the initial reviews. Nevertheless, the significant number of women in Bellamy and Nationalist Clubs helped to foster dis-cussions of the role of women in the *Nationalist* and *New Nation*, an inter-est that continued to grow during the twentieth century. This development and the continuity of interest in religion, equality, and utopia suggest that future readers will also share an interest in these topics. But the nature of the responses has and will, of course, continue to depend on the expecta-tions of interpretive reading communities, as well as each reader's gender, age, race, socioeconomic background, and geographical-cultural environ-ments. These factors will determine whether readers see too much God, no religion, or true and unselfish Christianity in *Looking Backward*; whether they classify Bellamy's women as practically invisible, hopefully envied, or relegated to a separate-but-definitely-not-equal status; whether they associate Bellamy's ideological hallmark—equality—with the nitty-gritty matters of who wears a flour-sack dress, which men get called "boy," and who goes to school and gets jobs or with abstract visions of universal brotherhood; and whether they perceive utopia as an unnatural mystery or as an all-American paradox—an impossibility Americans take for granted.

Bellamy would be disappointed with another element of my portrait: the inability or unwillingness of most of the modern readers to see that trans-forming his text transformed them. But Bellamy shouldn't be surprised or completely disheartened. The readers in my sample were doing what the first readers of *Looking Backward* had done and what readers of utopias al-ways have done and always will probably do. They responded to the some-times reassuring, sometimes threatening and insulting, and frequently de-familiarizing invitations of a utopian text with transformative associations that enabled them to give familiar personal and cultural meanings to the text. They performed transformative acts of personalized acculturation "on" utopia.

Bellamy would, I hope, be pleased that despite the enormous historical and cultural changes of the past century, contemporary readers can still perceive *Looking Backward* as relevant and provocative. That response is a testament to the power of West's narrative and to the jarring, stimulating impact of utopian literature. It is also a testament to the power and creativity of readers. True, my captive audiences of readers may have been sent off by me and the other professors on a forced march to utopia. Once they arrived, however, they demonstrated remarkable ingenuity in transforming many parts of a hundred-year-old text into personally meaningful images and concepts. These alien readers may draw maps of utopia that would baffle Bellamy and his original readers. But they can still navigate. They can still locate utopia.

# Afterword
## A Gathering of Utopian Audiences

Some arrived in mundane ways. They walked, rode bikes. One psychology professor was particularly suburban-bourgeois; he rode in a station wagon for the last few miles. Others boarded vehicles that stirred the imaginations of their contemporaries: sleek sailing ships, biplanes, monorails, and rocket ships. There were miraculous travelers. They came via one-hundred-year sleeps induced by mesmerism, chemicals, or deep freezes; they took mind voyages at the invitation of visitors from the future; they thrilled to visions and dreams. Then there were the hyper-techies who used enormous drills that uncovered underground worlds, instantaneous space-travel "ansibles," and time machines. Some historically determined guests rode the energies of Grand Revolutions or simply drifted with the currents of Grand Evolutions. One even rode the tail of a comet. Perhaps the most miraculous route of all, however, was practiced by practically all the visitors. They held a collection of pages filled with marks and moved their eyes back and forth, or up and down, over those silent inscriptions.

Their destination housed nowhere, but the house was definitely sometime and somewhere—springtime in Paris. To be more exact, these visitors were attending a secret preview of the wonderful *Utopie: la quête de la société idéale en Occident* exhibit in the Grande Salle and Petite Salle of the new Site François-Mitterand/Tolbiac on the banks of the Seine at the Bibliothèque nationale de France, which was open to the public from

April 4 to July 9, 2000. The exhibit included hundreds of books, beautiful illuminated manuscripts, extravagant maps, ornate globes, idealistic city plans, even a back-buttoning vest worn by a follower of Saint-Simon—for him dressing was a cooperative enterprise, unless he was a contortionist.[1]

Six groups of visitors packed the Grande and Petite Salles; each group had distinguished itself as (literal or metaphorical) readers of literary utopias. The most honored group consisted of the first readers, the authors of the books. After scrutinizing Lyman Tower Sargent's list of more than five thousand writers in English, supplemented by non-English authors, the exhibit committee invited a few hundred utopists and added several creators of website domains such as The Principality of Freedonia (inspired by Jefferson and Ayn Rand rather than the Marx Brothers) and one author (Joseph R. Myers) who had made a case for his status as Edward Bellamy's reincarnation.

The next group was much smaller—selected authors' living descendants who shared the legacies of their ancestors' utopian words. One subgroup of this contingent was particularly fascinating. Several of the descendants of Edward Bellamy contacted by his great-grandson, Michael Bellamy, had first gathered publicly on Saturday, October 15, 1994, at the nineteenth annual meeting of the Society for Utopian Studies in Toronto. There they commented on the ironies of public and private legacies: Edward Bellamy had envisioned a utopia free of financial and psychological worries, but his enthusiastic financial and personal commitments to Nationalism had left his own family with many financial worries, had helped to undermine his health, and had deprived his son Paul of a father in his early teens. Paul's namesake (who bore a striking resemblance to his ancestor) spoke of the effects of reading *Looking Backward* at different stages of his life. Richard told stories of meeting people all over the world who asked about *Looking Backward* when they heard his last name. The youngest descendant in attendance in 1994 admitted that she had not yet read the book. As she entered the Grande Salle six years later, one of her elders asked if she had finally read it. Her answer was lost in the bustle of the arrival of the other four groups.

One of these groups consisted of professional readers: book reviewers, book illustrators, literary critics, and scholars. Edward Bellamy immediately rushed over to shake hands with Frances Willard, one of the few nineteenth-century woman reviewers in attendance. Sally Kitch, Tom

Moylan, Susan Matarese, Ralph Pordzik, and Phillip Wegner, whose new books on utopia had just appeared or were soon to appear, debated the merits of seeking book-jacket blurbs from some of the grand names of criticism in attendance. A quote from Aristophanes would certainly gain attention, but, then again, Aristophanes hadn't always had kind words for utopian speculations.

The activist readers often shunned the critics and theorists. Inspired by visions of Owen, Cabet, Fourier, or more recently, Skinner, they had attempted to transform fiction and vision into communal fact; or hoped to transform Bellamy's Boston and Herzl's Altneuland into Massachusetts state laws and a model nation-state for Israel; or wished to transform Marxist treatises or the fiction of Ayn Rand and H. L. Hunt into inspiring socialist or capitalist societies.

The last two groups seemed out-of-place, either because they were not well known or because, well, they simply didn't exist. The former were 733 contemporary readers—most from seven states in the United States, but also small groups from Canada and Japan, and one Austrian reader. It seems that completing a previous forced academic march to utopia had qualified them for a free pass to the exhibit. Who could turn down a free "field trip" to Paris? The latter group was very difficult to see. They were best imagined. Most of them were famous voyagers to utopia whose "texts" had been their sightings of nowhere. These were the visitors who took the most exotic forms of transportation to the exhibit. Many had double personalities, such as Julian West's pre- and post-conversion-experience selves or the Owner of the Voice's present and parallel-world selves created by H. G. Wells; some came in groups—Hythloday-Giles-More's persona or Gilman's Terry, Van, and Jeff. The rest of this group were textual and cultural constructs created by the critics and scholars. Compared to the 733 real readers, they were frequently elusive. Fortunately they adhered to academic conventions and wore identity badges; some even subtitled their identities with catchy phrases, for example, "Implied Readers—We'll Fill The Gaps." The constructs labeled "Ideal" and "Competent Readers" initially shunned the 733 readers, but even the "Ideals" had to admit that there were some resemblances between them and the flesh-and-blood readers.

There were other, warmer connections among the groups. The utopists and critics rushed over to embrace their literary and theoretical creations.

The sympathies were sincere, though attempting to hug a fiction or a textual construct can be frustrating. As the day wore on, however, criticisms and disagreements seemed to outnumber sympathetic connections. The Japanese, African Americans, and several of the immigrants to Texas from the 733 readers wondered aloud about the exhibit's focus on the "Occident," which eliminated many possible selections from Asia, Africa, and Central and South America. Other members of the group of 733 modern readers puzzled over comments by their colleagues. The Canadian women from the University of Regina thought the Hood College students' preoccupation with women's issues in each exhibit was limiting. The Japanese students were dismayed that the elders in the group of 733, the readers from the Wesley Palms retirement community, abhorred Edith Leete. The Hood students were both concerned and moved by the women with farm and urban labor backgrounds who longed to live in Bellamy's utopia. The nineteenth-century American reviewers were stunned and a bit threatened by the attention lavished on women in utopia by the late twentieth-century critics. (Frances Willard couldn't hide her smile as she watched their puzzled faces.) Critical encounters were everywhere. William Morris's claims of extrapolating the one "serious essay" from each utopia seemed to fall on deaf poststructuralist ears. Small clusters championed reading utopia as critiques of our ability to imagine utopia, as thought experiments that create the space to imagine, as perception-changing experiences, and as representations that should inspire or even guide specific social changes. The activists agreed to avoid most of the critics, but they often disagreed on how to activate utopia. *Looking Backward* became a territorial point of controversy: an anarchist, a socialist, a labor leader, a suffragette, a retired general, a Christian Socialist, and an editor from *Good Housekeeping* each proclaimed that Bellamy was "their man."

That man was disappointed that *Looking Backward* was not displayed as part of the late nineteenth-century story of utopia, though he was delighted that his book still ignited passionate debate. But Bellamy couldn't help noticing that it was mainly the nineteenth-century guests who discussed the application of utopian fiction to the real world. There were significant exceptions in attendance: for example, the founders of intentional communes and the 1970s environmentalists inspired by Ernest Callenbach's *Ecotopia*. But many of the modern guests, including the 733 contemporary readers, not only thought that history had bypassed or disproved many utopian ideas, but also seemed not to see the literary utopias as invitations capable of changing either their self-images or their worlds. The reality Bellamy saw as he walked the streets and read newspapers before he entered the library also seemed to confirm this suspicion and the suspicion of one of his descendants. Back in 1994 in Toronto, Richard Bellamy had informally commented that "2000 is the payoff time for Bellamy's book." Here it was 2000, and utopia evidently had not arrived. "No utopian payoff?" Bellamy wondered.

The exhibit organizers wondered too. Overhearing the conversations suggested that a chorus of utopian readers can transform a library's Grande Salle into a Tower of Babel. What was the *point* of bringing all these diverse readers of utopia together at such great expense? (Renting an "ansible" doesn't come cheap.) One significant point demonstrated dramatically by this gathering was the obvious but sometimes ignored power of agents "outside" the book that shape reading: the life experiences before (and after) the reading; the adopted identity of the reader (reformer, author, reviewer, critic, student, curious reading-group member); the conventions of reading learned from both popular literature and academic writing and instruction; the community(ies) of readers heard in the "mind's ear" while reading; and the larger forces of gender, race, culture, and age all combined with the historical forces of the moment.

There was more to the point. There were some important points of agreement overheard in the conversations. For instance, these "strangers" who had voyaged to a "strange land" (to borrow the words of one of the attending critics, Peter Ruppert) valued familiar companionship on their journeys. The personified mediators—those fictional visitors—gave readers from backgrounds as different as rural Texas, urban Japan, a nineteenth-century book-review department, and feminist and poststructuralist classrooms convenient and reassuring ways of identifying with and vicariously experiencing utopia. This agreement, of course, flattered the egos of Hythloday, Gulliver, Julian West, Connie, and the other fictional travelers who attended the exhibit.

In a conversation among the voices of H. G. Wells, his Owner of the Voice, and the ideal Wells encountered on a parallel planet, one of the three spoke of another fundamental connection: the shared awareness of and fascination with the "silk-shot" hybrid nature of utopian literature. The evolving varieties of fiction and nonfiction literatures that come together in

utopian literature help to explain why the readers at the exhibit transformed the utopias they read with so many different varieties of experiential, emotional, ideological, and intellectual associations.

And yet if we compare readings as different as Aristophanes' satiric
dramas, utopists' readings and rereadings of their own works, nineteenth-
century reviews, mid-twentieth-century exposé/discovery analyses, late
twentieth-century poststructuralist interpretations, and the responses of
the 733 readers on their assigned trip to utopia, we hear an inclination to
value most highly the transformational associations relating to fundamental beliefs about the functions of language and literature, the presumed
and desired states of equality, the nature of human nature, and the possibility or impossibility of hope for humans. To borrow the verb used by many
of the reviewers, utopian literature has the power to "move" readers. The
movement takes on very different forms of expression from era to era, ranging from public activist to private contemplative. But the exchanges between the transformative powers of both readers and utopias have been
and remain lively reflections of attempts of humans to access their place in
the past, present, and future. So two more important "points" were that the
disagreements were not simply Babel, and the exhibit was not an elaborate
funeral for the death of book power and utopia. Indeed, at the end of the
preview day, one of the departing guests, Ursula K. Le Guin, was heard
quoting one of her books, *Always Coming Home*. The exhibit reminded her
that utopia should be an expansive "living room," inviting us to consider the
basics of "what if" and "what ought" from many different angles.

Of course, as Le Guin's fictional mediator Pandora reminded her months
later, that story acted out on a spring day in Paris was not the whole story
of the utopian "living box." The visitors to Paris enjoyed themselves so
much that they attended a reunion (again, a secret preview not covered by
the press) when the exhibit, in a modified form, moved to the New York
Public Library from October 14 through January 27, 2001. During the inter-
vening six months, life experiences (or in many of their cases after-life,
fictional, or theoretical life experiences) had altered their viewpoints and
hence modified their responses to the utopias exhibited. Furthermore, the
real whole story would have to include the responses of the general public
who viewed both exhibits after the secret previews, and then go on to tell
the tales of the responses of all the publics outside the library halls long
before and long after the exhibits were contemplated and forgotten.

This is a humbling thought, even more humbling than the opening of a book appearing not too long after the exhibits closed down. In the preface, the author contemplated how impossible it would be to fathom the actual responses of one solitary reader photographed in the Hospice de Beaune in France and then went on blithely with numerous words, some statistics, and a few book illustrations to speculate about the responses of many types of real and imagined readers to a literature that imagines the unreachable. A foolish journey indeed. But maybe the attempt will encourage others to follow with better books. Possibly his and their efforts will help us to understand the powers and limits of utopian speculation and the ways readers transform utopias and other forms of literature. Perhaps their attempts will even gain them invitations to the next gathering of utopian audiences.

# Characteristics of the Samples

COMBINED SAMPLES *(biographical information for 668)*

Biographical data were not collected from two UT Arlington classes: F '93, S '96 (50 students). For ethnic background, information was gathered from 513 readers; for marital status, 511. Five classes (155 students) from UT Arlington were not asked to provide information in these areas: F '83, S '84 (two classes), F '84, and S '87.

Sex [668]: F: 58% (388); M: 42% (280)

Age [668]: Avg.: 23 (low: 16; high: 89)

Raised [668]: Texas: 41% (272); Midwest: 22% (147; 66 from Minnesota); Northeast: 13% (85); South/Southeast: 7% (45; 14 from Kentucky); Southwest: 6% (41); West/Northwest: 2% (16); International: 9% (62; 23 in Japan)

Ethnicity [513]: Caucasian: 77% (397); Asian/Asian American: 9% (46; 23 Japanese); Native American: 6% (31); African American: 4% (20); Hispanic: 4% (19)

Marital Status [511]: Single: 80% (409); Married: 17% (86); Divorced: 2% (12); Widowed: 1% (4)

Employment [668]: Part-time: 58% (390); None: 32% (214; includes 8 retired); Full-time: 10% (64)

Level [668]: Sophomore: 29% (192); Junior: 23% (157); Senior: 23% (151); Freshman: 12% (78); High School: 6% (42); Graduate: 6% (40); Graduated: 1% (8)

Major: Liberal Arts: 41% (271); Business: 18% (122); Other: 16% (109); Engineering: 13% (84); Science: 12% (82)

INDIVIDUAL SAMPLES

*University of Texas at Arlington (biographical information for 383)*

Fourteen classes [383]: six sophomore-level American literature courses (F '83, S '84 (two classes) F '87, F '88, F '89); four upper-level "Build Your Own Utopia" (interdisciplinary) courses (F '84, S '87, S '89, F '90); one freshman honors American studies course (S '88); one upper-level "American Utopian Expressions" course (S '90); one graduate seminar, "Shapes of Utopia" (F '90); one late nineteenth-century American history course not taught by Roemer (S '91). Five classes (F '83, S '84 (two classes), F '84, S '87; 155 students) were not asked questions about ethnic background, marital status, or reading/viewing habits. The samples for these categories are 228.

Sex: F: 55% (210); M: 45% (173)

Age: Avg.: 23.4 (low: 18; high 74). 11% (42), above 30: 30–39 [32]; 40–49 [8]; 50–59 [1]; 60–69 [0]; 70–79 [1].

Raised: Texas: 60% (231); Midwest: 12% (46); Northeast: 7% (29); Southwest: 7% (27); South: 6% (22); West / Northwest: 3% (10); International (Great Britian, India, Honduras, Puerto Rico, Greece, Philippines, Germany, Malaysia, France, Vietnam, Pakistan): 5% (18)

Ethnicity [228]: Caucasian 74% (168); Native American: 10% (22); Hispanic: 7% (17); African American: 5% (12); Asian American: 4% (9)

Marital Status [228]: Single: 71% (161); Married: 25% (58); Divorced: 4% (9)

Employment: Part-time: 63% (242); None (includes 1 retired): 25% (96); Full-time: 12% (45)

Level: Sophomore: 30% (114); Junior: 24% (94); Senior: 23% (89); Freshman: 16% (60); Graduate: 7% (26)

Major: Liberal Arts: 44% (168); Business: 25% (94); Science: 11% (43); Engineering: 10% (40); Other: 10% (38)

*Arlington High (biographical information for 42)*

Two sections of a junior advanced placement American history course, S '91.

Sex: F: 52% (22); M: 48% (20)

Age: Avg.: 16.5 (low: 16; high: 17)

Raised: Texas: 90% (38); Midwest & West: 8% (3); Spain: 2% (1)

Ethnicity: Caucasian: 83% (35); Asian American: 12% (5); Native American: 5% (2)

Marital Status: Single: 100% (42)

Employment: None: 57% (24); Part-time: 43% (18)

Level: Junior: 98% (41); Senior: 2% (1)

Major: Undecided: 55% (23); 45% (19) equally divided: Liberal Arts, Science/Engineering, Fine Arts, Law, Business

*University of Minnesota (biographical information available for 95)*

"Utopianism, Society, and Culture in 18th- and 19th-Century America" (primarily sophomore-level American studies course), S '89, '90

Sex: F: 71% (67); M: 29% (28)

Age: Avg.: 20 (low: 17; high: 30)

Raised: Minnesota: 70% (66); Midwest: 24% (23); South, Southwest, West, and Northwest: each 1% (each 1); International (Canada, Germany): 2% (2)

Ethnicity: Caucasian: 88% (84); Asian American: 5% (5); Native American: 4% (4);
   Hispanic: 2% (2) [The other 1% was split almost equally among the groups.]
Marital Status: Single: 88% (84); Married: 11% (10); Divorced: 1% (1)
Employment: Part-time: 76% (72); None: 21% (20); Full-time: 3% (3)
Level: Sophomore: 50% (48); Junior: 20% (19); Senior: 16% (15); Freshman: 14% (13)
Major: Liberal Arts: 29% (28); Science (esp. psychology): 26% (25); Undecided: 17%
   (16); Business: 16% (15); Pre-Law, Agriculture, Education, Fine Arts: 12% (11)

*Hood College (biographical information available for 18)*

"The American Novel" (English, primarily juniors and seniors), F '89

Sex: F: 100% (18)
Age: Avg. of 16 of the 18: 21 (low: 19; high: 30); 2 others: 54 and 69
Raised: Northeast: 83.5% (15); Midwest: 5.5% (1); South: 5.5% (1); Japan: 5.5% (1)
Ethnicity: Caucasian: 89% (16); Asian American: 5.5% (1); Native American: 5.5% (1)
Marital Status: Single: 89% (16); Married: (11%) (2)
Employment: Part-time: 56% (10); None: 33% (6); Full-time: 11% (2)
Level: Senior: 44% (8); Junior: 39% (7); Sophomore: 17% (3)
Major: Liberal Arts: 78% (14); Business: 11% (2); Science: 5.5% (1); Education: 5.5% (1)

*RPI (biographical information for 51)*

"Utopia in Theory and Practice" (primarily sophomores and juniors), F '89; "Utopian Literature" (approximately half seniors), S '91

Sex: F: 25% (12); M: 75% (39)
Age: Avg.: 20 (low: 18; high: 23)
Raised: Northeast: 76% (39); Midwest: 6% (3); Southwest: 6% (3); South: 4% (2);
   West: 2% (1); International (Korea, Taiwan, Switzerland): 6% (3)
Ethnicity: Caucasian: 88% (45); Asian American: 8% (4); Native American: 4% (2)
Marital Status: Single: 98% (50); Married: 2% (1)
Employment: None: 59% (30); Part-time: 41% (21)
Level: Senior: 33% (17); Junior: 33% (17); Sophomore: 26% (13); Freshman: 8% (4)
Major: Science/Engineering: 86% (44); Liberal Arts: 10% (5); Architecture: 4% (2)

*University of Louisville (biographical information for 25)*

"Modern Political Thought" (Political science, primarily juniors and seniors), S '90

Sex: F: 56% (14) M: 44% (11)
Age: Avg.: 23 (low: 19; high: 33)
Raised: Kentucky: 56% (14); South: 12% (3); Midwest: 12% (3); Southwest: 8% (2);
   Northeast: 4% (1); International (Saudi Arabia, India, Japan): 8% (2)
Ethnicity: Caucasian: 80% (20); African American: 8% (2); Native American: 8% (2);
   Asian (Japanese): 4% (1)
Marital Status: Single: 88% (22); Married: 12% (3)
Employment: Part-time: 64% (16); Full-time: 20% (5); None: 16% (4)

Level: Senior: 52% (13); Junior: 32% (8); Sophomore: 12% (3); Other: 4% (1)
Major: Liberal Arts: 88% (22); Business: 12% (3)

*Harvard University Summer School (biographical information for 12)*

"Technology and the Future" (History of science, upper-level and graduate; mix of students from Harvard, MIT, Oberlin, Bard, and Lesley), S '90

Sex: F: 58% (7); M: 42% (5)
Age: Avg.: 25 (low: 19; high: 34)
Raised: Northeast: 42% (5); Midwest: 8% (1); Northwest: 8% (1); International (Africa, France, Germany, Jamaica, Japan): 42% (5)
Ethnicity: Caucasian: 67% (8); African American: 17% (2); Asian American: 8% (1); Native American: 8% (1)
Marital Status: Single: 83% (10); Married: 17% (2)
Employment: None: 50% (6); Full-time: 42% (5); Part-time: 8% (1)
Level: Senior: 42% (5); Graduate and Junior: each 25% (3 each); Sophomore: 8% (1)
Major: Liberal Arts: 33% (4); Business: 25% (3); 42% (5) equally divided: Math/Science, Engineering, Education, Fine Arts, Liberal Arts/Engineering

*Wesley Palms Retirement Community, San Diego (biographical information for 7),*
*S '91*

No course; volunteers interested in this project.

Sex: F: 100% (7)
Age: Avg: 80 (low: 72; high: 89)
Raised: Midwest: 28.5% (2); Northeast: 28.5% (2); Southwest: 14.3% (1); Northwest: 14.3% (1); International (Germany): 14.3% (1)
Ethnicity: Caucasian: 85.6% (6); Native American: 14.3% (1)
Marital Status: Widowed: 57% (4); Married: 28.6% (2); Divorced: 14.3% (1)
Employment: Retired: 85.6% (6); Full-time (writer): 14.3% (1)
Level: Graduated: 100% (7) (M.A. or M.S.: 3)
Major: Education/Public Administration: 43% (3); Liberal Arts: 28.3% (2); Library Science: 14.3% (1); Other: 14.3 (1)

*Women's Social/Reading Group, Arlington, Texas (biographical information for 6),*
*S '97*

No course; volunteers interested in the project.

Sex: F: 100% (6)
Age: Avg.: 54 (low: 49; high: 59)
Raised: Texas: 50% (3); Northeast: 33% (2); South: 17% (1)
Ethnicity: Caucasian: 100% (6)
Marital Status: Married: 83% (5); Divorced: 17% (1)
Employment: Part-time: 50% (3); Full-time: 33% (2); Retired: 17% (1)

Level: Graduate: 66% (4); Graduated: 17% (1); Sophomore: 17% (1)
Major: Science: 33% (2); Other: 33% (2); Business: 17% (1); Liberal Arts: 17% (1)

## INTERNATIONAL SAMPLES

*Campion College, University of Regina, Saskatchewan, Canada (biographical information for 8), W '90*

"Utopian Literature and Thought"; upper-level undergraduate humanities course; the class included men and women, but only eight women turned in completed questionnaires.

Sex: F: 100% (8)
Age: Avg. of 6 of 8: 20.5 (low: 19; high: 22); 2 others: 50 and 54
Raised: Canada (primarily Quebec, Manitoba, Saskatchewan): 100% (8)
Ethnicity: Caucasian: 100%
Marital Status: Single: 63% (5); Married: 25% (2); Divorced: 12% (1)
Employment: Part-time: 50% (4); None: 38% (3); Full-time: 12% (1)
Levels: Sophomore and Senior: each 38% (3 each); Junior: 12% (1); Other: 12% (1)
Major: Liberal Arts and Science: each 37.5% (3 each); Undecided: 25% (2)

*International Christian University, Mitaka, Tokyo, Japan (biographical information for 20), S '88*

"America as Utopia" (upper-level undergraduate American studies course). The sample includes 1 undergraduate student from Keio University and graduate students from Rikkyo University (4) and the University of Tokyo (1). The graduate students did not take the course; they read *Looking Backward* and completed the questionnaire "on their own."

Sex: F: 80% (16); M: 20% (4)
Age: Avg.: 22 (low: 19; high: 36)
Raised: Japan: 95% (19); Detroit: 5% (1)
Ethnicity: Asian (Japanese): 100%
Marital Status: Single: 95% (19); Married: 5% (1)
Employment: None: 90% (18); Part-time: 10% (2)
Level: Junior: 35% (7); Sophomore: 30% (6); Graduate: 25% (5); Senior and Freshman: each 5% (1 each)
Major: Liberal Arts: 95% (19); Biology: 5% (1)

*Institut fur Anglistik und Amerikanistik, Universität für Bildungswissenchaften, Klagenfurt, Austria (biographical information for 1), F '90*

Female; 24; Austria; Caucasian; Single; Part-time; Junior; English and American studies.

## THE SAMPLES OF READERS OF *LOOKING BACKWARD*

|  | TOTAL NO. OF TRANSFORMATIONAL ASSOCIATIONS | MOST IMPORTANT TRANSFORMATIONAL ASSOCIATIONS |
|---|---|---|
| *USA* | | |
| UT Arlington, '83-'93 | 2,184 | 395 |
| Arlington High, '91 | 197 | 43 |
| U of Minnesota, '89-'90 | 264 | 63 |
| Hood College, '89 | 69 | 17 |
| RPI, '89, '91 | 149 | 38 |
| U of Louisville, '90 | 77 | 18 |
| Harvard U, '90 | 50 | 12 |
| Wesley Palms, '91 | 31 | 6 |
| [Women's Reading Group, '97 See Sample-by-Sample Breakdown, below.] | 3,021 | Totals 592 |
| | | |
| *Other Countries* | | |
| Canada, '90 (U of Regina) | 32 | 7 |
| Japan, '88 (ICU, U of Tokyo, Rikkyo U) | 100 | 22 |
| Austria, '90 (Klagenfurt) | 5 | 1 |
| | 3,158 | Totals 622 |

Note: Instructors asked the students to identify five important "influences" that shaped their responses and to indicate which one was the most important. Thus, the total number should be five times greater than the most-important totals. The actual totals do not conform to this ratio exactly because quite a few UTA students identified more than five transformational associations, several non-UTA students identified fewer than five, two Japanese students each identified two "most important" transformational associations, and, most siginificantly, an entire class of 31 students at UTA ('87) did not identify most important transformational associations (i.e., *the actual number of readers who completed analyses of influences on their reading was* 622+31–2 (Japan)=651.

## SAMPLE-BY-SAMPLE BREAKDOWN

Key: AC=past academic courses; IC=immediate circumstance(s) while reading *Looking Backward*; RT=reading and viewing tastes, including mention of specific books and films; PE=nonacademic, nonreading personal experiences, including both events and people in the readers' lives; AB=attitudes and beliefs stated in general terms (i.e., not specifically associated with an event or person)

A plus sign indicates that the reader defined the response as positive; a minus sign indicates a negative response; a +/– sign indicates a mixture of positive and negative responses. The signs appear only in the indications of totals under their respective columns (first column=pluses, second=minuses, third=plus/minus. F=fall semester; S=spring semester).

*University of Texas at Arlington*

Thirteen English classes, one American studies class, one history class (1983-1993): six sophomore American literature classes primarily for non-English majors; seven upper-level utopian literature classes primarily for liberal arts majors; one honors America Studies class primarily for Liberal Arts majors; one upper-level history course primarily for history majors.

| | ALL TRANSFORMATIONAL ASSOCIATIONS | | | | | MOST IMPORTANT TRANSFORMATIONAL ASSOCIATIONS | | | | |
|---|---|---|---|---|---|---|---|---|---|---|
| 6% | AC | 129 ( | 67 | 61 | 1 ) | 3% | AC | 14 ( | 7 | 6 | 1 ) |
| 8% | IC | 169 ( | 98 | 68 | 3 ) | 7% | IC | 28 ( | 20 | 6 | 2 ) |
| 14% | RT | 308 ( | 162 | 137 | 9 ) | 9% | RT | 34 ( | 19 | 14 | 1 ) |
| 30% | PE | 665 ( | 449 | 199 | 17 ) | 29% | PE | 115 ( | 70 | 43 | 2 ) |
| 42% | AB | 913 ( | 383 | 503 | 27 ) | 52% | AB | 204 ( | 71 | 125 | 8 ) |
| 100% | | 2184 ( | 1159+ | 968– | 57+/–) | 100% | | 395 ( | 187+ | 194– | 14+/–) |
| | | | 53% | 44% | 3% | | | | 47% | 49% | 4% |

*Arlington High School*

Combined totals of two sections of a junior advanced placement American history course, S '91.

| | ALL TRANSFORMATIONAL ASSOCIATIONS | | | | | MOST IMPORTANT TRANSFORMATIONAL ASSOCIATIONS | | | | |
|---|---|---|---|---|---|---|---|---|---|---|
| 6% | AC | 11 ( | 6 | 5 | 0 ) | 7% | AC | 3 ( | 3 | 0 ) |
| 11% | IC | 22 ( | 10 | 12 | 0 ) | 14% | IC | 6 ( | 4 | 2 ) |
| 15% | PE | 30 ( | 12 | 18 | 0 ) | 16% | PE | 7 ( | 4 | 3 ) |

*(continued)*

ALL TRANSFORMATIONAL ASSOCIATIONS

| 18% | RT | 36 ( | 11 | 25 | 0 ) |
|---|---|---|---|---|---|
| 50% | AB | 98 ( | 48 | 49 | 1 ) |
| 100% | | 197 ( | 87+ | 109− | 1+/−) |
| | | | 44% | 55% | 1% |

MOST IMPORTANT TRANSFORMATIONAL ASSOCIATIONS

| 14% | RT | 6 ( | 1 | 5 ) |
|---|---|---|---|---|
| 49% | AB | 21 ( | 11 | 10 ) |
| 100% | | 43 ( | 23+ | 20− ) |
| | | | 53% | 47% |

## University of Minnesota

Two American studies classes: "Utopianism, Society, and Culture in 18th- and 19th-Century America"; primarily sophomores with some juniors and seniors and a few freshmen, S '89, S '90.

ALL TRANSFORMATIONAL ASSOCIATIONS

| 9% | IC | 23 ( | 5 | 17 | 1 ) |
|---|---|---|---|---|---|
| 11% | AC | 28 ( | 18 | 9 | 1 ) |
| 17% | PE | 46 ( | 31 | 14 | 1 ) |
| 18% | RT | 49 ( | 29 | 19 | 1 ) |
| 45% | AB | 118 ( | 62 | 53 | 3 ) |
| 100% | | 264 ( | 145+ | 112− | 7+/−) |
| | | | 55% | 42% | 3% |

MOST IMPORTANT TRANSFORMATIONAL ASSOCIATIONS

| 6% | IC | 4 ( | 3 | 1 | 0 ) |
|---|---|---|---|---|---|
| 8% | RT | 5 ( | 4 | 1 | 0 ) |
| 8% | PE | 5 ( | 4 | 1 | 0 ) |
| 10% | AC | 6 ( | 6 | 0 | 0 ) |
| 68% | AB | 43 ( | 21 | 19 | 3 ) |
| 100% | | 63 ( | 38+ | 22− | 3+/−) |
| | | | 60% | 35% | 5% |

## Hood College

"The American Novel": English, primarily juniors and seniors, F '89.

ALL TRANSFORMATIONAL ASSOCIATIONS

| 6% | IC | 4 ( | 2 | 2 | 0 ) |
|---|---|---|---|---|---|
| 20% | RT | 14 ( | 9 | 5 | 0 ) |
| 23% | PE | 16 ( | 9 | 7 | 0 ) |
| 25% | AC | 17 ( | 11 | 6 | 0 ) |
| 26% | AB | 18 ( | 10 | 7 | 1 ) |
| 100% | 69 | ( | 41+ | 27− | 1+/−) |
| | | | 59% | 39% | 2% |

MOST IMPORTANT TRANSFORMATIONAL ASSOCIATIONS

| 6% | RT | 1 ( | 1 | 0 | 0 ) |
|---|---|---|---|---|---|
| 18% | IC | 3 ( | 2 | 1 | 0 ) |
| 18% | PE | 3 ( | 3 | 0 | 0 ) |
| 23% | AB | 4 ( | 2 | 2 | 0 ) |
| 35% | AC | 6 ( | 3 | 3 | 0 ) |
| 100% | | 17 ( | 11+ | 6− | 0 ) |
| | | | 65% | 35% | 0% |

## RPI

"Utopia in Theory and Practice" (primarily sophomores and juniors with a few seniors and one freshman), F '89; "Utopian Literature"(approximately half seniors; only three freshmen), S '91. In both classes most of the students were engineering and science students.

ALL TRANSFORMATIONAL ASSOCIATIONS

| 8% | IC | 12 ( | 4 | 7 | 1 ) |
|---|---|---|---|---|---|
| 11% | AC | 16 ( | 11 | 5 | 0 ) |
| 11.5% | PE | 17 ( | 14 | 3 | 0 ) |
| 21.5% | RT | 32 ( | 20 | 12 | 0 ) |
| 48% | AB | 72 ( | 30 | 39 | 3 ) |
| 100% | 149 | ( | 79 | 66 | 4 ) |
| | | | 53% | 44% | 3% |

MOST IMPORTANT TRANSFORMATIONAL ASSOCIATIONS

| 5% | PE | 2 ( | 2 | 0 | 0 ) |
|---|---|---|---|---|---|
| 8% | IC | 3 ( | 1 | 1 | 1 ) |
| 8% | AC | 3 ( | 2 | 1 | 0 ) |
| 16% | RT | 6 ( | 4 | 2 | 0 ) |
| 63% | AB | 24 ( | 11 | 13 | 0 ) |
| 100% | | 38 ( | 20 | 17 | 1 ) |
| | | | 53% | 45% | 2% |

### University of Louisville

"Modern Political Thought": Political science, primarily juniors and seniors, S '90.

| ALL TRANSFORMATIONAL ASSOCIATIONS | | | | | | MOST IMPORTANT TRANSFORMATIONAL ASSOCIATIONS | | | | | |
|---|---|---|---|---|---|---|---|---|---|---|---|
| 3% | IC | 2 ( | 2 | 0 | 0 ) | 0% | IC | 0 ( | 0 | 0 | 0 ) |
| 9% | AC | 7 ( | 5 | 2 | 0 ) | 0% | AC | 0 ( | 0 | 0 | 0 ) |
| 16% | RT | 12 ( | 11 | 1 | 0 ) | 5% | RT | 1 ( | 1 | 0 | 0 ) |
| 27% | PE | 21 ( | 12 | 8 | 1 ) | 17% | PE | 3 ( | 2 | 1 | 0 ) |
| 45% | AB | 35 ( | 12 | 21 | 2 ) | 78% | AB | 14 ( | 5 | 8 | 1 ) |
| 100% | | 77 ( | 42+ | 32– | 3+/–) | 100% | | 18 ( | 8+ | 9– | 1+/–) |
| | | | 54.5% | 41.5% | 4% | | | | 44% | 50% | 6% |

### Harvard University

"Technology and the Future: Historical Perspectives": History of science, upper-level and graduate, mix from Harvard, MIT, Oberlin, Bard, and Lesley, Summer '90.

| ALL TRANSFORMATIONAL ASSOCIATIONS | | | | | | MOST IMPORTANT TRANSFORMATIONAL ASSOCIATIONS | | | | | |
|---|---|---|---|---|---|---|---|---|---|---|---|
| 2% | IC | 1 ( | 0 | 0 | 1 ) | 8% | IC | ( | 0 | 0 | 1 ) |
| 12% | AC | 6 ( | 4 | 2 | 0 ) | 8% | AC | 1 ( | 0 | 1 | 0 ) |
| 22% | RT | 11 ( | 9 | 2 | 0 ) | 8% | RT | 1 ( | 1 | 0 | 0 ) |
| 30% | AB | 15 ( | 8 | 4 | 3 ) | 34% | PE | 4 ( | 4 | 0 | 0 ) |
| 34% | PE | 17 ( | 13 | 4 | 0 ) | 42% | AB | 5 ( | 4 | 1 | 0 ) |
| 100% | | 50 ( | 34+ | 12– | 4+/–) | 100% | | 12 ( | 9+ | 2– | 1+/–) |
| | | | 68% | 24% | 8% | | | | 75% | 17% | 8% |

### Wesley Palms Retirement Community

This small group (6) volunteered to indicate their transformational associations. There was no course associated with their reading and responses, S '91.

| ALL TRANSFORMATIONAL ASSOCIATIONS | | | | | MOST IMPORTANT TRANSFORMATIONAL ASSOCIATIONS | | | | |
|---|---|---|---|---|---|---|---|---|---|
| 3% | IC | 1 ( | 1 | 0 ) | 0% | AC | 0 ( | 0 | 0 ) |
| 3% | RT | 1 ( | 0 | 1 ) | 0% | RT | 0 ( | 0 | 0 ) |
| 10% | AC | 3 ( | 1 | 2 ) | 17% | IC | 1 ( | 1 | 0 ) |
| 26% | AB | 8 ( | 2 | 6 ) | 33% | AB | 2 ( | 1 | 1 ) |
| 58% | PE | 18 ( | 11 | 7 ) | 50% | PE | 3 ( | 1 | 2 ) |
| 100% | | 31 ( | 15+ | 16– ) | 100% | | 6 ( | 3+ | 3– ) |
| | | | 48% | 52% | | | | 50% | 50% |

### Women's Social/Reading Group, Arlington, TX

This small reading group (6) was willing to be part of the project. Unfortunately, only two readers described their transformational associations. Since their responses did not necessarily reflect the views of the group, I decided not to include them in the statistical survey. Nevertheless, several aspects of the responses were interesting and deserve note. Both readers mentioned personal experience associations that shaped their responses to Bellamy's women. One (who responded negatively) indicated that women rarely based their selection of a man purely on rational evaluations of their work performance. The other (who had a mildly positive response) has a brother and a nephew who both attended The Citadel. She perceived the separate woman's section of the industrial army as an intriguing response to the issue of women in the military. The former reader had a very negative response to LB; all five of her described transformational associations (personal experience [1], reading tastes [2], and general beliefs [2]) inclined her toward negative responses. Her strong belief in capitalism was her most important association. The latter reader had a mixed reaction: immediate circumstances (1 +/−), past academic class (1−), and personal experience (2+, 1−). Two especially interesting associations were her personal experience as a speech pathologist (she was disappointed by the lack of change in language in Bellamy's future) and the association with The Citadel mentioned above, which was her most important association. S '97.

*Campion College, University of Regina, Canada$*
"Utopian Literature and Thought": Humanities, sophomores, juniors, seniors, Winter '90.

| ALL TRANSFORMATIONAL ASSOCIATIONS | | | | | | MOST IMPORTANT TRANSFORMATIONAL ASSOCIATIONS | | | | |
|---|---|---|---|---|---|---|---|---|---|---|
| 9% | IC | 3 ( | 2 | 1 | 0 ) | 0% | AC | 0 ( | 0 | 0 ) |
| 13% | AC | 4 ( | 2 | 2 | 0 ) | 0% | RT | 0 ( | 0 | 0 ) |
| 22% | PE | 7 ( | 4 | 2 | 1 ) | 43% | IC | 3 ( | 2 | 1 ) |
| 25% | AB | 8 ( | 2 | 6 | 0 ) | 28.5% | PE | 2 ( | 2 | 0 ) |
| 31% | RT | 10 ( | 5 | 5 | 0 ) | 28.5% | AB | 2 ( | 0 | 2 ) |
| 100% | | 32 ( | 15+ | 16− | 1+/−) | 100% | | 7 ( | 4+ | 3− ) |
| | | | 47% | 50% | 3% | | | | 57% | 43% |

*International Christian University, Mitaka, Tokyo, Japan*
"America as Utopia": Humanities, upper-level, ICU; also 5 graduate students, University of Tokyo [1], Rikkyo University [4]), '88

| ALL TRANSFORMATIONAL ASSOCIATIONS | | | | | | MOST IMPORTANT TRANSFORMATIONAL ASSOCIATIONS | | | | | |
|---|---|---|---|---|---|---|---|---|---|---|---|
| 2% | AC | 2 ( | 2 | 0 | 0 ) | 0% | AC | 0 ( | 0 | 0 | 0 ) |
| 9% | IC | 9 ( | 6 | 2 | 1 ) | 5% | IC | 1 ( | 1 | 0 | 0 ) |
| 16% | RT | 16 ( | 12 | 4 | 0 ) | 14% | RT | 3 ( | 3 | 0 | 0 ) |
| 16% | PE | 16 ( | 8 | 8 | 0 ) | 36% | PE | 8 ( | 5 | 3 | 0 ) |
| 57% | AB | 57 ( | 23 | 33 | 1 ) | 45% | AB | 10 ( | 2 | 7 | 1 ) |
| 100% | | 100 ( | 51+ | 47− | 2+/−) | 100% | | 22 ( | 11+ | 10− | 1+/−) |
| | | | 51% | 47% | 2% | | | | 50% | 46% | 4% |

*Universität für Bildungswissenschaften, Klagenfurt, Austria*
A utopian literature course in the Institut für Anglistik und Amerikanistik, F '90.

The one student who completed the course indicated three types of influences that helped her to understand and respond positively to *LB*: 1 reading taste, 1 personal experience, and 3 general attitudes about equality, opportunities for professional training, and nineteenth-century history (in the latter case the transformational associations helped shape a negative response). The most important influence was the personal experience, her treatment in a psychiatric ward.

# Questionnaire and Responses

Appendix C

The responses include the UTA classes from fall 1987 to spring 1996 (except for the fall 1993 class) and the classes from Arlington High School, U of Minnesota (two classes), Hood College, RPI (two classes), U of Louisville, Harvard Summer School, Campion College (U of Regina, Canada), and International Christian University (Japan), as well as the Wesley Palms retirement community in San Diego and a women's social/reading group in Arlington, Texas. For descriptions of the samples and the course titles, see appendix A, Characteristics of the Samples.

The number of responses varied slightly from question to question. For example, for the combined sample responses, the number of responses varied from a low of 526 to a high of 541. The number of responses to each question for each sample is indicated below. If a sample has fewer than twenty readers, the percentages are bracketed.

1. If someone who had not read *LB* asked you what it was "about," what would you tell him or her?

*(The responses were divided into two categories depending upon whether the answers focused on the plot, e.g., a man falls asleep for 113 years or on a concept, e.g., a socialistic utopia.)*

|  | PLOT | | CONCEPT | |
|---|---|---|---|---|
| Combined Sample (539) | 46% | (247) | 54% | (292) |
| UT Arlington (254) | 52% | (133) | 48% | (121) |
| Arlington High (43) | 51% | (22) | 49% | (21) |
| U of Minnesota (95) | 48% | (46) | 52% | (49) |
| Hood College (18) | [28%] | (5) | [72%] | (13) |
| RPI (51) | 39% | (20) | 61% | (31) |
| U of Louisville (25) | 4% | (1) | 96% | (24) |
| Harvard Summer (12) | [42%] | (5) | [58%] | (7) |
| Wesley Palms (6) | [17%] | (1) | [83%] | (5) |

*(continued)*

[ 245 ]

| | PLOT | | CONCEPT | |
|---|---|---|---|---|
| Women's Group (6) | [33%] | ( 2) | [67%] | ( 4) |
| Campion, Canada (8) | [37%] | ( 3) | [63%] | ( 5) |
| ICU, Japan (20) | 45% | ( 9) | 55% | ( 11) |
| Klagenfurt, Aus. (1) | | ( 0) | | ( 1) |

2. What type of book do you think *LB* is?

*(UF=utopian fiction/literature; the most common other designations were science fiction and historical fiction.)*

| | UF | | OTHER | |
|---|---|---|---|---|
| Combined Sample (540) | 74% | (397) | 26% | (143) |
| UT Arlington (256) | 71% | (183) | 29% | ( 73) |
| Arlington High (42) | 71% | ( 30) | 29% | ( 12) |
| U of Minnesota (95) | 71% | ( 67) | 29% | ( 28) |
| Hood College (18) | [83%] | ( 15) | [17%] | ( 3) |
| RPI (51) | 86% | ( 44) | 14% | ( 7) |
| U of Louisville (25) | 88% | ( 22) | 12% | ( 3) |
| Harvard Summer (12) | [58%] | ( 7) | [42%] | ( 5) |
| Wesley Palms (6) | 83%] | ( 5) | [17%] | ( 1) |
| Women's Group (6) | [83%] | ( 5) | [17%] | ( 1) |
| Campion, Canada (8) | [63%] | ( 5) | [37%] | ( 3) |
| ICU, Japan (20) | 65% | ( 13) | 35% | ( 7) |
| Klagenfurt, Aus. (1) | | ( 1) | | ( 0) |

3. Have you ever read a book like this before? If so, please list the title(s).

*The most frequently mentioned titles were* Nineteen Eighty-four *and* Brave New World. *Others mentioned with consistency were* Utopia *(More),* Time Machine, Walden Two, Animal Farm, Blithedale, Herland, Handmaid's Tale, *and* Woman on the Edge of Time. *Classes with strong female enrollment (e.g., Hood, Campion) emphasized the latter three.*

| | YES | | NO | |
|---|---|---|---|---|
| Combined Sample (530) | 48% | (253) | 52% | (277) |
| UT Arlington (247) | 38% | ( 93) | 62% | (154) |
| Arlington High (43) | 51% | ( 22) | 49% | ( 21) |
| U of Minnesota (93) | 43% | ( 40) | 57% | ( 53) |
| Hood College (18) | [89%] | ( 16) | [11%] | ( 2) |
| RPI ((51) | 73% | ( 37) | 27% | ( 14) |
| U of Louisville (25) | 60% | ( 15) | 40% | ( 10) |
| Harvard Summer (12) | [75%] | ( 9) | [25%] | ( 3) |
| Wesley Palms (6) | [67%] | ( 4) | [33%] | ( 2) |
| Women's Group (6) | [50%] | ( 3) | [50%] | ( 3) |
| Campion, Canada (8) | [63%] | ( 5) | [37%] | ( 3) |
| ICU, Japan (20) | 40% | ( 8) | 60% | ( 12) |
| Klagenfurt, Aus. (1) | | ( 1) | | ( 0) |

4. Would you like to read a book like this again? If so, why? If not, why?

*Most of the positive responses indicated interest in provoking thought about alternative views of society or the future or ideal worlds. Most of the negative responses described the book as boring or unrealistic.*

| | YES | | NO | |
|---|---|---|---|---|
| Combined Sample (536) | 75% | ( 402) | 25% | ( 134) |
| UT Arlington (250) | 75% | ( 187) | 25% | ( 63) |
| Arlington High (43) | 60% | ( 26) | 40% | ( 17) |
| U of Minnesota (96) | 79% | ( 76) | 21% | ( 20) |
| Hood College (18) | [ 78%] | ( 14) | [22%] | ( 4) |
| RPI (51) | 80% | ( 41) | 20% | ( 10) |
| U of Louisville (25) | 80% | ( 20) | 20% | ( 5) |
| Harvard Summer (12) | [ 83%] | ( 10) | [17%] | ( 2) |
| Wesley Palms (6) | [ 50%] | ( 3) | [50%] | ( 3) |
| Women's Group (6) | [ 67%] | ( 4) | [33%] | ( 2) |
| Campion, Canada (8) | [ 88%] | ( 7) | [12%] | ( 1) |
| ICU, Japan (20) | 65% | ( 13) | 35% | ( 7) |
| Klagenfurt, Aus. (1) | | ( 1) | | ( 0) |

5. How is this book "told," (1st person, 3rd person limited, 3rd person omniscient)?

| | FIRST PERSON | | OTHER | |
|---|---|---|---|---|
| Combined Sample (541) | 90% | ( 489) | 10% | ( 52) |
| UT Arlington (255) | 91% | ( 231) | 9% | ( 24) |
| Arlington High (43) | 95% | ( 41) | 5% | ( 2) |
| U of Minnesota (96) | 90% | ( 86) | 10% | ( 10) |
| Hood College (18) | [ 89%] | ( 16) | [11%] | ( 2) |
| RPI (51) | 88% | ( 45) | 12% | ( 6) |
| U of Louisville (25) | 88% | ( 22) | 12% | ( 3) |
| Harvard Summer (12) | [ 83%] | ( 10) | [17%] | ( 2) |
| Wesley Palms (6) | [100%] | ( 6) | [ 0%] | ( 0) |
| Women's Group (6) | [ 67%] | ( 4) | [33%] | ( 2) |
| Campion, Canada (8) | [100%] | ( 8) | [ 0%] | ( 0) |
| ICU, Japan (20) | 95% | ( 19) | 5% | ( 1) |
| Klangenfurt, Aus. (1) | | ( 1) | | ( 0) |

6. Are there any particular episodes that you
*a. especially liked—which one(s)?*

*Two most frequently mentioned: episodes involving West and Edith Leete, and West's dream return to 1887 near the conclusion. Other episodes mentioned consistently: West's awakening, the shopping tour.*

*b. especially disliked—which one(s)?*

*Two most frequently mentioned: Rev. Barton's sermon and the long talks between Dr. Leete and West. The dream, the shopping tour, and the Edith Leete–West episodes were mentioned with some consistency.*

7. In reference to the "love story" (West and Edith Leete), did you:
*a. dislike them; b. no particular like or dislike; c. like them?*

| | DISLIKE | | NO PARTICULAR LIKE OR DISLIKE | | LIKE | |
|---|---|---|---|---|---|---|
| Combined Sample (539) | 14% | ( 74) | 38% | (206) | 48% | (259) |
| UT Arlington (253) | 12% | ( 31) | 38% | ( 96) | 50% | (126) |

*(continued)*

| | DISLIKE | | NO PARTICULAR LIKE OR DISLIKE | | LIKE | |
|---|---|---|---|---|---|---|
| Arlington High (43) | 9% | ( 4) | 42% | ( 18) | 49% | ( 21) |
| U of Minnesota (96) | 6% | ( 6) | 37% | ( 35) | 57% | ( 55) |
| Hood College (18) | [ 33%] | ( 6) | [ 56%] | ( 10) | [ 11%] | ( 2) |
| RPI (51) | 25.5% | ( 13) | 45% | ( 23) | 29.5% | ( 15) |
| U of Louisville (25) | 12% | ( 3) | 24% | ( 6) | 64% | ( 16) |
| Harvard Summer (12) | [ 25%] | ( 3) | [ 50%] | ( 6) | [ 25%] | ( 3) |
| Wesley Palms (6) | [ 67%] | ( 4) | [16.5%] | ( 1) | [16.5%] | ( 1) |
| Women's Group (6) | [ 0%] | ( 0) | [ 33%] | ( 2) | [ 67%] | ( 4) |
| Campion, Canada (8) | [ 12%] | ( 1) | [ 25%] | ( 2) | [ 63%] | ( 5) |
| ICU, Japan (20) | 10% | ( 2) | 35% | ( 7) | 55% | ( 11) |
| Klagenfurt, Austria (1) | | ( 1) | | ( 0) | | ( 0) |

8. In reference to the talks West has with Dr. Leete, did you:
*a. dislike them; b. no particular like or dislike; c. like them?*

| | DISLIKE | | NO PARTICULAR LIKE OR DISLIKE | | LIKE | |
|---|---|---|---|---|---|---|
| Combined Sample (529) | 30% | (158) | 27% | (143) | 43% | (228) |
| UT Arlington (244) | 31% | ( 74) | 31% | ( 73) | 38% | ( 97) |
| Arlington High (42) | 48% | ( 20) | 16% | ( 7) | 36% | ( 15) |
| U of Minnesota (96) | 30% | ( 29) | 29% | ( 28) | 41% | ( 39) |
| Hood College (18) | [44.5%] | ( 8) | [ 11%] | ( 2) | [44.5%] | ( 8) |
| RPI (51) | 18% | ( 9) | 21% | ( 11) | 61% | ( 31) |
| U of Louisville (25) | 20% | ( 5) | 16% | ( 4) | 64% | ( 16) |
| Harvard Summer (12) | [ 33%] | ( 4) | [ 17%] | ( 2) | [ 50%] | ( 6) |
| Wesley Palms (6) | [ 50%] | ( 3) | [ 17%] | ( 1) | [ 33%] | ( 2) |
| Women's Group (6) | [ 17%] | ( 1) | [ 33%] | ( 2) | [ 50%] | ( 3) |
| Campion, Canada (8) | [ 12%] | ( 1) | [ 0%] | ( 0) | [ 88%] | ( 7) |
| ICU, Japan (20) | 20% | ( 4) | 65% | ( 13) | 15% | ( 3) |
| Klagenfurt, Austria (1) | | ( 1) | | ( 0) | | ( 0) |

9. In reference to West's dream return to 1887 near the end of the book, did you:
*a. dislike it; b. no particular like or dislike; c. like it?*

| | DISLIKE | | NO PARTICULAR LIKE OR DISLIKE | | LIKE | |
|---|---|---|---|---|---|---|
| Combined Sample (540) | 17% | ( 93) | 26% | (138) | 57% | (309) |
| UT Arlington (254) | 16.5% | ( 42) | 25.5% | ( 65) | 58% | (147) |
| Arlington High (43) | 33% | ( 14) | 20% | ( 9) | 47% | ( 20) |
| U of Minnesota (96) | 7% | ( 7) | 32% | ( 31) | 61% | ( 58) |
| Hood College (18) | [ 6%] | ( 1) | [ 11%] | ( 2) | [ 83%] | ( 15) |
| RPI (51) | 27% | ( 14) | 20% | ( 10) | 53% | ( 27) |
| U of Louisville (25) | 16% | ( 4) | 36% | ( 9) | 48% | ( 12) |
| Harvard Summer (12) | [ 8.5%] | ( 1) | [ 8.5%] | ( 1) | [ 83%] | ( 10) |
| Wesley Palms (6) | [ 33%] | ( 2) | [ 50%] | ( 3) | [ 17%] | ( 1) |
| Women's Group (6) | [ 17%] | ( 1) | [ 50%] | ( 3) | [ 33%] | ( 2) |
| Campion, Canada (8) | [ 25%] | ( 2) | [ 0%] | ( 0) | [ 75%] | ( 6) |
| ICU, Japan (20) | 25% | ( 5) | 20% | ( 4) | 55% | ( 11) |
| Klagenfurt, Austria (1) | | ( 0) | | ( 1) | | ( 0) |

10. In reference to the final paragraphs (West's return, tears, talk, reunion with Edith Leete), did you:

*a. dislike it; b. no particular like or dislike; c. like it?*

|  | DISLIKE | | NO PARTICULAR LIKE OR DISLIKE | | LIKE | |
|---|---|---|---|---|---|---|
| Combined Sample (539) | 16% | ( 88) | 29% | (157) | 55% | (294) |
| UT Arlington (254) | 15% | ( 38) | 25% | ( 64) | 60% | (152) |
| Arlington High (42) | 17% | ( 7) | 38% | ( 16) | 45% | ( 19) |
| U of Minnesota (96) | 8% | ( 8) | 26% | ( 25) | 66% | ( 63) |
| Hood College (18) | [ 17%] | ( 3) | [ 44%] | ( 8) | [ 39%] | ( 7) |
| RPI (51) | 41% | ( 21) | 33% | ( 17) | 26% | ( 13) |
| U of Louisville (25) | 16% | ( 4) | 32% | ( 8) | 52% | ( 13) |
| Harvard Summer (12) | [ 17%] | ( 2) | [ 33%] | ( 4) | [ 50%] | ( 6) |
| Wesley Palms (6) | [ 33%] | ( 2) | [ 33%] | ( 2) | [ 33%] | ( 2) |
| Women's Group (6) | [33.3%] | ( 2) | [33.3%] | ( 2) | [33.3%] | ( 2) |
| Campion, Canada (8) | [ 0%] | ( 0) | [ 12%] | ( 1) | [ 88%] | ( 7) |
| ICU, Japan (20) | 5% | ( 1) | 45% | ( 9) | 50% | ( 10) |
| Klagenfurt, Austria (1) | | ( 0) | | ( 1) | | ( 0) |

11. Did you like or dislike the following characters?

*a. Julian West*

|  | LIKE | | DISLIKE | |
|---|---|---|---|---|
| Combined Sample (533) | 91% | (484) | 9% | ( 49) |
| UT Arlington (251) | 88% | (221) | 12% | ( 30) |
| Arlington High (42) | 90% | ( 38) | 10% | ( 4) |
| U of Minnesota (95) | 97% | ( 92) | 3% | ( 3) |
| Hood College (18) | [ 83%] | ( 15) | [17%] | ( 3) |
| RPI (51) | 94% | ( 48) | 6% | ( 3) |
| U of Louisville (25) | 100% | ( 25) | 0% | ( 0) |
| Harvard Summer (12) | [ 92%] | ( 11) | [ 8%] | ( 1) |
| Wesley Palms (5) | [ 80%] | ( 4) | [20%] | ( 1) |
| Women's Group (6) | [ 83%] | ( 5) | [17%] | ( 1) |
| Campion, Canada (8) | [ 88%] | ( 7) | [12%] | ( 1) |
| ICU, Japan (19) | [ 89%] | ( 17) | [11%] | ( 2) |
| Klagenfurt, Aus. (1) | | ( 1) | | ( 0) |

*b. Dr. Leete*

|  | LIKE | | DISLIKE | |
|---|---|---|---|---|
| Combined Sample (533) | 74% | (397) | 26% | (136) |
| UT Arlington (252) | 74% | (186) | 26% | ( 66) |
| Arlington High (42) | 67% | ( 28) | 33% | ( 14) |
| U of Minnesota (95) | 75% | ( 72) | 25% | ( 23) |
| Hood College (18) | [ 61%] | ( 11) | [39%] | ( 7) |
| RPI (51) | 82% | ( 42) | 18% | ( 9) |
| U of Louisville (25) | 88% | ( 22) | 12% | ( 3) |
| Harvard Summer (12) | [ 58%] | ( 7): | [42%] | ( 5) |
| Wesley Palms (5) | [ 80%] | ( 4) | [20%] | ( 1) |

*(continued)*

|  | LIKE | | DISLIKE | |
|---|---|---|---|---|
| Women's Group (6) | [100%] | ( 6) | [ 0%] | ( 0) |
| Campion, Canada (8) | [ 50%] | ( 4) | [50%] | ( 4) |
| ICU, Japan (18) | [ 78%] | ( 14) | [12%] | ( 4) |
| Klagenfurt, Aus. (1) | | ( 1) | | ( 0) |

*c. Edith Leete*

|  | LIKE | | DISLIKE | |
|---|---|---|---|---|
| Combined Sample (535) | 78% | (415) | 22% | (120) |
| UT Arlington (254) | 76% | (193) | 24% | ( 61) |
| Arlington High (42) | 74% | ( 31) | 26% | ( 11) |
| U of Minnesota (95) | 89% | ( 85) | 11% | ( 10) |
| Hood College (18) | [ 56%] | ( 10) | [44%] | ( 8) |
| RPI (51) | 69% | ( 35) | 31% | ( 16) |
| U of Louisville (25) | 88% | ( 22) | 12% | ( 3) |
| Harvard Summer (12) | [ 67%] | ( 8) | [33%] | ( 4) |
| Wesley Palms (5) | [ 40%] | ( 2) | [60%] | ( 3) |
| Women's Group (6) | [ 83%] | ( 5) | [17%] | ( 1) |
| Campion, Canada (8) | [ 88%] | ( 7) | [12%] | ( 1) |
| ICU, Japan (18) | [ 94%] | ( 17) | [ 6%] | ( 1) |
| Klagenfurt, Aus.(1) | | ( 0) | | ( 1) |

*d. Other Characters*

Not many of the readers indicated likes and dislikes of other characters. Of those who did, there was a consistent dislike of Rev. Barton and mixed responses to Mrs. Leete: she was described either as being too stereotypically Victorian or as deserving a larger role.

12. Are there any particular ideas/theories/etc. that you:

*a. especially liked (specify)?*

*Despite the diversity of responses to this question, there was a consistent approval for equality of opportunity.*

*b. especially disliked (specify)?*

*No dominant trends, but there was a dislike of absolute economic equality and the authoritative nature of the industrial army. The separate status of women was noted by students in almost every sample.*

13. What do you think Bellamy's primary criticism of the nineteenth century was?
*Inequality and selfishness dominated; also frequently mentioned: poverty and labor problems.*

14. What do you think Bellamy liked best about the new world that West sees when he wakes up in the year 2000?
*Equality; also frequently mentioned: increase in cooperation and a decrease in strikes and poverty.*

15. What, *in your opinion*, was/is the worst characteristic of:

*a. the nineteenth century?*

*Labor problems and poverty dominated the responses.*

*b. the twentieth century?*

No dominant trends, though materialism, poverty, and environmental problems were mentioned consistently. Responses often related to current events. For instance, during the Gulf War, there were more comments about war, and during the later 1980s, there were more comments about homelessness as this problem gained publicity.

16. What, *in your opinion*, is the most significant improvement you'd like to see in the twenty-first century?

Increased equality of opportunity and decreased poverty were mentioned consistently. Of the numerous other types of responses many related to increased environmental protection and increased international cooperation.

17. Do you think *LB* is: a. still relevant; b. out of date?

|  | RELEVANT | | OUT OF DATE | |
|---|---|---|---|---|
| Combined Sample (535) | 81% | (435) | 19% | (100) |
| UT Arlington (250) | 83% | (207) | 17% | ( 43) |
| Arlington High (43) | 74% | ( 32) | 26% | ( 11) |
| U of Minnesota (96) | 82% | ( 79) | 18% | ( 17) |
| Hood College (18) | [ 83%] | ( 15) | [17%] | ( 3) |
| RPI (51) | 82% | ( 42) | 18% | ( 9) |
| U of Louisville (25) | 84% | ( 21) | 16% | ( 4) |
| Harvard Summer (12) | [ 75%] | ( 9) | [25%] | ( 3) |
| Wesley Palms (6) | [ 83%] | ( 5) | [17%] | ( 1) |
| Women's Group (5) | [ 40%] | ( 2) | [60%] | ( 3) |
| Campion, Canada (8) | [100%] | ( 8) | [ 0%] | ( 0) |
| ICU, Japan (20) | 70% | ( 14) | 30% | ( 6) |
| Klagenfurt, Aus. (1) | | ( 1) | | ( 0) |

18. Do you think *LB* should be read as:

*a. a realistic and practical social criticism and model for actual reform?*

*b. a speculative work with some possible applications?*

*c. a "thought experiment" with little value for application?*

*d. other: e.g., an adventure/love story, a fantasy?*

|  | REALISTIC | | SPECULATIVE | | THOUGHT | | OTHER | |
|---|---|---|---|---|---|---|---|---|
| Combined Sample (538) | 9% | (49) | 63% | (338) | 23% | (123) | 5% | (28) |
| UT Arlington (256) | 11% | (28) | 61% | (157) | 22% | (57) | 6% | (14) |
| Arlington High (40) | 5% | ( 2) | 50% | (20) | 45% | (18) | 0% | ( 0) |
| U of Minnesota (96) | 14% | (13) | 59% | (57) | 20% | (19) | 7% | ( 7) |
| Hood College (18) | [ 6%] | ( 1) | [72%] | (13) | [22%] | ( 4) | [ 0%] | ( 0) |
| RPI (51) | 0% | ( 0) | 80% | (41) | 18% | ( 9) | 2% | ( 1) |
| U of Louisville (25) | 8% | ( 2) | 72% | (18) | 16% | ( 4) | 4% | ( 1) |
| Harvard Summer (12) | [ 17%] | ( 2) | [50%] | ( 6) | [25%] | ( 3) | [ 8%] | ( 1) |
| Wesley Palms (6) | [ 0%] | ( 0) | [83%] | ( 5) | [17%] | ( 1) | [ 0%] | ( 0) |
| Women's Group (6) | [ 0%] | ( 0) | [17%] | ( 1) | [83%] | ( 5) | [ 0%] | ( 0) |
| Campion, Canada (8): | [ 12%] | ( 1) | [88%] | ( 7) | [ 0%] | ( 0) | [ 0%] | ( 0) |
| ICU (19) | [ 0%] | ( 0) | [68%] | (13) | [11%] | ( 2) | [21%] | ( 4) |
| Klag. (1) | | ( 0) | | ( 0) | | ( 1) | | ( 0) |

19. Do you think Bellamy primarily wanted to:

a. *change social systems?*

b. *change individual readers' feelings and thoughts?*

c. *both of the above equally?*

d. *neither of the above; he had other intents (specify)?*

| | SYSTEMS | INDIVIDUALS | BOTH | NEITHER |
|---|---|---|---|---|
| Combined Sample (534) | 8% (43) | 34% (184) | 55% (291) | 3% (16) |
| UT Arlington (253) | 7% (18) | 35% (89) | 56% (141) | 2% ( 5) |
| Arlington High (40) | 10% ( 4) | 30% ( 12) | 60% (24) | 0% ( 0) |
| U of Minnesota (95) | 12% ( 11) | 29% (28) | 53% (50) | 6% ( 6) |
| Hood College (18) | [16%] ( 3) | [28%] ( 5) | [ 50%] ( 9) | [ 6%] ( 1) |
| RPI (51) | 8% ( 4) | 41% ( 21) | 49% (25) | 2% ( 1) |
| U of Louisville (25) | 0% ( 0) | 44% ( 11) | 56% (14) | 0% ( 0) |
| Harvard Summer (12) | [16%] ( 2) | [16%] ( 2) | [ 68%] ( 8) | [ 0%] ( 0) |
| Wesley Palms (6) | [ 0%] ( 0) | [33%] ( 2) | [ 67%] ( 4) | [ 0%] ( 0) |
| Women's Group (5) | [ 0%] ( 0) | [20%] ( 1) | [ 40%] ( 2) | [ 40%] ( 2) |
| Campion, Canada (8) | [ 0%] ( 0) | [75%] ( 6) | [12.5%] ( 1) | [12.5%] ( 1) |
| ICU, Japan (20) | 5% ( 1) | 30% ( 6) | 65% (13) | 0% ( 0) |
| Klagenfurt, Austria (1) | ( 0) | ( 1) | ( 0) | ( 0) |

20. Did reading *LB* change your views about:

a. *society (if so, how?)*

*For those answering "yes," there was an emphasis on increasing awareness of flaws in their present society.*

| | YES | NO |
|---|---|---|
| Combined Sample (534) | 40% (214) | 60% (320) |
| UT Arlington (250) | 38% ( 96) | 62% (154) |
| Arlington High (43) | 51% ( 22) | 49% ( 21) |
| U of Minnesota (94) | 46% ( 43) | 54% ( 51) |
| Hood College (18) | [44%] ( 8) | [56%] ( 10) |
| RPI (51) | 33% ( 17) | 67% ( 34) |
| U of Louisville (25) | 44% ( 11) | 56% ( 14) |
| Harvard Summer (12) | [25%] ( 3) | [75%] ( 9) |
| Wesley Palms (6) | [17%] ( 1) | [83%] ( 5) |
| Women's Group (6) | [33%] ( 2) | [67%] ( 4) |
| Campion, Canada (8) | [25%] ( 2) | [75%] ( 6) |
| ICU, Japan (20) | 45% ( 9) | 55% ( 11) |
| Klagenfurt, Austria (1) | ( 0) | ( 1) |

b. *yourself (if so, how?)*

*For those responding "yes," the primary emphasis was on a need to find ways to help improve society (implications of guilt feelings). Fewer students responded to this question than to any other question, reinforcing the impression given by the low percentage responding "yes" that they did not believe LB altered there self perceptions.*

| | YES | NO |
|---|---|---|
| Combined Sample (526): | 27% (144) | 73% (382) |
| UT Arlington (241) | 32% ( 77) | 68% (164) |

(continued)

| | YES | | NO | |
|---|---|---|---|---|
| Arlington High (43) | 28% | ( 12) | 72% | ( 31) |
| U of Minnesota (95) | 22% | ( 21) | 78% | ( 74) |
| Hood College (18) | [22%] | ( 4) | [ 78%] | ( 14) |
| RPI (51) | 12% | ( 6) | 88% | ( 45) |
| U of Louisville (25) | 32% | ( 8) | 68% | ( 17) |
| Harvard Summer (12) | [25%] | ( 3) | [ 75%] | ( 9) |
| Wesley Palms (6) | [ 0%] | ( 0) | [100%] | ( 6) |
| Women's Group (6) | [50%] | ( 3) | [ 50%] | ( 3) |
| Campion, Canada (8) | [37%] | ( 3) | [ 63%] | ( 5) |
| ICU, Japan (20) | 30% | ( 6) | 70% | ( 14) |
| Klagenfurt, Austria (1) | | ( 1) | | ( 0) |

21. Would you recommend this book to someone else?
*a. if so, why?; if not, why?*

*The most frequent positive response was that LB provoked thought about alternative possibilities, worlds, societies, etc. Negative comments were often expressed in modifiers such as "boring" or "unrealistic," or by stating that there were "better" examples of utopian literature.*

| | YES | | NO | |
|---|---|---|---|---|
| Combined Sample (532) | 77% | (409) | 23% | (123) |
| UT Arlington (247) | 79% | (195) | 21% | ( 52) |
| Arlington High (43) | 70% | ( 30) | 30% | ( 13) |
| U of Minnesota (96) | 75% | ( 72) | 25% | ( 24) |
| Hood College (18) | [83%] | ( 15) | [ 17%] | ( 3) |
| RPI (51) | 71% | ( 36) | 29% | ( 15) |
| U of Louisville (25) | 88% | ( 22) | 12% | ( 3) |
| Harvard Summer (12) | [92%] | ( 11) | [ 8%] | ( 1) |
| Wesley Palms (6) | [83%] | ( 5) | [ 17%] | ( 1) |
| Women's Group (5) | [60%] | ( 3) | [ 40%] | ( 2) |
| Campion, Canada (8) | [75%] | ( 6) | [ 25%] | ( 2) |
| ICU, Japan (20) | 65% | ( 13) | 35% | ( 7) |
| Klagenfurt, Austria (1) | | ( 1) | | ( 0) |

Question 22 presented the instructions for describing the transformational associations. For summaries of responses to this question, see appendix B. For a summary of a specific sample, see appendix D. Here is the question: "What five types of influences (e.g., personal experiences; economic, social, or political attitudes; knowledge of other people; reading preferences; immediate situation of the reading experience; past courses; etc.) were particularly important in shaping your responses to *Looking Backward*? Be specific: describe the influence, which part or parts of the book affected you, and the nature of the response (e.g., positive, negative, mixture of positive and negative). List the most important influence last. Use the back of this sheet for the list of influences, parts of the text, and responses." Note: UTA students wrote a paper to answer this question.

Questions 23 through 50 related to general reading habits. These questions were not used for most of the samples. Questions 51 through 62 related to biographical background. For a summary of this information, see appendix A.

# Sample List of Transformational Associations

The following sample list of transformational associations is based on reading analyses written in 1983 at the University of Texas at Arlington. The number in parentheses indicates how many times the association was mentioned.

*Previous Academic Experiences 9 (7+, 2–) [+ indicates a positive response; – a negative response]*

SPECIFIC COURSES:
History (read *LB,* so the surprise end was no surprise; 1–); U.S. history (1+); Psychology (1–); Political science "equality" (1+); English (wrote a similar story, though better: (1+); Art (1+); Economics (1+); Government (1+)

GENERAL EXPERIENCE: ENJOYS STUDYING HISTORY (1+)

*Reading/Viewing Tastes 30 (20+, 10–)*

GENERAL PREFERENCES
Likes: science fiction (2+); romances (2+); surprise endings (1+); Gothic romances with class differences (1–); imagery/symbolism (1+); happy endings with romance (1+); utopian literature (1+)

Dislikes: science fiction (1–); exciting cover blurbs and dull historical openings (1–); wordiness (1–); formula endings (1+); overly detailed descriptions (1–) Marxist/Communist books (1–); dystopias (1+); futuristic works (1–); foreign language books (1–)

SPECIFIC WRITTEN OR VIDEO WORKS
*Utopia* (1–); *Nineteen Eighty-four* (1+, 1–); *Animal Farm* (1+); *The Jungle* (1+); "House of Usher" (1+); "Rip Van Winkle" (1+); favorite ghost story (1+); biblical prophesies

(1+); *The Jetsons* (1+); favorite space comedy (1+); historical documentary on late nineteenth century (1+)

## Circumstances While Reading 34 (18+, 16−)

### PHYSICAL ENVIRONMENT

alone/late night (identify with West's isolation; 3+); quiet/night (2+, 1−); cold/quiet (identify with West, 1+); private study (1+); library (1−); comfortable univ. center area (1+)

### EFFECT OF ASSIGNMENT/SCHOOL

forced to look for influences (1+, 1−); lack confidence in paper writing ability (1−); heavy paper-writing load (1−); English class low priority (1+, 1−); required to read Bellamy (2−)

### OTHER EXPERIENCES

reading the book twice (2−); rereading specific paragraphs (2+); watching boyfriend's sister (1+); live in a house for the "needy" (1−); upset about ill pet (1−); bad weather (1−); sunny winter day (1−); fight with boyfriend (1+); sick (1−); living in Chinese community (1+); conversation about sports salaries (1+); reading *The Jungle* (1+); dreamlike state while reading (1+); upset about oversleeping (1−)

## Previous Personal Experiences 37 (32+, 5−)

### KNOWING PEOPLE WITH CHARACTERS OR SITUATIONS SIMILAR TO BELLAMY'S
### CHARACTERS

Girlfriend (1−); fiancee (1+); handicapped uncle (1+); friend who visited another country (1+); friend in a coma for a year (1+); woman who suddenly became wealthy (1+); member of a minority (1−); meeting a person similar to a past acquaintance (1+);

### CHARACTERISTICS OF SELF (THE READER)

mixture of realism and idealism (1+); guided by "middle-age practical" goals (1−); role as mother (1+)

### OTHER EXPERIENCES

King of the Mountain childhood game (1+); discussions with friend about Marxism (1−); return to hometown (1+); receiving unfair wages (1+); live in socialist Germany (1+); education exp. (1+); collect records (1+); job experience (4+, 1−); impact of dreams (1+); high school graduation (1+); college experience (1+); moving to new locales (3+); tight finances (1+); playing Monopoly (1+); disorientations after waking up from surgery, etc. (3+); frustrations about Christmas shopping (1+); desire to be a coach but know how low the pay can be (1+); difficulty explaining a new-found truth to friends (1+)

## Attitudes/Beliefs 68 (30+, 34−, 4+/−)

### LIKES AND DISLIKES

Likes: capitalism (3−); education (2+); time travel imaginatively (1+); music (4+); hypnosis (1+); individual freedom (1−); competition (2−); peace (1+); animals (1−);

homes with personality (1–); time to travel (1+); interesting personal relationships (1+); politics (1+); science/technology (1+, 1–); statistics (1+)

Dislikes: TV religion (1–); trends in our society (1+); expensive concerts (1+); sermons (1–); socialism (3–, 1+); any talk about unions (2–); commercial competition (1+); preaching not based on the Bible (1–); middlemen (1+); lawyers (1+); communism (2–); selfishness (1+); threat of physical punishment as motivation (1–); hypnosis (1–)

General Attitudes About: concept of an ideal society (2+, 1–, 1+/–); human motivation (2–); Braniff failure (1+); shopping (1–); social interdependence (1+); twentieth-century women (2+, 3–, 1+/–); inability of humans to achieve high ideals (1–); the poor (1+); social security (1+, 1+/–); relationship between achievement and reward (1+); the economies of N. and S. Vietnam (2–); national differences (1–); U.S. as military peacekeeper (1–); family relations (1 +/–); menial jobs (1–).

# Notes

Preface

    1. Except where specifically indicated, all page references will be to John L. Thomas's excellent Belknap-Harvard edition of *Looking Backward*.

Introduction

    1. See Edward Rothstein's 5 February 2000, *New York Times* article "Paradise Lost" for evidence of renewed interest in utopian studies. The exhibit catalogue, *Utopia: The Search for the Ideal Society in the Western World*, was edited by Roland Schaer, Gregory Claeys, and Lyman Tower Sargent. Several of the important bibliographies include Moichi's "Japanese Utopian Literature" and Sargent's "Australian Utopian Literature," *New Zealand Utopian Literature*, and "Utopian Literature in English Canada." Six of the important works published since 2000 include Kitch's *Higher Ground: From Utopianism to Realism in American Feminist Thought and Theory*; Moylan's *Scraps of the Untainted Sky: Science Fiction, Utopia, and Dystopia*; Matarese's *American Foreign Policy and the Utopian Imagination*; Pordzik's *The Quest for Postcolonial Utopia*; Wegner's *Imaginary Communities: Utopia, the Nation and the Spacial Histories of Modernity*; and Parrinder's collection *Learning from Other Worlds*, which focuses more on science fiction than on literary utopias. For recent studies of the late nineteenth- and early twentieth-century period, see Matarese, as well as Lewes, Peyser, and Shor (*Utopianism*) in the Works Cited list. The best evaluative source for recent books is the extensive book review section of *Utopian Studies*. Very recent titles are listed in *Utopus Discovered*, the newsletter of the Society for Utopian Studies, and on the newsletter website: www.coloradocollege/edu/Dep/EN/Utopus/.

    2. For general bibliographies, see Lewis, Negley, and especially Sargent's *British and American Utopian Literature*. For an excellent example of a single-author bibliography, see Widdicombe's *Edward Bellamy*.

3. For examples, see Cornet, Fitting ("Positioning and Closure"), Khanna ("Reader in *Looking Backward*" and "Text as Tactic"), Shor ("Ideological Matrix"), Widdicombe ("Edward Bellamy's Utopian Vision"), and several of my articles ("Contexts and Texts," "Getting 'Nowhere,'" "Literary Domestication," "Perceptual Origins," and "Prescriptions for Readers").

4. See Angenot's, Spencer's, and McKnight's articles in the Works Cited list, and Moylan's *Scraps of the Untainted Sky*, especially 3–8.

5. One of the essays in Boyarin's *Ethnography of Reading* that is especially relevant to this study is Elizabeth Long's "Textual Interpretation as Collective Action" (180–211).

6. Harris offered an indication of her work in progress in her MLA paper, "Literary Hostesses."

7. The minister of education, who later became minister of labor, was William Pember Reeves. The prime minister was John Ballance. See Bowman, *Bellamy Abroad*, 236. For discussions of the impact of late nineteenth-century utopian literature in America, see Forbes, Matarese, Pfaelzer (*Utopian Novel*), Parrington, Roemer (*Obsolete Necessity* and *America as Utopia*), Simmons, and Shor (*Utopianism*). For the impact abroad, see Bowman (*Bellamy Abroad*), Sargent (*New Zealand*), Shor ("Ideological Matrix"), and Toth. For a recent study of Bellamy's and other utopists' influence throughout the English-speaking world, see Pordzik's *The Quest for Postcolonial Utopia*.

Chapter 1

1. Of the many discussions of definitions of literary utopias, three are especially relevant to this study: Suvin, *Metamorphoses*, 37–62; Sargent, "Three Faces," 5–13; and Roemer, *America as Utopia*, 1–15.

2. Sargent, *British and American Utopian Literature, 1516–1975* and *British and American Utopian Literature, 1516–1985*; Negley, *Utopian Literature*; Winter, *Compendium Utopiarum*; and Lewis, *Utopian Literature*.

3. Overviews of the themes can be found in standard studies such as Manuel and Manuel, *Utopian Thought in the Western World,* and Kumar, *Utopia and Anti-Utopia in Modern Times* and *Utopianism,* and also in the brief annotations in Sargent's bibliographies and the full annotations in Lewis's bibliography.

4. See Sargent, "Capitalist Eutopias in America" and Fitting, "Utopia beyond Our Ideals."

5. For example, see Atkinson, "Visions of Peach Blossom Spring," and Fung, "Notes on the Make-Do Garden."

6. For an excellent discussion of the role of romance narratives in utopian literature, see Jacobs, "*Islandia*: Plotting Utopian Desire."

Chapter 2

1. For reviews of other well-known and obscure late nineteenth-century American utopias, see Roemer, *Obsolete Necessity,* 186–208.

2. For valuable surveys of the scholarship, see Sargent's first bibliography, *British and American Utopian Literature, 1516–1975,* 167–290; Widdicombe, "Early Histories of Uto-

pian Thought," 1–38; and the extensive review section of each issue of *Utopian Studies*. For one of the few discussions of "real" readers, see Roemer, "Utopian Literature, Empowering Students, and Gender Awareness," 395–97.

3. The Society for Utopian Studies has a particularly useful website with important links and information about listservs (www.utoronto.ca/utopia/). The society's newsletter, *Utopus Discovered,* carries information about relevant websites.

4. Rimmer discussed the title change in a public letter dated January 1979 and entitled "DON'T LET THE COVER AND THE BACK COPY OF MY NEW NOVEL *LOVE ME TOMORROW* mislead you!" He mailed out the letter at his own expense.

5. The respectable number of farmers may in part be explained by the promotion by the Farmers' Alliance of an inexpensive Houghton Riverside edition of *Looking Backward* (Kopp, "Looking Back" 3).

6. For example, see Schneekloth, 18–21 and Jacob, 103–19.

7. See David, "The Unexpurgated *A Connecticut Yankee*," 99–117, and Inge, "Mark Twain and Dan Beard's Collaborative *Connecticut Yankee*," 169–227.

8. Kopp, "Looking Back" 4; Kopp "Looking Back . . . Exhibit" 3. Griffith does list one other edition, published by the World Publishing Company in 1946, as having "decorations" (8). There is an illustrated edition of a long excerpt from *Equality* that was published by Charles H. Kerr (n.d.) as part of the Pocket Library of Socialism. The title is *The Parable of the Water Tank*. The line drawings depict figures in Greco-Roman attire to enhance the allegorical-mythic nature of the parable. One of the evil soldiers has a dollar sign imprinted on his breastplate (23).

9. Pagination for the introduction was designated in lowercase letters. Information about the number of copies printed appeared on an unpaginated page after Bellamy's postscript. Easton Press published a fine edition reprint in 1981.

10. Kopp, "Looking Back . . . Exhibit" 10. *Art Index* offers three brief references for Elise Cavanna; they are exhibition reviews for the Forsythe Gallery and Heller Gallery in California, published in 1950 and 1954 in *Art Digest* and *Art News*. (See especially Millier.) The 1950 Forsythe Gallery exhibition included line drawings, lithographs, and textile designs. Cavanna evidently remarried. In 1954 she was cross-referenced as Mrs. James B. Welton. After the name change, there are no further references to her.

11. As is the case with all page references to the text of *Looking Backward,* this page refers to Thomas's 1962 Belknap edition. The page references to illustrations in the previous paragraphs refer to the 1941 Hollywood edition.

12. See especially her "Non-Euclidean View of California as a Cold Place to Be," 80–100, which she wrote while she was working on *Always Coming Home*.

13. In a personal letter to me dated 19 May 1991, she specifically mentioned five scholars: Dell Hymes, Karl Kroeber, Jarold Ramsey, Barre Toelken, and Melville Jacobs.

14. In letters dated 4 December 1991 and 7 February 1995, she specifically mentions Leslie Marmon Silko's *Ceremony* and Linda Hogan's poetry. In her 19 May 1991 letter she mentions that contemporary Native American literature "especially by women . . . is a miracle and delight to me."

15. See the special section of *Utopian Studies* 2.1 and 2 (1991), 1–60, which is devoted to Le Guin.

16. One sad irony of the publishing history is that, *Always Coming Home* was out of print, for several years. Fortunately, University of California Press reprinted it in 2001.

17. Another obvious point of compatibility is Iser's concept of a form of negation that invokes "familiar and determinate elements of knowledge only to cancel them out" (*Prospecting* 34).

18. This trend is particularly clear in Levitas's *Concept of Utopia* (see especially 198–200).

19. In *Always Coming Home*, Le Guin repeatedly makes effective use of the hinge metaphor.

20. For example, see Khanna, "Text as Tactic," 39; Morson, 92; Suvin, *Metamorphoses*, 49, 53–58; Pfaelzer, "Immanence," 51; Wegner's discussion of Marin, "Horizons," 63; and Ruppert, 4–5.

21. See Roemer, "Nowhere beyond the Pale," 5–6.

Chapter 3

1. For discussion of and bibliographic information about early American literary utopias, see Nydahl, Parrington, and Sargent's second bibliography, *British and American Utopian Literature, 1516–1985*. For discussions of other forms of early utopian expression, see Fogarty, Eberwein, Mohawk, Sweet, and Sargent, "Utopianism in Colonial America."

2. Segal and Lipow emphasize this sense of loss within the contexts of technological utopianism and the Nationalist movement. Wiebe places his discussion of the desire for order within the general contexts of historical developments from 1877 to 1920.

3. The desire for order was especially obvious in the utopists' descriptions of economic and governmental systems, city plans, and daily activities. See Roemer, *Obsolete Necessity* 91–93, 100, 136–38, 151–52, 160–61, 172–73, 175, 180.

4. See Auerbach 32–34, 37–39; Kumar, *Utopia and Anti-Utopia* 149, 158–59.

5. Harben's *Land of the Changing Sun* is a dystopia; hence, he offered a negative view of these vast technological developments.

6. The "technological" utopias described by Segal 19–32, the "progressive" utopias described by Pfaelzer, *Utopian Novel* 26–51, and many of the "cooperative" utopias described by Rooney 102–11, strongly reflect these values, as do most of the other late nineteenth-century utopias (Roemer, "Utopia and Victorian Culture" 315–20). Significant exceptions are the "conservative" utopias (e.g., Wheeler's *Our Industrial Utopia*, 1895) and the agrarian utopias, such as Howells's *Altrurian Romances,* as well as the few utopias that advocate premarital sex (e.g., Howard's *The Milltillionaire,* 1895).

7. See Sargent, "Capitalist Eutopias," and Fitting, "Utopia beyond Our Ideals."

8. For example, see Rooney 19–36, Segal 56–73, Nydahl 237–51, and Manuel and Manuel 33–63, 413–531, 697–756, 773–87.

9. These include the scholars listed in note 1, as well as Perry Miller, Ernest Lee Tuveson, Sacvan Bercovitch, David Smith, and Paul Boyer.

10. In *American Foreign Policy and the Utopian Imagination* Susan Matarese repeatedly stresses that the late nineteenth-century utopian depictions of international relations were decidedly nationalistic. If they bothered to pay any attention to global per-

spectives, the authors typically perceived the rest of the world evolving along the lines of an American utopia. For example, see *Looking Forward* (1899), which was written by Arthur Bird, an ex-vice consul-general of America at Port-au-Prince, Haiti.

11. These scholars include Pfaelzer, Quissell, Lewes, Kessler, Patai, and me. Although Jacobs focuses on Austin Tappan Wright's *Islandia*, she offers excellent insights about the use of romantic plots in *Looking Backward* (e.g., 79). In their discussions of eighteenth- and nineteenth-century fiction Herbert Brown tends to use "sentimental"; Kelley uses "domestic"; Baym uses "woman's fiction"; and Susan Harris uses "exploratory." Here and in chapter 4 "domestic" and "sentimental" are the most appropriate for my comparisons.

12. For a more detailed description of the desire for unity as expressed in late nineteenth-century utopian literature, see Roemer, *Obsolete Necessity* 91–93, 136–38, 151–52, 160–61, 172–73.

13. For example, see Hart 306–10.

14. See Schiffman 716–32; Rooney 24–27, 152–56; Thomas, *Alternative America* 237–61; and Roemer *Obsolete Necessity* 22–25, 32, 44, 50, 59, 87–88, 95–101.

Chapter 4

1. See Kelley, *Private Woman* viii. Even eighteenth-century works such as Susanna Rowson's *Charlotte Temple* (1791) and Hannah Foster's *The Coquette* (1797) "remained steady sellers into the last half of the nineteenth century" (Davidson, *Revolution* 135). As indicated in note 11 for chapter 3, the terms *domestic* and *sentimental* fiction suit my comparisons better than *woman's fiction* or *exploratory* fiction.

2. Besides the scholars mentioned in chapter 3, several other scholars have made brief comments about the relationships between *Looking Backward* and works such as *Uncle Tom's Cabin*. For example, see Aaron 101, Bowman, *Year 2000* 116, 117, Elliott 108–10, Fromm v, Hart 183, Khanna, "Reader" 69, Lipow 30, Lokke 124, 142, Schweninger 107–09, Tichi 8, Towers 52. More extended discussions of connections between domestic and utopian fiction that are particularly relevant to this chapter include Pfaelzer, *Utopian Novel* 28–39, Roemer, "Perceptual Origins" 17–20, Quissell, "Sentimental," especially 131–41, 163–81, Dowst, esp. 95–106, and Kolmerten, "Texts and Contexts" 108–09, 117–25.

3. Bellamy's early novels, especially *Miss Ludington's Sister* (1884), demonstrate his knowledge of some of the sentimental and domestic fiction conventions, as do several of his short stories (see Griffith 11–14) and literary notices in the *Springfield Daily Union* (see Griffith 17–34). Sylvia Bowman notes that in an August 15, 1877, *Springfield Daily Union* essay entitled "What Reading for the Young," Bellamy conceded that "mushy stories filled with lifeless morality could do little harm" to adolescents (qt. in *Edward Bellamy* 93).

4. See Morgan's *Plagiarism in Utopia,* and Suvin, *Metamorphoses* 177.

5. Pagination in Michael Bellamy's unpublished manuscript appears either by chapter or by parts within each chapter.

6. For more detailed discussion of this scene, see Ruppert 64–65, and Roemer, "Contexts and Texts" 220–21.

7. For example, see Dupont 759–63, Roemer, *Obsolete Necessity* 60–62, Thomas, *Alternative America* 238–41, Towers 52–63, Wilson xxxii–xxxiii, Winters 29–36.

8. Michael Bellamy notes that there is an earlier Bellamy character named West—

the Rev. Stephen West in *Duke of Stockbridge*, which was serialized in 1879. This character seems backward-looking; he sides with the moneyed powers during the time of
Shay's Rebellion (ch. 5, pt. 1, 1).

## Chapter 5

1. For example, see my survey "Utopian Studies," and Khanna ("The Reader"; "Truth
and Art"), Ruppert, Somay, Suvin ("Concept" and *Metamorphoses*), Levitas (*Concept of
Utopia*), Tom Moylan, Wegner, and the Fredric Jameson special issue of *Utopian Studies*
9.2 (1998).

2. In this particular discussion I have been especially influenced by Wolfgang Iser
(*Implied Reader, Act of Reading, Prospecting*), Jonathan Culler ("Literary Competence"),
Robert DeMaria, and Stanley Fish (*Is There a Text in This Class?*).

3. For example, see Dupont, Lewis ("Utopian Dreams"), Quissell ("Sentimental"),
Thomas (*Alternative America*), and Towers.

4. See Ruppert 64–65, 72, and Roemer ("Contexts and Texts" 220–21).

5. For a convincing discussion of parallels between Bellamy's beliefs and Puritan
concepts, see Hall's "The Religious Ethics of Edward Bellamy and Jonathan Edwards."

6. See Griffith's bibliography of reviews and articles (16–34).

## Chapter 6

1. There are numerous references to the book-length responses to *Looking Backward* in the following studies. The page references are highly selective: Parrington 69–
78; Rooney 93–140; Pfaelzer, *Utopian Novel* 86–92; Lewes 12, 28–29, 36–37; Shor, *Utopianism* 3–26; and Roemer, *Obsolete Necessity* 6–7, 56–83.

2. *The Boston Evening Transcript* review, "The Millennium of Socialism," also suggested that Bellamy was guilty of plagiarism (6), a charge that Bellamy ignored in his
postscript.

3. For example, see "The Millennium of Socialism," *Boston Evening Transcript* review
(6); see also Morgan, *Plagiarism in Utopia*, and Suvin, *Metamorphoses* 71.

## Afterword

1. The vest was displayed at both the Paris and New York exhibits. I attended in
New York. For a detailed review of both exhibits and the exhibit catalogue, see Fitting,
"Representing Utopia."

# Works Cited

Aaron, Daniel. *Men of Good Hope: A Story of American Progressives*. New York: Galaxy-Oxford UP, 1961.

Akutagawa, Ryunosuke. *Kappa: A Novel*. Trans. Geoffrey Bownas. 1927. Tokyo: Tuttle, 1971.

Amory, Hugh, and David D. Hall, eds. *A History of the Book in America: The Colonial Book in the Atlantic World*. Vol. 1. New York: Cambridge UP, 2000.

Andreä, Johann Valentin. *Reipublicae Christianopolis descripto*, 1619. New Haven: Research Publications, 1970.

Angenot, Marc. "The Absent Paradigm: An Introduction to the Semiotics of Science Fiction." *Science-Fiction Studies* 6 (1979): 9–19.

Aristophanes. *Ecclesiazusae*. Ed. R. G. Usser. Oxford: Clarendon, 1973.

Astor, John Jacob. *A Journey in Other Worlds. A Romance of the Future*. New York: Appleton, 1994.

Atkinson, Alan. "Visions of Peach Blossom Spring: Artistic Recreations of a Fourth-Century Chinese Utopia." Society for Utopian Studies Conference. Menger Hotel, San Antonio. 12 Nov. 1999.

Atwood, Margaret. *The Handmaid's Tale*. Boston: Houghton, 1986.

Auerbach, Jonathan. "'The Nation Organized': Utopian Impotence in Edward Bellamy's *Looking Backward*." *American Literary History* 6 (1994): 24–47.

Ballance, John. "The Altruistic State." Rev. of *Looking Backward, 2000–1887*, by Edward Bellamy. *Monthly Review* Apr. 1890: 217–19.

Baxter, Sylvester. "The Author of *Looking Backward*." *New England Magazine* ns 1 (1889): 92–98.

Baym, Nina. *Novels, Readers and Reviewers: Responses to Fiction in Antebellum America*. Ithaca: Cornell UP, 1984.

————. *Woman's Fiction: A Guide to Novels by and about Women in America, 1820–1870.* Ithaca: Cornell UP, 1978.

"Beauties of Bellamism." Rev. of *Looking Backward, 2000–1887,* by Edward Bellamy. *Liberty* 25 Jan. 1890: 7.

Bellamy, Charles J. *An Experiment in Marriage. A Romance.* Albany: Albany Book Co., 1889.

Bellamy, Edward. *Dr. Heidenhoff's Process.* New York: Appleton, 1880.

————. *The Duke of Stockbridge.* 1879. Ed. Joseph Schiffman. Cambridge: Belknap-Harvard UP, 1962.

————. *Equality.* New York: Appleton, 1897.

————. "How and Why I Wrote *Looking Backward.*" *America as Utopia.* Ed. Kenneth M. Roemer. New York: Burt Franklin, 1981. 22–27.

————. "How I Came to Write *Looking Backward.*" *Nationalist* May 1889: 1–4.

————. "How I Wrote *Looking Backward.*" *Ladies Home Journal* Apr. 1894: 2.

————. "*Looking Backward* Again." *North American Review* Mar. 1890: 351–63.

————. *Looking Backward, 2000–1887.* 1888. New York: Limited Editions Club, 1941.

————. *Looking Backward, 2000–1887.* 1941. Norwalk: Easton, 1981.

————. *Looking Backward, 2000–1887.* 1888. Ed. John Thomas. Cambridge: Belknap-Harvard UP, 1967.

————. "A Love Story." *Century* May 1888: 26–38.

————. *Miss Ludington's Sister.* Boston: Osgood, 1884.

————. *The Parable of the Water Tank.* No. 18, Pocket Library of Socialism. Chicago: Charles H. Kerr, n.d.

————. "The Religion of Solidarity." *The Philosophy of Edward Bellamy.* Ed. Arthur E. Morgan. New York: King's Crown, 1945. 7–25.

————. "Woman in the Year 2000." *Ladies Home Journal.* Feb. 1891. 3.

Bellamy, Michael. *"Pleasure Reconciled to Virtue": Edward Bellamy's Utopian Quest.* Ts.

Bennett, Tony. "Texts in History: The Determination of Readings and Their Texts." *Post-Structuralism and the Question of History.* Ed. Derek Attridge, et al. Cambridge: Cambridge UP, 1987. 63–81.

Bercovitch, Sacvan. "The Typography of America's Mission." *American Quarterly* 30 (1978): 135–55.

Bird, Arthur. *Looking Forward: A Dream of the United States of the Americas in 1999.* Utica: Childs, 1899.

Blathwayt, Raymond. "'Looking Forward': A Talk with the Author of *Looking Backward.*" *Great Thoughts from Master Minds* 8 Jan. 1892: 8–10.

Bleich, David. "Epistemological Assumptions in the Study of Response." *Reader-Response Criticism: From Formalism to Post-Structuralism.* Ed. Jane P. Tompkins. Baltimore: Johns Hopkins UP, 1980. 134–63.

————. "Eros and Bellamy." *American Quarterly* 16 (1964): 445–59.

————. "Gender Interests in Reading and Language." *Gender and Reading: Essays on Readers, Texts, and Contexts.* Ed. Elizabeth Flynn and Patrocinio Schweickart. Baltimore: Johns Hopkins UP. 234–66.

———. *Subjective Criticism.* Baltimore: Johns Hopkins UP, 1978.

"Book-Talk." *Lippincott's* July 1889: 136.

Bourdieu, Pierre. *Distinction: A Social Critique of the Judgment of Taste.* Trans. Richard Nice. Cambridge: Harvard UP, 1984.

Bowman, Sylvia. "Edward Bellamy." *American Literary Realism* 1 (1967): 7–12.

———. *Edward Bellamy.* Boston: Twayne, 1986.

———. *The Year 2000: A Critical Biography of Edward Bellamy.* New York: Bookman, 1958.

———, et al. *Bellamy Abroad: An American Prophet's Influence.* New York: Twayne, 1962.

Boyarin, Jonathan, ed. *The Ethnography of Reading.* Berkeley: U of California P, 1993.

Boyer, Paul. *When Time Shall Be No More: Prophecy Belief in Modern American Culture.* Cambridge: Harvard UP, 1992.

Brown, Gillian. "Getting in the Kitchen with Dinah: Domestic Politics in *Uncle Tom's Cabin.*" *American Quarterly* 36 (1984): 503–23.

Brown, Herbert Ross. *The Sentimental Novel in America 1789–1860.* 1940. New York: Octagon, 1975.

Bryan, Clark W. "Edward Bellamy." Rev. of *Looking Backward, 2000–1887,* by Edward Bellamy. *Good Housekeeping* 21 Dec. 1889: 95–96.

Budd, Louis, ed. *A Listing of and Selection from Newspaper and Magazine Interviews with Samuel L. Clemens, 1874–1910.* Arlington: American Literary Realism, 1977.

Butler, Octavia E. *The Parable of the Sower.* New York: Warner, 1993.

———. *The Parable of the Talents.* New York: Seven Stories P, 1998.

Butler, Samuel. *Erewhon; or, Over the Range.* London: Trübner, 1872.

———. *Erewhon Revisited Twenty Years Later, Both by the Original Discoverer and by His Son.* London: Richards, 1901.

Cabet, Étienne. *Voyage en Icarie.* 1840. 5th ed. Paris: Au bureau du Populaire, 1848.

Callenbach, Ernest. *Ecotopia: The Notebooks and Reports of William Weston.* Berkeley: Banyan Tree Books, 1975.

———. *Ecotopia Emerging.* Berkeley: Banyan Tree Books, 1981.

Campanella, Tommaso. *La città del sole: dialogo poetico. The City of the Sun: A Poetical Dialogue.* 1619. Trans. Daniel J. Donno. Berkeley: U of California P, 1981.

Carlson, Scott. "Minority Students Posted Slight Increase in College Enrollment in 1997, Report Says." *Chronicle of Higher Education* 17 Dec. 1999: A53.

Cary, John, ed. *The Farber Book of Utopias.* London: Farber and Farber, 1999.

Cavallo, Guglielmo, and Roger Chartier, eds. *A History of Reading in the West.* Trans. Lydia G. Cochrane. Amherst: U of Massachusetts P, 1999.

Chernyshevsky, Nikolai G. *What Is to Be Done? Tales about New People.* 1863. Trans. Benjamin R. Tucker. New York: Random House, 1961.

Cocteau, Jean. *Les enfants terribles, roman.* Paris: Bernard Grasset, 1925.

Cooper, James Fenimore. *The Crater; or, Vulcan's Peak. A Tale of the Pacific.* New York: Burgess, Stringer, 1847.

Cornet, Robert J. "Rhetorical Strategies in *Looking Backward*." *Markham Review* 4.3 (1974): 53–58.

Cowie, Alexander. "The Vogue of the Domestic Novel, 1850–1870." *South Atlantic Quarterly* 41 (1942): 416–24.

Culler, Jonathan. "Literary Competence." *Reader-Response Criticism: From Formalism to Post-Structuralism.* Ed. Jane P. Tompkins. Baltimore: Johns Hopkins UP, 1980. 101–17.

———. "Prolegomena to a Theory of Reading." *The Reader in the Text: Essays on Audience and Interpretation.* Ed. Susan R. Suleiman and Inge Crosman. Princeton: Princeton UP, 1980. 46–66.

———. *Structuralist Poetics: Structuralism, Linguistics and the Study of Literature.* Ithaca: Cornell UP, 1975.

Cummins, Maria Susanna. *The Lamplighter.* Boston: Jewett, 1854.

Danky, James P., and Wayne A. Wiegand, eds. *Print Culture in a Diverse America.* Urbana: U of Illinois P, 1998.

David, Beverly R. "The Unexpurgated *A Connecticut Yankee*: Mark Twain and His Illustrator Daniel Carter Beard." *Prospects* 1 (1975): 99–117.

Davidson, Cathy. *Revolution and the Word: The Rise of the Novel in America.* New York: Oxford UP, 1986.

———, ed. *Reading in America: Literature and Social History.* Baltimore: Johns Hopkins UP, 1989.

Defoe, Daniel. *Robinson Crusoe.* 1719. New York: Knopf, 1992.

Delany, Samuel R. *Triton.* New York: Bantam, 1976.

de Laveleye, Emile. "Two New Utopias." Rev. of *Looking Backward, 2000–1887,* by Edward Bellamy, and *Études Sociales,* by Charles Secrétan. *Eclectic Magazine* Apr. 1890: 433–45.

DeMaria, Robert, Jr. "The Ideal Reader: A Critical Fiction." *PMLA* 93 (1978): 463–74.

Donnelly, Ignatius. *Caesar's Column: A Story of the Twentieth Century.* Chicago: Schult, 1890.

Dostoyevsky, Fyodor Mikhaylovich. *Notes from Underground and the Grand Inquisitor.* 1864. Trans. Ralph E. Matlaw. New York: Dutton, 1960.

Dowst, Kenneth. "The Rhetoric of Utopian Fiction." Diss. U of Pittsburgh, 1979.

Dupont, V. *L'Utopie et le roman utopique dans la litterature anglaise.* Cahors: Coueslant; Paris: Didier, 1941.

Eagleton, Terry. *Literary Theory: An Introduction.* Minneapolis: U of Minneapolis P, 1983.

Eberwein, Jane Donahue. "Looking Further Backward: Puritan and Revolutionary American Utopias." *CEA Critic* 52. 1 and 2 (1989, 1990): 87–96.

"Edward Bellamy." *People* 29 May 1898: 2.

Elliott, Robert C. *The Shape of Utopia: Studies in a Literary Genre.* Chicago: U of Chicago P, 1970.

Emerson, Ralph Waldo. "The Young American." *The Collected Works of Ralph Waldo*

*Emerson*. Vol. 1. *Nature, Addresses, and Lectures*. Introd. and notes, Robert
    Spiller. Text established by Alfred R. Ferguson. Cambridge: Belknap-Harvard
    UP, 1971. 217–44.

Escarpit, Robert. *Sociology of Literature*. Trans. Ernest Pick. Plainesville: Lake Erie
    College Press, 1965.

Esrock, Ellen J. *The Reader's Eye: Visual Imaging as Reader Response*. Baltimore: Johns
    Hopkins UP, 1994.

Evans, Augusta J. *St. Elmo: A Novel*. 1867. North Stratford: Ayer, 1975.

Fawcett, E. Douglas. "*Looking Backward* and the Socialist Movement." Rev. of *Looking
    Backward, 2000–1887*, by Edward Bellamy. *Theosophist* June 1890: 475–85.

Feagin, Susan. *Reading with Feeling: The Aesthetics of Appreciation*. Ithaca: Cornell UP,
    1996.

Ferns, Chris. *Narrating Utopia: Ideology, Gender, Form in Utopian Literature*. Liverpool:
    Liverpool UP, 1999.

Fetterley, Judith. *The Resisting Reader: A Feminist Approach to American Fiction*.
    Bloomington: Indiana UP, 1978.

Fish, Stanley. *Is There a Text in This Class? The Authority of Interpretive Communities*.
    Cambridge: Harvard UP, 1980.

———. "Literature in the Reader: Affective Stylistics." *Reader-Response Criticism:
    From Formalism to Post-Structuralism*. Ed. Jane P. Tompkins. Baltimore: Johns
    Hopkins UP, 1980. 70–100.

Fiske, Amos K. *Beyond the Bourn [ . . . ]*. New York: Fords, Howard & Hulbert, 1891.

Fitting, Peter. "The Concept of Utopia in the Work of Fredric Jameson." *Utopian
    Studies* 9.2 (1998): 8–17.

———. "Positioning and Closure: On the 'Reading Effect' of Contemporary Utopian
    Fiction." *Utopian Studies*. Vol. 1. Ed. Gorman Beauchamp and Kenneth M.
    Roemer. Washington: UP of America, 1987. 23–36.

———. "Utopia beyond Our Ideals: The Dilemma of the Right-Wing Utopia." *Utopian
    Studies* 2: 1 and 2 (1991): 95–109.

Flynn, Elizabeth. "Gender and Reading." *Gender and Reading: Essays on Readers, Texts,
    and Contexts*. Ed. Elizabeth Flynn and Patrocinio Schweickart. Baltimore:
    Johns Hopkins UP, 1986. 267–88.

———, and Patrocinio Schweickart, eds. *Gender and Reading: Essays on Readers, Texts,
    and Contexts*. Baltimore: Johns Hopkins UP, 1986.

Fogarty, Robert. *Dictionary of American Communal and Utopian History*. Westport,
    Conn.: Greenwood P, 1980.

Forbes, Allyn B. "The Literary Quest for Utopia, 1880–1900." *Social Forces* 6 (1927):
    179–89.

Fortunati, Vita, and Raymond Trousson, eds. *Dictionary of Literary Utopias*. Paris:
    Honoré Champion, 2000.

Foster, Susan Lynch. "Romancing the Cause: Fourierism, Feminism, and Free Love in
    *Papa's Own Girl*." *Utopian Studies* 8.1 (1997): 31–54.

*Fredric Jameson*. Spec. issue of *Utopian Studies* 9.2 (1998): 1–77.

Freeman, William. "Looking Backward, 2000–1887." Rev. of *Looking Backward,*
    *2000–1887,* by Edward Bellamy. *Zealandia* Nov. 1889: 296–97.

"A French Opinion of *Looking Backward.*" Rev. of *Looking Backward, 2000–1887,*
    by Edward Bellamy. *Review of Reviews* Nov. 1890: 457.

Freund, Elizabeth. *The Return of the Reader: Reader-Response Criticism.* London:
    Methuen, 1987.

Fromm, Eric. Forward. *Looking Backward, 2000–1887.* By Edward Bellamy. New York:
    New American Library, 1960. v–xx.

Fung, Stanislaus. "Notes on the Make-Do Garden." *Utopian Studies* 9.1 (1998):
    142–48.

Garrison, Dee. "Immoral Fiction in the Late Victorian Library." *American Quarterly* 26
    (1976): 71–89.

"General Gossip of Authors and Writers." *Current Literature* Mar. 1890: 185.

George, Henry. *Progress and Poverty: An Inquiry [ . . . ].* 1879. New York: Modern
    Library-Random House, n.d.

———. Rev. of *Looking Backward, 2000–1887. Standard* 31 Aug. 1889: 1–2.

Gervereau, Laurent. "Symbolic Collapse: Utopia Challenged by Its Representations."
    *Utopia: Search for the Ideal World in the Western World.* Ed. Roland Schaer,
    Gregory Claeys, and Lyman Tower Sargent. New York: Oxford UP, 2000.
    357–67.

Gillette, King C. *The Human Drift.* 1894. Facsim. ed. Introd. Kenneth M. Roemer.
    Delmar: Scholars' Facsimiles & Reprints, 1976.

———. *The People's Corporation.* New York: Boni and Liveright, 1924.

———. *"World Corporation."* Boston: New England News, 1910.

Gilman, Charlotte Perkins. *Herland.* 1915. Introd. Ann J. Lane. New York: Pantheon-
    Random, 1979.

Gilman, Nicholas P. "Nationalism in the United States." *Quarterly Journal of Economics*
    4 (1889): 50–76.

———. "The Way to Utopia." Rev. of *Looking Backward, 2000–1887,* by Edward
    Bellamy. *Unitarian Review* July 1890: 48–66.

Gilmore, William. *Reading Becomes a Necessity of Life: Material and Cultural Life in
    Rural New England.* Knoxville: U of Tennessee P, 1989.

Griffith, Mary. "Three Hundred Years Hence." *Camperdown; or, News from Our
    Neighborhood.* Philadelphia: Carey, 1836. 9–92.

Griffith, Nancy Snell. *Edward Bellamy: A Bibliography.* Metuchen: Scarecrow, 1986.

Gronlund, Laurence. *Coöperative Commonwealth in Its Outlines: An Exposition in
    Modern Socialism.* 1884. Ed. Stow Persons. Cambridge: Belknap-Harvard UP,
    1965.

Guarneri, Carl J. *The Utopian Alternative: Fourierism in Nineteenth-Century America.*
    Ithaca: Cornell UP, 1991.

Guttin, Jacques. *Epigone, histoire du siècle futur.* Paris: Lamy, 1659.

Hall, David D. *Cultures of Print: Essays in the History of the Book.* Amherst: U of
    Massachusetts P, 1996.

Hall, Richard A. S. "The Religious Ethics of Edward Bellamy and Jonathan Edwards."
    *Utopian Studies* 8.2 (1997): 13–31.
Haller, John S., Jr., and Robin M. Haller. *The Physician and Sexuality in Victorian
    America*. Urbana: U of Illinois P, 1974.
Hansot, Elisabeth. *Perfection and Progress: Two Modes of Utopian Thought*. Cambridge:
    MIT P, 1974.
Harben, Will N. *The Land of the Changing Sun*. New York: Merriam, 1894.
Harrington, James. *Common-wealth of Oceana*. London: Streater, 1656.
Harris, Neil. "Utopian Fiction and Its Discontents." *Uprooted Americans: Essays to
    Honor Oscar Handlin*. Ed. Richard L. Bushman, et al. Boston: Little Brown,
    1979. 209–44.
Harris, Susan K. "Literary Hostesses: Annie Adams Fields and Mary Gladstone Drew."
    MLA Convention. Hyatt Regency, Chicago. 29 Dec. 1999.
———. *19th-Century American Women's Novels: Interpretive Strategies*. Cambridge:
    Cambridge UP, 1990.
Harris, W. T. "Edward Bellamy's Vision." Rev. of *Looking Backward, 2000–1887*, by
    Edward Bellamy. *Forum* Oct. 1889: 199–208.
Hart, James D. *The Popular Book: A History of American Literary Taste*. Berkeley: U of
    California P, 1961.
Hartman, Matthew. "Utopian Evolution: The Sentimental Critique of Social
    Darwinism by Bellamy and Peirce." *Utopian Studies* 10.1 (1999): 26–41.
Hawthorne, Nathaniel. *The Blithedale Romance*. Boston: Ticknor, 1852.
Hayden, Dolores. *The Grand Domestic Revolution: A History of Feminist Designs for
    American Homes, Neighborhoods, and Cities*. Cambridge: MIT P, 1981.
Hayes, Kevin J. "The Book in American Utopia Literature." *Visible Language* 31.1 (1997):
    64–85.
Heinemann, William. "The Revolt Against the Rule of the Rich: or, An American Short
    Cut to the Millennium." Rev. of *Equality* and *Looking Backward, 2000–1897*,
    by Edward Bellamy. *Review of Reviews* Aug. 1897: 191–200.
Herzl, Theodor. *Altneuland, Roman*. 1902. *Gesammelte Zionistische Werke*. Vol. 5.
    Tel Aviv: Hozaah Ivrith, 1935.
———. *The Jewish State*. 1896. New York: Dover, 1989.
Higgs, William. "Some Objections to Mr. Bellamy's Utopia." Rev. of *Looking Backward,
    2000–1887*, by Edward Bellamy. *New Englander and Yale Review* Mar. 1890:
    231–39.
Hildreth, Charles. Rev. of *Looking Backward, 2000–1887*, by Edward Bellamy. *Belford's
    Magazine* Jan. 1890: 291.
Hills, William. "Literary News and Notes." *Author* 15 Nov. 1889: 156–60.
Hochman, Barbara. *Getting at the Author: Reimagining Books and Reading in the Age
    of American Realism*. Amherst: U of Massachusetts P, 2001.
Holland, Norman N. *5 Readers Reading*. New Haven: Yale UP, 1975.
Housekeeper. "A Plain Talk with Mr. Bellamy." *Good Housekeeping* 1 Mar. 1890:
    213–15.

Howard, Albert Waldo. *The Milltillionaire*. Boston: Author, 1895.

Howe, Daniel Walker. "American Victorianism as Culture." *American Quarterly* 27 (1975): 507–32.

———, ed. *Victorian America*. Philadelphia: U of Pennsylvania P, 1976.

Howe, Ron. "Reconsidering Edward Bellamy in the Year 2000." *Revising the Legacy of Edward Bellamy (1850–1898), American Author and Social Reformer*. Ed. Toby Widdicombe and Herman Preiser. Lewiston: Mellen, 2002. 417–32.

Howells, William Dean. *The Altrurian Romances*. Ed. Clara Kirk and Rudolf Kirk. Bloomington: Indiana UP, 1968.

———. "Editor's Study." Rev. of *Looking Backward, 2000–1887*, by Edward Bellamy. *Harper's* June 1888: 154–55.

———. "Edward Bellamy." *Atlantic* Aug. 1898: 253–56.

———. *A Traveler from Altruria*. New York: Harper, 1894.

Hunt, H. L. *Alpaca*. Dallas: Hunt, 1960.

———. *Alpaca Revisited*. Dallas: H. L. H. Products, 1967.

Huxley, Aldous. *Ape and Essence*. New York: Harper, 1948.

———. *Brave New World*. Garden City: Doubleday-Doran, 1932.

———. *Island*. New York: Harper & Row, 1962.

[Illustrations for *Looking Backward*.] *Boston Globe* 4 May 1890: 25.

Inge, M. Thomas. "Mark Twain and Dan Beard's Collaborative Connecticut Yankee." *Author-ity and Textuality: Current Views of Collaborative Writing*. Ed. James S. Leonard, et al. West Cornwall: Locust Hill P, 1994. 169–227.

Iser, Wolfgang. *The Act of Reading: A Theory of Aesthetic Response*. Baltimore: Johns Hopkins UP, 1978.

———. *The Implied Reader: Patterns of Communication in Prose Fiction from Bunyan to Beckett*. Baltimore: Johns Hopkins UP, 1974.

———. *Prospecting: From Reader Response to Literary Anthropology*. Baltimore: Johns Hopkins UP, 1989.

J. A. M. "Looking Backward." Rev. of *Looking Backward, 2000–1887*, by Edward Bellamy. *Knox College Monthly and Presbyterian Magazine* 10.4 (1889): 209–12.

Jacob, Johanna. "Calvino's Reality: Designer's Utopia." *Utopian Studies* 9.1 (1998): 103–19.

Jacobs, Naomi. "*Islandia*: Plotting Utopian Desire." *Utopian Studies* 6.2 (1995): 75–89.

Jameson, Fredric. "Comments." *Utopian Studies* 9.2 (1998): 74–77.

———. "'If I find one good city, I will spare the man': Realism and Utopia in Kim Stanley Robinson's *Mars* Trilogy." *Learning from Other Worlds: Estrangement, Cognition, and the Politics of Science Fiction and Utopia*. Ed. Patrick Parrinder. Durham: Duke UP, 2001. 208–32.

———. Progress versus Utopia; or, Can We Imagine the Future?" *Science-Fiction Studies* 9 (1982): 147–58.

———. "Of Islands and Trenches: Neutralization and the Production of Utopian Discourse." *Diacritics* 7.2 (1977): 2–21.

Jauss, Hans Robert. "Literary History as a Challenge to Literary Theory." *New Literary History* 2 (1970): 7–37.

Jenkins, Henry. *Textual Poachers: Television Fans and Participatory Culture.* New York: Routledge, 1992.

Kaestle, Carl F., et al. *Literacy in the United States: Readers and Reading since 1880.* New Haven: Yale UP, 1991.

Kaledin, Eugenia. "Teaching Bellamy in China." Society for Utopian Studies Conference. Emerson College, Boston. 1 Oct. 1988.

Karp, Andrew. "Utopian Tension in L. Frank Baum's Oz." *Utopian Studies* 9.2 (1998): 103–21.

Kelley, Mary. *Private Woman, Public Stage: Literary Domesticity in Nineteenth-Century America.* New York: Oxford UP, 1984.

———. "The Sentimentalists: Promise and Betrayal in the Home." *Signs* 4 (1979): 434–46.

Kessler, Carol Farley, ed. *Daring to Dream: Utopian Stories by United States Women, 1836–1919.* Rev. ed. Syracuse: Syracuse UP, 1995.

Khanna, Lee Cullen. "The Reader and *Looking Backward.*" *Journal of General Education* 33 (1981): 69–79.

———. "Text as Tactic . . ." *Looking Backward, 1988–1888: Essays on Edward Bellamy.* Ed. Daphne Patai. Amherst: U of Massachusetts P, 1988. 37–50.

———. "Truth and Art in Women's Worlds: Doris Lessing's *Marriages between Zones Three, Four, and Five.*" *Women and Utopia: Critical Interpretations.* Ed. Marleen Barr and Nicholas Smith. Washington: UP of America, 1983. 121–34.

Kitch, Sally L. *Higher Ground: From Utopianism to Realism in American Feminist Thought.* Chicago: U of Chicago P, 2000.

Kolmerten, Carol A. *Women in Utopia: The Ideology of Gender in the American Owenite Communities.* Bloomington: Indiana UP, 1990.

———. "Texts and Contexts: American Women Envision Utopia, 1890–1920." *Utopian and Science Fiction by Women: Worlds of Difference.* Syracuse: Syracuse UP, 1994. 107–25.

Kopp, James J. "Looking Back at *Looking Backward:* Collecting Edward Bellamy's Utopian Novels." Society for Utopian Studies Conference. Vancouver. 21 Oct. 2000.

———. "Looking Back at *Looking Backward:* Collecting Edward Bellamy's Utopian Novels: Exhibit Catalogue." Portland: Lewis and Clark College, 2000.

Kroeber, A. L. *Handbook of the Indians of California.* Bulletin 78, Bureau of American Ethnography of the Smithsonian Institution. Washington: Government Printing Office, 1925.

Kuhlman, Hilke. "The Reception of *Walden Two* in Intentional Communities in North America." Diss. Albert Ludwigs U zu Freiburg. 1999–2000.

Kumar, Krishan. *Utopia and Anti-Utopia in Modern Times.* Oxford: Basil Blackwell, 1987.

———. *Utopianism.* Minneapolis: U of Minnesota P, 1991.

Lane, Mary E. *Mizora: A Prophecy.* New York: Dillingham, 1889.

Le Guin, Ursula K. *Always Coming Home.* New York: Harper & Row, 1985.

———. *The Dispossessed.* New York: Harper & Row, 1974.

———. *The Left Hand of Darkness.* New York: Ace, 1969.

———. Letter to the author. 19 May 1991.

———. Letter to the author. 25 June 1995.

———. Letter to the author. 29 Feb. 2000.

———. "A Non-Euclidean View of California as a Cold Place to Be." *Dancing at the Edge of the World: Thoughts on Words, Women, Places.* New York: Grove, 1989. 80–100.

———. "The Ones Who Walk Away from Omelas." *New Directions* 3. Ed. Robert Silverberg. Garden City: Nelson Doubleday, 1973. 1–8.

Leibacher-Ouvrard, Lise. "*Epigone, Histoire du siècle futur* (1659): Reflexions sur l'histoire, le temps et la littérature." Society for Utopian Studies Conference. Montreal, 16 Oct. 1998.

Leslie, Marina. *Renaissance Utopias and the Problem of History.* Ithaca: Cornell UP, 1998.

Lessing, Doris. *The Marriages between Zones Three, Four, and Five.* New York: Knopf, 1980.

Levitas, Ruth. *The Concept of Utopia.* Syracuse: Syracuse UP, 1990.

———. "Who Holds the Hose: Domestic Labour in the Work of Bellamy, Gilman, and Morris." *Utopian Studies* 6.1 (1995): 65–84.

Lewes, Darby. *Dream Revisionaries: Gender and Genre in Women's Utopian Fiction 1870–1920.* Tuscaloosa: U of Alabama P, 1995.

Lewis, Arthur O., Jr. "The Utopian Dream." *Directions in Literary Criticism.* Ed. Stanley Weintraub and Philip Young. University Park: Pennsylvania State UP, 1973. 190–200.

———. *Utopian Literature in the Pennsylvania State University Libraries: A Selected Bibliography.* University Park: Pennsylvania State U Libraries, 1984.

Lipow, Arthur. *Authoritarian Socialism in America: Edward Bellamy and the Nationalist Movement.* Berkeley: U of California P, 1982.

Lloyd, Henry Demarest. *Wealth against Commonwealth.* New York: Harper, 1894.

Lloyd, John Uri. *Etidorhpa; or, The End of Earth.* Cincinnati: Lloyd, 1895.

Lokke, Virgil L. "The American Utopian Anti-Novel." *Frontiers of American Culture.* Ed. Ray B. Browne, et al. West Lafayette: Purdue UP, 1968. 123–53.

London, Jack. *The Iron Heel.* New York: Macmillan, 1908.

Long, Elizabeth. "Textual Interpretation as Collective Action." *The Ethnography of Reading.* Ed. Jonathan Boyarin. Berkeley: U of California P, 1993. 180–211.

"A Look Ahead." Rev. of *Looking Backward, 2000–1887,* by Edward Bellamy. *Literary World* 17 Mar. 1888: 85–86.

"'Looking Backward': A Socialistic Dream." Rev. of *Looking Backward, 2000–1887,* by Edward Bellamy. *Christian Union* 17 May 1888: 617–18.

Lyons, Martyn. "New Readers in the Nineteenth Century." *A History of Reading in the*

*West*. Ed. Guglielmo Cavallo and Roger Chartier. Trans. Lydia G. Cochrane. Amherst: U of Massachusetts P, 1999. 313–44.

Mabie, Hamilton W. "The Most Popular Novels in America." *Forum* Dec. 1893: 508–16.

MacNair, Everett. *Edward Bellamy and the Nationalist Movement, 1889 to 1994*. Milwaukee: Fitzgerald, 1957.

Machor, James L. *Readers in History: Nineteenth-Century American Literature and Contexts of Response*. Baltimore: Johns Hopkins UP, 1993.

Macnie, John. *The Diothas: or, a Far Look Ahead*. New York: Putnam's, 1883.

Maher, Michael. "A Socialist's Dream." Rev. of *Looking Backward, 2000–1887*, by Edward Bellamy. *Month* Jan. 1891: 1–19; Feb. 1891: 173–88.

Mailloux, Steven. *Interpretive Conventions: The Reader in the Study of American Fiction*. Ithaca: Cornell UP, 1982.

Manguel, Alberto. *A History of Reading*. New York: Viking, 1996.

———, and Gianni Guadalupi. *The Dictionary of Imaginary Places*. Rev. ed. New York: Harcourt, 2000.

Manuel, Frank, and Fritzi Manuel. *Utopian Thought in the Western World*. Cambridge: Belknap-Harvard UP, 1979.

Marin, Louis. *Utopics: Spatial Play*. Trans. Robert A. Vollrath. Atlantic Highlands: Humanities, 1984.

Martin, Terence. "The Negative Structures of American Literature." *American Literature* 57 (1985): 1–22.

Martyn, Carlos. "The Success of *Looking Backward*." Rev. of *Looking Backward, 2000–1887*, by Edward Bellamy. *Knights of Labor* 6 Feb. 1890: n.pag.

Matarese, Susan M. *American Foreign Policy and the Utopian Imagination*. Amherst: U of Massachusetts P, 2001.

McClung, W. A. "Designing the Text: An Interdisciplinary Experiment." *Humanities in the South* 65 (1987): 8–11.

McKnight, Ed. "Reader-Response Theory and Science Fiction." *SFRA Review* 247 (2000): 13–17.

M'Cready, Mr. Rev. of *Looking Backward, 2000–1887*, by Edward Bellamy. *Standard* 2 June 1888: 8.

Melville, Herman. *Typee* [ . . . ]. London: Murray, 1846.

Mercier, Louis-Sébastien. *Memoirs of the Year 2500*. 1771. New York: Gregg, 1977.

Merriam, Alexander R. "Some Literary Utopias." *Hartford Seminary Record* May 1898: 203–26.

Merrill, Albert Adams. *The Great Awakening*. Boston: George Book, 1899.

Meyrick, Geraldine. "The Ethics of Nationalism." Rev. of *Looking Backward, 2000–1887*, by Edward Bellamy. *Overland Monthly* June 1890: 566–68.

Michaelis, Richard C. *Looking Further Forward, An Answer to* Looking Backward *by Edward Bellamy*. Chicago: Rand, McNally, 1890.

"The Millennium of Socialism." Rev. of *Looking Backward, 2000–1887*, by Edward Bellamy. *Boston Evening Transcript* 30 Mar. 1888: 6.

Miller, Perry. *Errand into the Wilderness*. 1956. New York: Harper Torchbook, 1964.

Millier, Arthur. "Los Angeles Events." *Art Digest* June 1950: 21.

Mohawk, John. *Utopian Legacies: A History of Conquest and Oppression in the Western World.* Santa Fe: Clear Light, 1999.

Moichi, Yoriko. "Japanese Utopian Literature from the 1870s to the Present and the Influence of Western Utopianism." *Utopian Studies* 10.2 (1999): 89–97.

Moore, David A. *The Age of Progress [ . . . ].* New York: Sheldon, 1856.

Moorer, Zoe W. Re: "Married Students at UTA." E-mail to the author. 9 Aug. 1999.

More, Thomas. [ . . . ] *Insul Utopia.* Frankfurt am Main: Henning Grossens Buchhandlung, 1704.

———. *Utopia: A New Translation, Backgrounds, Criticism.* Ed. and trans. Robert M. Adams. New York: Norton, 1975.

Morgan, Arthur E. *Edward Bellamy.* New York: Columbia UP, 1944.

———. *Nowhere Was Somewhere; How History Makes Utopias and How Utopias Make History.* Chapel Hill: U of North Carolina P, 1946.

———. *Plagiarism in Utopia [ . . . ].* Yellow Springs: Morgan, 1944.

Morris, William. "Looking Backward." Rev. of *Looking Backward, 2000–1887,* by Edward Bellamy. 1889. *Science-Fiction Studies* 8 (1976): 287–89.

———. *News from Nowhere; or, An Epoch of Rest, Being Some Chapters from a Utopian Romance.* Boston: Roberts Bros., 1890.

Morson, Gary Saul. *The Boundaries of Genre. Dostoevsky's Diary of a Writer and the Traditions of Literary Utopia.* Austin: U of Texas P, 1981.

Mott, Frank Luther. *Golden Multitudes: The Story of Best Sellers in the United States.* New York: Bowker, 1960.

Moylan, Michele, and Lane Stiles, eds. *Reading Books: Essays on the Material Text and Literature in America.* Amherst: U of Massachusetts P, 1996.

Moylan, Tom. *Demand the Impossible: Science Fiction and the Utopian Imagination.* New York: Methuen, 1986.

———. *Scraps of Untainted Sky: Science Fiction, Utopia, and Dystopia.* Boulder: Westview, 2000.

Myers, Joseph R. *Edward Bellamy Writes Again.* N.p.: Author, 1997.

"Nationalism and Modern Romance." Rev. of *Looking Backward, 2000–1887,* by Edward Bellamy. *New Nation* 23 Jan. 1892: 57.

Negley, Glenn. *Utopian Literature: A Bibliography with a Supplementary Listing of Works Influential in Utopian Thought.* Lawrence: Regents P of Kansas, 1977.

Neihardt, John G. *Black Elk Speaks: Being the Life Story of a Holy Man of the Oglala Sioux.* 1932. Introd. Vine Deloria, Jr. Lincoln: U of Nebraska P, 1979.

"The New Utopia." Rev. of *Looking Backward, 2000–1887,* by Edward Bellamy. *Pilot* 7 Apr. 1888: 1.

"New Utopia: What Might Be in the Twentieth Century." Rev. of *Looking Backward, 2000–1887,* by Edward Bellamy. *New York Tribune* 5 Feb. 1888: 10.

"Novels." Rev. of *Looking Backward, 2000–1887,* by Edward Bellamy. *Saturday Review* 24 Mar. 1888: 356–57.

"Novels." Rev. of *Looking Backward, 2000–1887,* by Edward Bellamy. *Saturday Review* 27 Apr. 1889: 508–09.

Nydahl, Joel. "Early Fictional Futures: Utopia, 1798–1864." *America as Utopia.* Ed. Kenneth M. Roemer. New York: Burt Franklin, 1981. 254–91.

———. "From Millennium to Utopia Americana." *America as Utopia.* Ed. Kenneth M. Roemer. New York: Burt Franklin, 1981. 237–53.

Oates, Joyce Carol. "Pleasure, Duty, Redemption Then and Now: Susan Warner's *Diana.*" *American Literature* 59 (1987): 422–27.

Ong, Walter J. "The Writer's Audience Is Always Fiction." *PMLA* 90 (1975): 9–21.

Orwell, George. *Nineteen Eighty-Four.* London: Secker & Warburg, 1949.

"Our Weekly News-Letter." *Twentieth Century* 28 May 1898: 14.

Papashvily, Helen Waite. *All the Happy Endings: A Study of the Domestic Novel in America, the Women Who Wrote It, the Women Who Read It, in the Nineteenth Century.* New York: Harper, 1956.

Parrinder, Patrick. "Eugenics and Utopia: Sexual Selection from Galton to Morris." *Utopian Studies* 8.2 (1997): 1–12.

———, ed. *Learning from Other Worlds: Estrangement, Cognition, and the Politics of Science Fiction and Utopia.* Durham: Duke UP, 2001.

Parrington, Vernon Louis, Jr. *American Dreams: A Study of American Utopias.* Providence: Brown UP, 1947.

Patai, Daphne. "British and American Utopias by Women (1836–1979): An Annotated Bibliography." *Alternative Futures* 4 (1981): 184–206.

———, ed. *Looking Backward, 1988–1888. Essays on Edward Bellamy.* Amherst: U of Massachusetts P, 1988.

Pawley, Christine. *Reading on the Middle Border: The Culture of Print in Late Nineteenth-Century Osage, Iowa.* Amherst: U of Massachusetts P, 2001.

Peebles, H. P. "The Utopias of the Past Compared with the Theories of Bellamy." *Overland Monthly* June 1890: 574–77.

Petter, Henri. *The Early American Novel.* Columbus: Ohio State UP, 1971.

Peyser, Thomas. *Utopia and Cosmopolis: Globalization in the Era of American Literary Realism.* Durham: Duke UP, 1998.

Pfaelzer, Jean. "Immanence, Interdeterminance, and the Utopian Pun in *Looking Backward.*" *Looking Backward, 1988–1888: Essays on Edward Bellamy.* Ed. Daphne Patai. Amherst: U of Massachusetts P, 1988. 51–67.

———. *The Utopian Novel in America, 1886–1896: The Politics of Form.* Pittsburgh: U of Pittsburgh P, 1984.

"Philanthropic Fiction." *Literary World* 25 May 1889: 176–77.

Piercy, Marge. *He, She, and It.* New York: Knopf, 1991.

———. *Woman on the Edge of Time.* New York: Knopf, 1976.

Plato. *The Republic.* Rev. ed. Trans. Desmond Lee. New York: Viking-Penguin, 1995.

Pordzik, Ralph. *The Quest for Postcolonial Utopia: A Comparative Introduction to the Utopian Novel in New English Literature.* New York: Lang, 2001.

Poulet, Georges. "Criticism and the Experience of Interiority." *Reader-Response Criticism: From Formalism to Post-Structuralism.* Ed. Jane P. Tompkins. Baltimore: Johns Hopkins UP, 1980. 41–49.

Prettyman, Gib. "Gilded Age Utopias of Incorporation." *Utopian Studies* 12.1 (2001): 19–40.

Prince, Gerald. "Notes on the Text as Reader." *The Reader in the Text: Essays on Audience and Interpretation.* Ed. Susan R. Suleiman and Inge Crosman. Princeton: Princeton UP, 1980. 225–40.

Putnam, J. Pickering. *Architecture under Nationalism.* Boston: Nationalist Educational Assn., 1890.

Quissell, Barbara. "The New World That Eve Made: Feminist Utopias Written by Nineteenth-Century Women." *America as Utopia.* Ed. Kenneth M. Roemer. New York: Burt Franklin, 1981. 148–74.

———. "The Sentimental and Utopian Novels of Nineteenth Century America: Romance and Social Issues." Diss. U of Utah, 1973.

Rabinowitz, Peter J. *Before Reading: Narrative Conventions and the Politics of Interpretation.* Ithaca: Cornell UP, 1987.

———. "Truth in Fiction: A Reexamination of Audiences." *Critical Inquiry* 4 (1977): 121–41.

Radway, Janice. *Reading the Romance: Women, Patriarchy, and Popular Literature.* New introd., Radway. Chapel Hill: U of North Carolina P, 1991.

Ramsey, Milton Worth. *Six Thousand Years Hence.* Minneapolis: Roper, 1891.

Rand, Ayn. *Atlas Shrugged.* New York: Random, 1957.

"Recent American Fiction." Rev. of *Looking Backward, 2000–1887,* by Edward Bellamy. *Atlantic* June 1888: 845–46.

"Recent Books." Rev. of *Looking Backward, 2000–1887,* by Edward Bellamy. *New York Times* 27 Feb. 1888: 3.

"Recent Fiction." Rev. of *Looking Backward, 2000–1887,* by Edward Bellamy. *Independent* 29 Mar. 1888: 16.

"Recent Fiction." Rev. of *Looking Backward, 2000–1887,* by Edward Bellamy. *Overland Monthly* Aug. 1888: 214.

"Recent Novels." Rev. of *Looking Backward, 2000–1887. Nation* 29 Mar. 1888: 266.

Reeves, William Pember. "Socialist Millennium." Rev. of *Looking Backward, 2000–1887,* by Edward Bellamy. *Lyttelton Times* 5 Aug. 1889: n.pag.

Reynolds, Mack. *Equality: In the Year* 2000. New York: Ace, 1977.

Richards, I. A. *Practical Criticism.* New York: Harcourt Brace, 1929.

Rimmer, Robert. *The Harrad Experiment.* 1966. Buffalo: Prometheus, 1990.

———. Letter to the public. Jan. 1979.

———. *Love Me Tomorrow.* New York: Signet-New American Library, 1978.

———. *The Premar Experiments.* New York: Signet-New American Library, 1975.

———. *Proposition 31.* New York: Signet-New American Library, 1968.

Roberts, J. W. *Looking Within. The Misleading Tendencies of* Looking Backward *Made Manifest.* New York: Barnes, 1893.

Robinson, Kim Stanley. *The Gold Coast.* New York: Tor, 1988.

———. *Pacific Edge.* New York: Ace, 1990.

Roemer, Kenneth M. "Contexts and Texts: The Influence of *Looking Backward.*" *Centennial Review* 27 (1983): 204–23.

———. "Getting 'Nowhere' beyond Stasis: A Critique, a Method, and a Case." *Looking*

*Backward, 1988–1888: Essays on Edward Bellamy.* Ed. Daphne Patai. Amherst: U of Massachusetts P, 1988. 126–46.

———. "The Literary Domestication of Utopia: There's No Looking Backward without Uncle Tom and Uncle True." *American Transcendentalist Quarterly* ns 3 (1989): 101–22.

———. "Nowhere beyond the Pale." Society for Utopian Studies Convention. Toronto. 21 Oct. 1995.

———. *The Obsolete Necessity: America in Utopian Writings, 1888–1900.* Kent: Kent State UP, 1976.

———. "104 + 1 Readers Reading Utopia." Society for Utopian Studies Conference. St. Louis. 7 Oct. 1984.

———. "Perceptual Origins: Preparing American Readers to See Utopian Fiction." *Utopian Thought in American Literature.* Ed. Arno Heller, et al. Tübingen: Gunter Narr Verlag, 1988. 7–24.

———. "Prescriptions for Readers (and Writers) of Utopias." Rev. of *Reader in a Strange Land,* by Peter Ruppert. *Science-Fiction Studies* 15 (1988): 88–93.

———. "Technology, Culture, and Utopia: Gillette's Unity Regained." *Technology and Culture* 26 (1985): 560–70.

———. "Utopia and Victorian Culture." *America as Utopia.* Ed. Roemer. New York: Burt Franklin, 1981. 305–32.

———. "Utopian Literature, Empowering Students, and Gender Awareness." *Science-Fiction Studies* 23 (1996): 393–405.

———. "Utopian Studies: A Fiction with Notes Appended." *Extrapolation* 24 (1984): 318–34.

———, ed. *America as Utopia.* New York: Burt Franklin, 1981.

Rooney, Charles J., Jr. *Dreams and Visions: A Study of American Utopias, 1865–1917.* Westport, Conn.: Greenwood P, 1985.

Rosemont, Franklin. "Bellamy's Radicalism Reclaimed." *Looking Backward, 1988–1888: Essays on Edward Bellamy.* Ed. Daphne Patai. Amherst: U of Massachusetts P, 1988. 147–209.

Rosenblatt, Louise. *Literature as Exploration.* 5th ed. New York: MLA, 1995.

———. *The Reader, the Text, the Poem: The Transactional Theory of the Literary Work.* 1978. Carbondale: Southern Illinois UP, 1994.

Rothstein, Edward. "Paradise Lost: Can Mankind Live without Its Utopias?" *New York Times* 5 Feb. 2000, natl. ed.: B1+.

Rowson, Susanna Haswell. *Charlotte Temple.* 1791. Ed. Cathy N. Davidson. New York: Oxford UP, 1986.

Ruppert, Peter. *Reader in a Strange Land: The Activity of Reading Literary Utopias.* Athens: U of Georgia P, 1986.

Russ, Joanna. *The Female Man.* New York: Bantam, 1975.

Russell, Addison Peale. *Sub-Coelum.* Boston: Houghton Mifflin, 1893.

Ryan, Barbara, and Amy M. Thomas, eds. *Reading Acts: U.S. Readers' Interactions with Literature, 1800–1950.* Knoxville: U of Tennessee P, 2002.

Sargent, Lyman Tower. "Australian Utopian Literature: An Annotated Chronological
        Bibliography, 1667–1999." *Utopian Studies* 10.2 (1999): 138–73.

———. *British and American Utopian Literature, 1516–1975. An Annotated Bibliography*.
        Boston: G. K. Hall, 1979.

———. *British and American Utopian Literature, 1516–1985*. New York: Garland. 1988.

———. "Capitalist Eutopias in America." *America as Utopia*. Ed. Kenneth M. Roemer.
        New York: Burt Franklin, 1981. 192–205.

———. *New Zealand Utopian Literature. An Annotated Bibliography*. Occasional Paper
        97/1. Wellington: Stout Research Center, Victoria U of Wellington, 1996.

———. "Re: Utopias Count." E-mail to the author. 6 Feb. 2003.

———. "The Three Faces of Utopianism Revisited." *Utopian Studies* 5.1 (1994): 1–37.

———. "Utopian Literature in English Canada: An Annotated Chronological
        Bibliography." *Utopian Studies* 10.2 (1999): 174–206.

———. "Utopianism and the Creation of New Zealand National Identity." *Utopian
        Studies* 12.1 (2001): 1–18.

———. "Utopianism in Colonial America." *History of Political Thought* 4 (1983):
        483–522.

———, and Gregory Claeys, eds. *The Utopia Reader*. New York: New York UP, 1999.

Sargisson, Lucy. *Contemporary Feminist Utopianism*. London: Routledge, 1996.

Saxton, Mark. *The Isar: A Narrative of Lang III*. Boston: Houghton, 1969.

"Science Fiction in Academe." Spec. sec. of *Science-Fiction Studies* 23 (1996): 371–528.

Schiffman, Joseph. "Edward Bellamy's Religious Thought." *PMLA* 68 (1953): 716–32.

Schindler, Solomon. *Young West: A Sequel to Edward Bellamy's Celebrated Novel
        Looking Backward*. Boston: Arena, 1894.

Schneekloth, Lynda H. "Unredeemably Utopian: Architecture and Making/Unmaking
        the World." *Utopian Studies* 9.1 (1998): 1–25.

Scholes, Robert. *Protocols of Reading*. New Haven: Yale UP, 1989.

Schweninger, Lee. "The Building of the City Beautiful: The Motif of the Jeremiad in
        Three Utopian Novels." *American Literary Realism* 18 (1985): 107–119.

Segal, Howard P. *Technological Utopianism in American Culture*. Chicago: U of
        Chicago P, 1985.

Serafini, Luigi. *Codex Seraphinianus*. Milan: Ricci, 1981.

Shakespeare, William. *The Tempest*. Ed. Northrop Frye. Baltimore: Penguin, 1959.

Sharp, William. Rev. of *Looking Backward, 2000–1887*, by Edward Bellamy. *Academy* 27
        Apr. 1889: 284.

Sheldon, Charles M. *In His Steps: "What Would Jesus Do?"* Chicago: Advance, 1897.

Shor, Francis. "The Ideological Matrix of Reform in Late 19th-Century America and
        New Zealand: Reading Edward Bellamy's *Looking Backward*." *Prospects* 17
        (1992): 29–58.

———. *Utopianism and Radicalism in a Reforming America, 1888–1918*. Westport,
        Conn.: Greenwood P, 1997.

Shortt, Adam. Rev. of *Looking Backward, 2000–1887*, by Edward Bellamy. *Presbyterian
        and Reformed Review* 2.6 (1891): 272–81.

Shurter, Robert. Introd. *Looking Backward, 2000–1887*. By Edward Bellamy. New York: Modern Library, 1951. v–xxi.

———. "The Utopian Novel in America, 1865–1900." Diss. Case Western Reserve U, 1936.

Shuttleworth, H. C. "Present Day Utopias, Utopias, Ancient and Modern." *Monthly Packet* Dec. 1895: 655–60.

Sibley, Mulford Q. *Technology and Utopian Thought*. Minneapolis: Burgess, 1971.

Sicherman, Barbara. "Reading and Middle-Class Identity in Victorian America: Cultural Consumption, Conspicuous and Otherwise." *Reading Acts: U.S. Readers' Interactions with Literature, 1800–1950*. Ed. Barbara Ryan and Amy M. Thomas. Knoxville: U of Tennessee P, 2002. 137–60.

Simmons, James R. "Utopian Cycles: Trends in American Visions of the Alternative Society." *Extrapolation* 39 (1998): 199–218.

Simpson, William. *The Man from Mars*. San Francisco: Bacon, 1891.

Skinner, B. F. *Shaping of a Behaviorist*. New York: Knopf, 1979.

———. *Walden Two*. 1948. Introd., Skinner. New York: Macmillan, 1976.

Smith, David E. "Millenarian Scholarship in America." *American Quarterly* 17 (1965): 535–49.

Smith, Goldwin. "Prophets of Unrest." Rev. of *Looking Backward, 2000–1887*, by Edward Bellamy. *Forum* Aug. 1890: 599–614.

Smith-Rosenberg, Carroll. "The Hysterical Woman: Sex Roles and Role Conflict in Nineteenth-Century America." *Social Research* 39 (1972): 652–78.

Spencer, Kathleen L. "'Red Sun Is High, the Blue Low': Towards a Stylistic Description of Science Fiction." *Science-Fiction Studies* 10 (1983): 35–49.

Somay, Bulent. "Towards an Open-Ended Utopia." *Science-Fiction Studies* 11 (1984): 25–38.

Steig, Michael. *Stories of Reading: Subjectivity and Literary Understanding*. Baltimore: Johns Hopkins UP, 1989.

Stowe, Harriet Beecher. *Uncle Tom's Cabin*. 1852. Facsim. ed. Introd. Howard Mumford Jones. Columbus: Merrill, 1969.

Straus, Sylvia. "Gender, Class, and Race in Utopia. *Looking Backward, 1988–1888: Essays on Edward Bellamy*. Ed. Daphne Patai. Amherst: U of Massachusetts P, 1988. 68–90.

Stupple, A. James. "Utopian Humanism in America, 1888–1900." Diss. Northwestern University, 1971.

Suleiman, Susan R., and Inge Crosman, eds. *The Reader in the Text: Essays on Audience and Interpretation*. Princeton: Princeton UP, 1980.

Suvin, Darko. "Anticipating the Sunburst—Dream and Vision: The Exemplary Case of Bellamy and Morris." *America as Utopia*. Ed. Kenneth M. Roemer. New York: Burt Franklin, 1981. 57–77.

———. "The Concept of Possible Worlds (Locus, Horizon, and Orientation) as a Key to Utopian Studies." Teorie e Prassi Utopiche Nell'età Moderna e Postmoderna Conference. Rome-Reggio Calabria. 22 May 1986.

———. *Metamorphoses of Science Fiction: On the Poetics and History of a Literary Genre*. New Haven: Yale UP, 1979.

———. "Utopianism from Orientation to Agency: What Are We Intellectuals under Post-Fordism to Do?" *Utopian Studies* 9.2 (1998): 162–90.

Sweet, Thomas. "Economy, Ecology, and *Utopia* in Early Colonial Promotional Literature." *American Literature* 71 (1999): 399–427.

Swift, Jonathan. *Gulliver's Travels*. 1726. New York: Limited Editions Club, 1950.

Thomas, Chauncey. *The Crystal Button, or, Adventures of Paul Prognosis in the Forty-Ninth Century*. Ed. George Houghton. Boston: Houghton Mifflin, 1891.

Thomas, John. *Alternative America: Henry George, Edward Bellamy, Henry Demarest Lloyd, and the Adversary Tradition*. Cambridge: Belknap-Harvard UP, 1983.

———. Introd. *Looking Backward, 2000–1887*. By Edward Bellamy. Ed. Thomas. Cambridge: Belknap-Harvard UP, 1967. 1–88.

Thorp, Willard. "Defenders of Ideality." *Literary History of the United States: History*. 3rd ed. rev. Ed. Robert E. Spiller, et al. New York: Macmillan, 1963. 809–26.

Tichi, Cecelia. Introd. *Looking Backward, 2000–1887*. By Edward Bellamy. Middlesex: Penguin, 1982. 7–27.

Tompkins, Jane P. *Sensational Designs: The Cultural Work of American Fiction 1790–1860*. New York: Oxford UP, 1985.

———, ed. *Reader-Response Criticism: From Formalism to Post-Structuralism*. Baltimore: Johns Hopkins UP, 1980.

Toth, Csaba. "Utopianism as Americanism." *American Quarterly* 45 (1993): 649–58.

———. "The Transatlantic Dialogue: 19th-Century American Utopianism and Europe." Diss. U of Minnesota, 1992.

Towers, Tom H. "The Insomnia of Julian West." *American Literature* 47 (1975): 52–63.

Travis, Molly Abel. *The Construction of Readers in the Twentieth Century*. Carbondale: Southern Illinois UP, 1998.

Tuveson, Ernest Lee. *Redeemer Nation*. Chicago: U of Chicago P, 1968.

Twain, Mark. *A Connecticut Yankee in King Arthur's Court*. 1889. Ed. Bernard L. Stein. Introd. Henry Nash Smith. Berkeley: U of California P, 1979.

Utter, Jack. *American Indians: Answers to Today's Questions*. 2nd. ed. Norman: U of Oklahoma P, 2001.

Vassos, John. Letter to the author. 11 Oct. 1978.

———, and Ruth Vassos. *Ultimo: An Imaginative Narration of Life under the Earth*. New York: Dutton, 1930.

Vinton, Arthur Dudley. *Looking Further Backward [ . . . ]*. Albany: Albany Book Co., 1890.

Walker, Francis A. "Mr. Bellamy and the Nationalist Party." Rev. of *Looking Backward, 2000–1887*, by Edward Bellamy. *Atlantic* Feb. 1890: 248–62.

Wallace, William. Rev. of *Looking Backward, 2000–1887*, by Edward Bellamy. *Academy* 24 Mar. 1888: 203.

Warhol, Robyn R. *Gendered Interventions: Narrative Discourse in the Victorian Novel*. New Brunswick: Rutgers UP, 1989.

Warner, Susan. *The Wide, Wide World.* 1850. Afterword, Jane P. Tompkins. Old
    Westbury: Feminist P, 1986.

Wegner, Phillip E. "Horizons, Figures, and Machines: The Dialectic of Utopia in the
    Work of Fredric Jameson." *Utopian Studies* 9.2 (1998): 58–73.

———. *Imaginary Communities: Utopia, the Nation, and the Spatial Histories of
    Modernity.* Berkeley: U of California P, 2002.

Wells, H. G. *A Modern Utopia.* 1905. Introd. Mark R. Hillegas. Lincoln: U of Nebraska,
    1967.

———. *Scientific Romances* [ . . . ]. Introd. Wells. London: Gollancz, 1933.

Wheeler, David H. *Our Industrial Utopia [ . . . ].* Chicago: McClurg, 1895.

White, Craig. "A Utopia of 'Spheres and Sympathies': Science and Society in The
    Blithedale Romance and at Brook Farm." *Utopian Studies* 9.2 (1998): 78–102.

Whiting, Lilian. "Boston Days." Rev. of *Looking Backward, 2000–1887,* by Edward
    Bellamy. *Times-Democrat* 5 Feb. 1888: pt. 2: 11.

Widdicombe, Richard Toby. "Early Histories of Utopian Thought (to 1950)." *Utopian
    Studies* 3.1 (1992): 1–38.

———. *Edward Bellamy: An Annotated Bibliography of Secondary Criticism.* New York:
    Garland, 1988.

———. "Edward Bellamy's Utopian Vision: An Annotated Check List of Reviews."
    *Extrapolation* 29 (1988): 5–20.

———, and Herman Preiser, eds. *Revising the Legacy of Edward Bellamy (1850–1898),
    American Author and Social Reformer: Uncollected and Unpublished Writings,
    Scholarly Perspectives for a New Millennium.* Lewiston: Mellen, 2002.

Wiebe, Robert H. *The Search for Order, 1877–1920.* New York: Hill and Wang, 1967.

Willard, Frances E. "An Interview with Edward Bellamy." *Household Guest* 4 (1889):
    539–42.

Wilson, R. Jackson. Introd. *Looking Backward, 2000–1887.* By Edward Bellamy. New
    York: Modern Library, 1982. vii–xxxv.

Winter, Michael. *Compendium Utopiarum: Typologie und Bibliographie literarischer
    Utopien.* Vol. 1. Stuttgart: Metzler, 1978.

Winters, Donald E. "The Utopianism of Survival: Bellamy's *Looking Backward* and
    Twain's *A Connecticut Yankee.*" *American Studies* 21 (1980): 23–38.

Wright, Austin Tappan. *Islandia.* New York: Holt, Rinehart, and Winston, 1942.

Young, Alexander. "The Author of 'Looking Backward.'" *Book News Monthly*
    Nov. 1889: 68.

———. "Boston Letter." *Critic* 29 June 1898: 322–23.

———. "Boston Letter." *Critic* 7 Dec. 1889: 289.

Zboray, Ronald. *A Fictive People: Antebellum Economic Development and the American
    Reading Public.* New York: Oxford UP, 1993.

# Index

KENNETH M. ROEMER was raised in East Rockaway, New York. He received his B.A. in English from Harvard and his M.A. and Ph.D. in American Civilization from the University of Pennsylvania. He has taught at the University of Texas at Arlington since 1971 and is currently a Distinguished Teaching Professor and President of the Society for Utopian Studies. His fellowships and grants include awards from the National Endowment for the Humanities, the American Council of Learned Societies, and the Japan Society for the Promotion of Science. His books include *The Obsolete Necessity* (1976), which was nominated for a Pulitzer; *America as Utopia*, ed. (1981); *Approaches to Teaching Momaday's* The Way to Rainy Mountain, ed. (1988); *Native American Writers of the United States*, ed. (1997), which won a Writer of the Year award from the Wordcraft Circle of Native Writers and Storytellers; and *Michibata de Deatta Nippon* [A Sidewalker's Japan] (2002). Professor Roemer lives in Arlington, Texas, with his wife, Micki.